The VOICE of the CHILD in American Literature

The VOICE of the CHILD in American Literature

Linguistic Approaches to Fictional Child Language

MARY JANE HURST

THE UNIVERSITY PRESS OF KENTUCKY

Copyright © 1990 by The University Press of Kentucky

Scholarly publisher for the Commonwealth,
serving Bellarmine College, Berea College, Centre
College of Kentucky, Eastern Kentucky University,
The Filson Club, Georgetown College, Kentucky
Historical Society, Kentucky State University,
Morehead State University, Murray State University,
Northern Kentucky University, Transylvania University,
University of Kentucky, University of Louisville,
and Western Kentucky University.

Editorial and Sales Offices: Lexington, Kentucky 40508-4008

Library of Congress Cataloging-in-Publication Data
Hurst, Mary Jane, 1952-
    The voice of the child in American literature : linguistic
approaches to fictional child language / Mary Jane Hurst.
      p.   cm.
    Includes bibliographical references.
    ISBN 978-0--8131-5315-5
    1. American literature—History and criticism. 2. Language and
languages in literature. 3. Children in literature. 4. Speech in
literature. 5. Children—Language. I. Title.
PS169.L36H8   1990
810.9'352054—dc20   90-33190

This book is printed on acid-free paper meeting
the requirements of the American National Standard
for Permanence of Paper for Printed Library Materials. ♾

For my family

Contents

List of Tables ix

Acknowledgments xi

1. Introduction 1
2. Basic Structures in Child Speech: Sounds, Word Forms, and Syntax 8
3. Case Grammar: Role Structures of Child Speech 19
4. Functions of Child Speech 42
5. Parent-Child Discourse 64
6. Children's Narratives 95
7. Gender and Fictional Children's Language 114
8. Conclusion: "That Evening Sun" 136

Notes 149

Bibliography 154

Index 177

Tables

1. A Description of Selected Case Frames   21
2. Case Roles in Lolita's Speech   30
3. Case Frames of Lolita's Speech   32
4. Case Roles in Maisie's Speech   36
5. Case Frames of Maisie's Speech   39
6. Communicative and Noncommunicative Functions of Child Speech   44
7. Functional Categories in the Speech of Miles and Flora in "The Turn of the Screw"   53
8. Functional Categories in the Speech of Regan in *The Exorcist*   54
9. Children's Speech Functions in Chapters 25 and 26 of *Uncle Tom's Cabin*   57
10. Children's Speech Functions in Two *Whilomville Stories*   59
11. Functions of Child Speech in Five Works   62
12. Functions of Adult Speech to Pearl in *The Scarlet Letter*   72
13. Gender-Related Characteristics of Speech in *My Ántonia*   129
14. Gender-Related Characteristics of Speech in *Shadows on the Rock*   130
15. Gender-Related Characteristics of Speech in *The Red Pony*   131
16. Gender-Related Characteristics of Speech in *The Grapes of Wrath*   132
17. Speech Differences between Male and Female Children   133
18. Speech Differences between Male and Female Children Created by Male and Female Authors   134
19. Gender Differences in Child Speech Related to Authors' Gender   135
20. Functions of Child and Adult Speech in "That Evening Sun"   141
21. Self-Referencing Case Frames in "That Evening Sun"   142

Acknowledgments

The research behind this project began when I was a graduate student at the University of Maryland, and I am indebted to Mary Rita Miller for guiding me throughout my graduate studies. I thank the following members of the University of Maryland faculty who provided helpful comments about my earlier linguistic studies of literature: Mary Rita Miller, Richard B. Hovey, Harold Herman, Eugene Hammond, Lewis Lawson, and William DeLorenzo. More recently, M. Jimmie Killingsworth of Texas A&M University and Laurie Ricou of the University of British Columbia gave me expert advice, and I thank them for their valuable suggestions.

At numerous conferences during the past eight years, I have met other people who are interested in subjects relevant to this study. So many individuals at these conferences have given me feedback about my ideas that I am able to offer only a general but genuine thank you to everyone. I would especially like to express my appreciation to the Linguistic Society of America for sponsoring Summer Institutes. The 1982 Institute at the University of Maryland and the 1987 Institute at Stanford University expanded my horizons and fueled my research. I am grateful to the University of Maryland and to Texas Tech University for providing funding that facilitated my travel and research.

My family's love and support have enabled me to carry out my work. Even with the demands of his medical practice, my husband, Daniel L. Hurst, patiently and generously read and reread my manuscript, and I thank him for his thoughtful responses. My daughter,

Katherine Jane Hurst, stimulated my interest in child language in the first place, and I am delighted to say she has grown into a most articulate person despite my excessive attention to her speech patterns.

I thank all the individuals and institutions who have helped me complete *The Voice of the Child in American Literature*. Any errors of fact or judgment which may remain in this book are my responsibility alone.

1. Introduction

In a well-known section of "Song of Myself," Walt Whitman uses the voice of a child to raise some of the central issues in his poem. Whitman's presentation of this speaking child typifies the ways in which children and child language often appear in American literature:

> A child said, *What is the grass?* fetching
>   it to me with full hands;
> How could I answer the child? I do
>   not know what it is any more than he.
>   [*Leaves of Grass* lines 98-100]

Here the child asks the primary question of the poem, penetrating with deadly accuracy to the heart of the subject. The child's utterance, simply formed with a state-of-being verb and a concrete noun, requests information and clarification. The charm of the question derives from its innocence, simplicity, and literalism, but beneath the surface lurks a tangle of more complicated questions about reality and perception and understanding. Knowing that he cannot answer all of those questions, the narrator of the poem, behaving in the same manner as so many other adult figures in American literature, does not respond to the query. Not only does the adult not know the answer, he even suspects the child is better equipped than he to solve the riddle. By casting the child as a deceptively innocent inquisitor whose capac-

2   The Voice of the Child

ity to ask questions exceeds the ability of his elders to provide answers, Whitman is weaving with a primary thread of our nation's literary fabric.

Just as we may not at first think of Whitman as a poet of childhood experience, we may not immediately think of American literature as including many child characters. However, when we begin counting children in literature, we find that they appear in the writings of nearly all American authors from all time periods. Perhaps our lack of notice is actually due, as Leslie Fielder has suggested ("The Invention of the Child" 22), to our total saturation with literary children: they are so numerous we fail to see them. The overwhelming number of children in our literature may reflect our cultural concern for innocence and the problem of lost innocence, key American themes, but our apparent ambivalence toward children, in literature as well as in life, suggests that the reasons behind their prominence in our literary tradition must be complex.

We as adults are reflected in our children, those in our literature as well as those in our families, and so it is natural to want to examine their presence among us. Children and child speech are important literary elements which merit careful critical analysis. Surprisingly, comprehensive studies of the child in American fiction have not been previously attempted, and fictional child speech, even that of individual characters, has been almost totally ignored. Nevertheless, the language of fictional children warrants attention for several reasons. First, language and language acquisition are primary issues for children, much as sex and sexual development are primary issues for adolescents. Second, because vast linguistic efforts have been directed toward language acquisition research, a broad base of concrete information exists with which to explore the topic. And, third, language is a key which opens many doors. An understanding of fictional children's language leads to discoveries about various critical questions, sociological and psychological as well as textual and stylistic.

This study examines the presentation of children and child language in American fiction by applying general linguistic principles as well as specific findings from child language acquisition research to children's speech in literary texts. It clarifies, sorts, and assesses the representations of child speech in American fiction. It tests on fictional discourse linguistic concepts heretofore applied exclusively to naturally occurring child language. The aim is not to evaluate the degree of realism in writers' presentations of child language, for that would be a simplistic and reductive enterprise. Rather, the overall object is to analyze fictional child language using linguistic methods to arrive at a better understanding of the language itself, of the fictional children who speak the language, of the texts in which the children appear, of the authors who have created the texts, and of the culture from which these authors and their works have emerged. Remembering that fictional children's utterances have been composed by adult authors rather than by child speakers, we must also recognize that writers are not required to create speaking child characters. The development of young characters in a work of fiction must, then, either attach some thematic significance to children or else indicate some special interest by the author in children. This study, in short, is motivated by a desire to understand the voice of the child and the role of the child in American fiction.

As a universal subject, literary children have previously been the focus of only six books. Horace Scudder's 1895 *Childhood in Literature and Art* provides a chronological review of selected child characters, mostly from Greek, Roman, Hebrew, early Christian, and medieval art and literature. Peter Coveney's 1967 *The Image of Childhood* concentrates on English literature, dating childhood as a literary theme from the poetry of Blake and Wordsworth. Robert Pattison's 1978 *The Child Figure in English Literature* argues that English literary children are figurative symbols in religious discussions. In his 1982 *Corruption in Paradise: The Child in Western Literature*, Reinhard Kuhn searches through the poetry and prose of all Western literatures, discovering two strands in the presentation of children: childhood as heavenly with children as innocent or, on the other hand, childhood as hellish with children as evil. Richard N. Coe's 1984 *When the Grass Was Taller* offers a poetic review of the fictional autobiography of childhood, drawing mainly on English, Australian, and European traditions, with some references to American and African literature. Laurie Ricou's 1987 *Everyday Magic: Child Languages in Canadian Literature* examines children's points of view and children's languages in Canadian literature; his is the first book-length study to recognize the significance of literary children's language.

Not one of these six English-language books deals exclusively or even extensively with children in American literature. Offhand remarks about fictional child characters are sprinkled throughout critical studies of American literature, and a few articles have attempted broad-ranging critiques of the American literary child, but the subject cannot be adequately managed in a short study.[1] Of course, dozens of articles, dissertations, and books have been written about specific fictive children. Some, such as Anne Tropp Trensky's "The Saintly Child in Nineteenth-Century American Fiction," limit themselves to particular time periods. Others, such as Earl Rovit's "Fathers and Sons in American Fiction," trace certain themes. Still others, such as Albert E. Stone's 1961 *The Innocent Eye: Childhood in Mark Twain's Imagination* or Muriel Shine's 1969 *The Fictional Children of Henry James*, treat child characters in a particular author's canon. In addition to containing a list of works cited, the present book's bibliography also includes references for much of this criticism.

With some exceptions, literary criticism has not given attention to children's conversations, a shocking lapse given that, at the very least, the language of children effectively and vividly portrays their characterizations. The numerous examinations of language and style in fiction have mostly ignored the presence of child language, and even when critics have discussed child speakers, they have generally not touched on the topic of child speech. The few studies which have centered on child language, such as Laurie Ricou's *Everyday Magic* or Naomi Sokolof's "Discoveries of Reading: Stories of Childhood by Bialik, Shahar, and Roth," differ from the present one because they do not approach a range of fiction from the United States and, while they do make reference to some linguistic ideas, their work does not directly utilize linguistic methodologies in the analysis of dialogue.

Linguistics, the study of language, may be subclassified in many ways, but as an academic discipline it is often divided into the following five areas: phonology, the study of sounds; morphology, the study of word units; syntax, the study of phrase and sentence structure; semantics, the study of meaning; and pragmatics, the study of language use. Besides these five descriptive areas, a number of subfields of applied linguistics use linguistic principles in other endeavors. For example, some linguists work to distinguish various types of dialects, others compare language systems, and others unravel how one language has evolved. Many linguists are drawn to child language acquisition because in a relatively short period of time the language-learning child masters the sound system, the vocabulary, the grammar, and all the social rules for language; therefore, the years during which language is acquired provide a window for directly observing the processes of language and how an individual constructs the parts of language into meaningful discourse. Too, linguistics can be joined with other disciplines such as neurology or sociology to form separate branches of scholarship including neurolinguistics, the study of brain and language, or sociolinguistics, the study of language in a social context. Interdisciplinary work in linguistics often serves practical purposes, as when a speech therapist might help a recovering stroke victim regain lost language function or when a literary critic might identify authorship of a newly discovered poem according to word patterns or grammatical structures.

Examining a written text by studying its language is hardly a new idea, but with the enormous twentieth-century advances in linguistic science, certain aspects of the relationship between literature and linguistics have flourished. M.A.K. Halliday, a practitioner of linguistic approaches to literature, says in "The Linguistic Study of Literary Texts" that "it is part of the task of linguists to describe texts; and all texts, including those, prose and verse, which fall within any definition of literature, are accessible to linguistic analysis" (217). Of course, some linguists and some literary critics alike object to approaching literature through linguistics, but movement within both disciplines shows increasing acceptance of properly managed studies connecting the two fields.[2] Within the last decade, for example, linguists have turned more directly to the study of conversations to form a linguistic theory accounting for language as it actually occurs in everyday discourse, and, for some, this trend has resulted in increased interest in literary discourse. As Deborah Tannen has said in her *Language* article on "Repetition in Conversation," "Ordinary conversation and literary discourse have more in common than has been commonly thought, as both depend for their effect on interpersonal involvement" (575), and linguists working on conversations analyze their data in ways similar to those used by literary critics studying literature, watching for repetition, metaphor, imagery, sound play, or other notable patterns of language.

Bakhtin writes that "the speaking person and his discourse is . . . what makes a novel a novel, the thing responsible for the uniqueness of the genre" (*Dialogic Imagination* 333). The spoken words of child characters in American fiction have received almost no critical attention, so in studying them we are not only reviewing an aspect of literature essential to the definition of fiction, but we are also covering new territory. Moreover, in breaking new ground, this present study aims to answer some old criticisms of linguistic approaches to literature. That is, this study does not presuppose that all literary interpretation can be facilitated by linguistic analysis, and, although areas of linguistics are separated here for purposes of explanation and definition, separating the parts does not imply that individual areas are unrelated. Furthermore, while the nature of literature prohibits total objectivity in any discussion of it, this study is grounded in the belief that linguistic analysis supplies a degree of objectivity because it deals with concrete and measurable facets of language. Linguistic analysis of these concrete and measurable aspects of literary texts helps the reader articulate points about characters and situations that otherwise seem intuitive or uncertain. And, finally, this study deals with a specific aspect of literature, fictional dialogue, which is in some ways comparable to actual speech.

The relationship between literary speech and actual conversations remains a matter for debate. One philosophical position holds that literary language is imitative and unreal. However, Mary Rita Miller, a linguist, concludes in "Attestations of American Indian Pidgin English in Fiction and Nonfiction," that "language structure cannot be manufactured at the whim of the author" (144). Norman Page's *Speech in the English Novel* presents many examples of fictional dialogue operating in exactly the same ways as its naturally occurring counterpart. Mary Louise Pratt's *Toward a Speech Act Theory of Literary Discourse* shows on both theoretical and practical grounds that it is a fallacy to differentiate between literary language and naturally occurring language. This point of view is supported by the analysis of conversational transcripts done by sociolinguists such as William Labov. While literary dialogue may look cleaner than transcripts of oral dialogue, partly because the false starts and interruptions normal in oral speech would be highly annoying for readers who are used to certain written conventions, the essence of the two types of speech is probably close. In fact, as shown later, many authors produce children's language with a high level of correspondence to linguistic field data.

As one of the foremost linguists of the twentieth century, Leonard Bloomfield, has said, "the most difficult step in the study of language is the first step" (*Language* 21). We have now taken that first step by examining some background issues for this project. Chapter Two begins the analysis of texts with a look at basic elements of language—sounds, word forms, and grammatical structures—as they appear in fictional children's speech. Subsequent chapters then turn to broader concepts of discourse—case grammar, speech functions, parent-child communication, and gender differences in language—as they are relevant to the portrayal of fictional children's voices. The final chapter concludes the study by applying all the approaches from previous chapters in a discussion of William Faulkner's "That Evening Sun." In this manner, features of language are introduced in the approximate order in which children are thought to acquire them and in which linguists usually explore them.

This project is not, however, meant to be just an exercise in linguistics. Language is the common ground shared by both linguistics and literature, and here we survey one portion of that common ground, fictional child language. The organization of this book is constructed around linguistics, but the areas of research selected for application—phonology, morphology, syntax, case grammar, speech functions, parent-child communication, and gender differences in language—are those that can be most readily and relevantly applied to the analysis of literature. While individual chapters are arranged around linguistic topics, at the heart of each chapter are discussions of several selections of literature.

The general parameters of the discussions to follow are easily stated. First, while Reinhard Kuhn has described a child as one who has "not yet sensed the irreversible and ineluctable impoverishment which leads to adulthood" (*Corruption in Paradise* 6), here a child is defined less poetically as a person under the age of thirteen. Childhood does not uniformly end at specific time, but people under the age of thirteen have usually not faced the life questions, mostly associated with death and sex, which shape adult thoughts and attitudes, and, in addition, many social, biological, and philosophical precedents support placing the upper limit of childhood at age thirteen. Linguistic evidence is variable, but research often follows Piaget's divisions of intellectual development, placing the final stage of development, the period of formal operations, somewhere between the ages of eleven and fifteen. The second parameter limits this project to spoken discourse, language which has traditionally been set off by quotation marks. Thoughts of characters, indirect discourse, or segments of prose intended as stream of consciousness are eliminated from review except as background material. Third, only American literature is considered. Fourth, the voices of children in fiction rather than in poetry are emphasized because linguistic approaches have the more relevance for the larger chunks of language found in fictional dialogue. And, finally, children's literature is not examined except for cases in which fiction written for a juvenile audience has since become an enduring part of our larger literary and cultural heritage.

2. Basic Structures in Child Speech
Sounds, Word Forms, and Syntax

Children often pronounce and form words differently than adults, saying, for example, "free" rather than "three" or "bringed" rather than "brought." These expressions appear in child speech for various reasons. Sometimes they occur in identifiable stages as a child begins to learn a particular form. The child who says "bringed," for instance, has learned to add an -ed ending to verbs referring to past action and is applying that knowledge to all verbs. Sometimes these childish utterances relate to the degree of difficulty associated with making a particular sound; sound combinations such as "free" or "tree," for example, may be easier to pronounce than "three." Though common in the productions of living children, such distinctive phonological (related to sounds) and morphological (related to word formations) features of speech seldom appear in literature. When they do occur, they stand out because they are unusual, and, therefore, we might suspect the author has included them to serve some purpose.

In J.D. Salinger's "Uncle Wiggly in Connecticut," little Ramona introduces her imaginary companions with phonological creativity as "Jimmy Jimmereeno" (26) and "Mickey Mickeranno" (37), which is just how a small child might double and repeat sounds. What significance could this have? In the first place it emphasizes that the speaker is a young child. Furthermore, within the story, Ramona's mother withdraws emotionally from her daughter, so the child must either entertain herself or devise a way to win her mother's attention. Such utterances accomplish both ends; by playing with language, Ramona can amuse herself while she irritates her mother enough to notice her. Thus, within the story Salinger uses this speech to indicate the relationship between characters and, in addition, as a tool to heighten his audience's feeling for the child by underlining her age and, by extension, her vulnerability.

In Harper Lee's *To Kill a Mockingbird*, the children's speech frequently contains collapsed phrases such as "Smatter?" for "What is the matter?" Children in this novel also commonly drop the final g as in, "Nothin' to it. I swear, Scout, sometimes you act so much like a girl it's mortifyin'" (42). Attributing such formations to dialect might seem logical, since the novel is set in the deep South, but the children's father, a lawyer who is a native Southerner, does not speak so casually. Other adults in the novel, though, are attributed such pronunciations, including the lower-class Mr. Ewell who says on the witness stand, "Well, the night of November twenty-one I was comin' in from the woods with a load o'kindlin' and just as I got to the fence I heard Mayella screamin' like a stuck hog inside the house—" (175). Surely, though, the author does not intend to connect the innocent children to Ewell, the novel's embodiment of malevolence. Nor is it likely that the author carelessly distributed her characters' speech, for Lee herself grew up in the South and within the novel she makes a point of elaborating on language use, as when Calpurnia explains to the youngsters why she talks differently in the black church on Sunday than she does while working in their white household during the week.

A possible interpretation of the child speech in *To Kill a Mockingbird* may, as in the Salinger story, have to do with drawing the readers' attention to the age of the characters. By speaking in an identifiably casual way, the children show they are different from the adults. Saying "nothin'" rather than "nothing" may be the verbal equivalent of carrying a teddy bear or baseball bat instead of a briefcase. Similar, though more complicated, examples of this nature can be found in the speech of William Faulkner's literary children. For instance, in Faulkner's *The Hamlet*, Eck Snopes's son says of a wild pony, "There he is! There's ourn!" (301). In this novel, the entire Snopes family is designated as lower class and usually speaks differently than do members of the yeoman or aristocratic classes. Yet Faulkner's distinction between adult and child speech is like Harper Lee's in that, in both artists' work, child characters have more freedom in their forms and pronunciation than adults, even though the children say nothing that might not be attributed to geographical or social dialect. Thus, age more than, or at least as well as, dialect affects how individuals talk. Preadolescent children seem to have a license to speak freely, and the features of their speech serve as a badge of their youth.

These examples of distinctive phonological features of child speech in the works of Faulkner, Lee, and Salinger are, to be sure, rare and scattered literary glimpses of what is common in life. However, these examples illustrate that the very appearance of child speech adds meaning and depth to fiction.

A more extended exception to the general absence of childlike phonological features in fictional dialogue occurs in Nathaniel Hawthorne's infrequently studied tale "The Snow-Image: A Childish Miracle." An unusual instance of Hawthorne using orthographic means to convey pronunciations, the story tells of two children who build a snowman or, in this case, snow-sister who comes to life and plays with them. Within the text, the speech of the two children, Violet and Peony, constitutes about 95 percent of the dialogue in the short story; they are thus not only among the earliest speaking children in American literature, but they are also among the most talkative.

As an earlier essay of mine, "The Language of Children in 'The Snow-Image,'" has shown, Hawthorne's creation of Violet and Peony was influenced by his experiences with his own children, for this story contains several linguistic parallels to a passage in Hawthorne's journal (*The American Notebooks*, 19 March 1848) describing his daughter Una and his son Julian. In the story, the little brother, Peony, refers many times to the snow-image as a "'ittle girl" or as his "'ittle sister," always dropping the first letter in his pronunciation of *little*. This pronunciation is like Julian Hawthorne's pronunciation of the word *walk* as recorded in his father's journal. In the journal, Julian is delighted at the prospect of a walk and cries, "'alk; ok," dropping the first letter of *walk*. Peony's word *little* begins with *l* and Julian's *walk* with *w*, but small children, probably including twenty-one-month-old Julian in 1848, do not usually say "little," but rather "wittle," substituting *w* for *l*. Thus, both boys were probably dropping the *w* sound in both words. The substitution of glides (/w/ and /y/) for liquids (/l/ and /r/) seems to be a universal phonological process in child language (de Villiers and de Villiers 44). Though not formally described until 1968 by Roman Jakobson, this process in children's speech was recorded in Hawthorne's journal and in Hawthorne's fiction more than one hundred years earlier. The deletion of initial sounds ("alk" for "walk") is also a common phenomenon in young children, so Julian probably did say "alk" for "walk," and Peony's "ittle" rather than "wittle" or its standard adult form of "little" is likewise reasonable.

In addition to phonological representation, many other notable aspects of child speech appear in both "The Snow-Image" and Hawthorne's journals. Overall, an awareness of the fictional children's language helps us understand the story and its place in the Hawthorne canon. That Hawthorne would have used lifelike child speech in a story with supernatural portent, combining romanticism with realism, reflects his typically complex style.

A more recent and more extended illustration of rendering the sounds of child speech in fiction appears in Henry Roth's *Call It Sleep*. This novel contains multiple language layers, with characters speaking various immigrant dialects and languages as well as assorted class and ethnic dialects of English. The characters' talk is also age-graded; that is, age related speech differences can be observed between the interaction of five-year-old David with his mother and the talk of men working in factories, between the babble of adults at markets and the play of children in streets, and between the words exchanged among the rabbis and among the boys at cheder. Frances Kleederman's dissertation on *Call It Sleep* examines much of the novel's language in detail, but remarks little on how noisy the book is, full of the sounds of life. Roth's concern for conveying sounds is shown in onomatopoetic coinages such as *klang, swank, s-s-s-s*. Speech is punctuated with *unghs* and *uphs*. Some sounds of children's speech are not much different from adults' except the child talk is freer, more playful and less self-conscious. "Yowooee!" cry the boys, for example, as they slide down a fire escape (220). Roth's ear and eye for noticing and then capturing on paper the sounds of speech and of life were probably nurtured by his personal exposure to a varied language environment when he was a child growing up in an immigrant area.

One concentrated example of speech sounds represented in written dialogue in *Call It Sleep* occurs when Leo expresses amazement at David's ignorance of the symbols of Catholicism: "Dat's a scapiller, see? An' dat's a pitcher o' de holy Mudder an' Chil'. Cheez! Doncha know de Woigin Mary w'en yuh sees 'er?" (305). Sounds of speech are also emphasized when David is trapped on the dock by older boys and out of fear denies he is a Jew:

"I'm a Hungarian. My mudder 'n' fodder's Hungarian. We're de janitors."
"W'y wuz yuh looking upstairs?"
"Cause my mudder wuz washin' de floors."

"Talk Hungarian," challenged the first lieutenant.
"Sure like dis. Abashishishabababyo tomama wawa. Like dot."
"Aa, yuh full o' shit!" sneered the second lieutenant angrily. "C'mom, Pedey, let's give 'im 'is lumps."
"Yea!" the other freckled one urged. "C'mon. He ain' w'ite. Yi! Yi! Yi!" He wagged his palms under his chin. [250]

The sounds of these excerpts, especially Leo's "Cheez!" and David's fake Hungarian and the "Yi! Yi! Yi!" taunts, add to the childlike flavor of the episode.

Few purely morphemic variations characteristic of child speech are found in American literature. More likely are variants of a combined phonological and morphological nature. For example, at the end of J.D. Salinger's *Catcher in the Rye*, Holden Caulfield waits at the museum for his younger sister when two little boys approach him:

"Where're the mummies, fella?" the kid said again. "Ya know?"
I horsed around with the two of them a little bit. "The mummies? What're they?" I asked the one kid.
"You know. The *mummies*—them dead guys. That get buried in them toons and all."
Toons. That killed me. He meant tombs. [203]

On one level, the replacement of *tomb* with *toon*, perhaps related to *cartoon*, identifies the speaker as a child who either mispronounces or misforms the word. It is the kind of error adults smile over, which is Holden's response, and Holden, in a manner characteristic of his behavior throughout the novel, belabors the humor by drawing attention to the mistake, noting his own reaction, and then translating the boy's meaning. The incident has a serious side, too, for it reinforces our perception of Holden as a language-oriented person with a special affection for children. Again, then, the author's handling of child speech has significance not only for the relationship between characters, but also for the readers' perceptions of those characters and, by extension, for the readers' responses to the entire novel.

In discussing his poem "The Flight," Theodore Roethke expresses concern about representations of child speech degenerating into "cutesy prattle . . . a suite in goo-goo" ("Open Letter" 70), but American writers cannot be accused of writing goo-goo. Of course, many speaking children in literature are older than six, beyond the stage of

Basic Structures in Child Speech   13

phonological and morphological productions strikingly distinctive from adult forms, but, still, the reluctance of writers to use the actual sounds and forms of children's speech points to a certain conservatism in literature. However, orthographical variations in a text can make reading difficult, and, as Jane Raymond Walpole explains in "Eye Dialect in Fictional Dialogue," employing eccentric spellings to indicate pronunciation offends some readers.

Of course, writers can employ more sophisticated ways of rendering phonology without resorting to idiosyncratic orthography. In her study of "Intonation Patterns of Sermons in Seven Novels," Dolores Burton says that "fictional utterances have a potential phonological dimension that has psychological reality for the reader and enables him to actualize this dimension by producing an appropriate contour when confronted with certain textual signals. These signals may be mechanical ones such as dashes or other marks of punctuation that graphemically surrogate pauses, or they may be syntactic clues inherent in the word order, the type of verb mood, the use of repetition, or the kind of sentence" (217-18). Readers are generally attuned to the more obvious authorial techniques for controlling the flow of dialogue. For example, a bit of direct discourse may be interrupted with a marker such as "he remarked thoughtfully and then added," and then be followed by more direct discourse by the same speaker. Interrupting the quotation in this way would give the impression of a slower conversation, of a definite pause in the interaction between characters.

Sensitive writers, evidently aware of intonation patterns in speech, modify the sound patterns in their dialogues to suit the personalities of their characters. For example, in Henry James's *What Maisie Knew*, Maisie's mother abuses her daughter mercilessly and then declares herself good. The poor child says sweetly, "That was what the Captain said to me that day, mamma" (158). But the mother, who has been through many lovers since the Captain, cannot even remember him and snaps, "The Captain? What Captain?" (159). The phrasing, sound, and rhythm of the mother's speech make her sound like a squawking parrot, whereas the gentle sing-song cadence and soft vowels of Maisie's speech ("That was what the captain said to me that day, mamma") make her sound like an innocent young child. Ending her sentence with the term of address *mamma* gives a deferential tone to the utterance that runs counter to the heavier beat and lowered pitch of its last syllable. The sounds of Maisie's words indicate her gentleness, but her speech also shows a firmness of character. That is, people who end sentences with a rising intonation give the impression of being uncertain or powerless, but the lowered pitch at the end of Maisie's sentence suggests a degree of strength. Indeed, Maisie's measure of strength allows her to survive emotionally amid the bitter disputes and passionate triangles of the adults around her.

Examining this one sentence from *What Maisie Knew* gives us insight into Maisie's character and into James's fictional technique. While telling a story shockingly realistic for its time, Henry James manages to portray his main character's speech with poetic sensitivity. Moreover, in this instance, as in others described above, when notable characteristics appear in the speech of literary children, those speech features accomplish more than or even something different from the representation of "real" child language. Furthermore, the portrayal of child speech can be rendered through distinctive orthography or through a subtle sensitivity to speech patterns, and the author's choice of representation provides clues about that author's style and fictional intent.

Syntax

The child's development of syntax may be the most scrutinized aspect of language acquisition, but it remains a controversial topic. Syntax deals with the construction of language above the level of an isolated word and at or below the level of a single sentence. Lively debates have centered on how children come to put words together. Some language specialists argue that children in a single word stage express phrases and sentences. That is, for example, when a young child is saying "Cookie," he or she might be thinking, "I want a cookie" or "This cookie tastes delicious!" This theory, while hard to refute, is nearly impossible to prove. In any case, the complex nature of syntax, whether involved before or only after children begin uttering strings of words together, can be appreciated by observing the difficulty adults have acquiring a second language. Learning a new vocabulary, a set of words, is not too hard, but learning to put those words together in the order, form, and context used by fluent speakers in spontaneous conversation is extremely difficult for most adults.

In general, most linguists agree that the human child comes "prewired" for language. In other words, the ability to learn a language is thought to be an innate human quality, while the acquisition of a specific language is thought to be a learned behavior. Furthermore, the learning of a specific language seems to occur best before some critical period, probably around the age of six, although the process of language acquisition, including the development of syntax, continues into adolescence. Linguistic analyses have also determined that the length and syntactic complexity of children's utterances increase predictably with age. This, too, is hardly new information to parents who know that their children begin to understand and use various constructions such as negatives or "why" questions in definite stages.

The literary question for us is to see how writers have portrayed the syntax of their speaking child characters. Overall, just as children's phonological and morphological usages are modestly represented in literature, so their syntax is usually not distinctive. As a notable exception, in Eudora Welty's *Losing Battles*, fourteen-month-old Lady May ends Part Five of the novel with "the first sentence of her life: 'What you huntin', man?'" (353). Her only utterance in the entire book, this is certainly an unusual, if not incredible, account of a child's first words, even in a novel filled with outrageous adult talk. Generally, literary children, even precocious youngsters such as Hawthorne's Pearl or Salinger's Teddy, speak in short simple or compound sentences uncluttered by modifying phrases and clauses. Their utterances are built primarily around action verbs with simple subjects and objects or around state-of-being verbs referring to themselves as in the following examples: "I'm tired" ("Teddy" 174); "'I am my mother's child,' answered the scarlet vision, 'and my name is Pearl!'" (*The Scarlet Letter* 109); and "The widder eats by a bell; she goes to bed by a bell; she gits up by a bell—everything's so awful reg'lar a body can't stand it" (*Tom Sawyer* 216).

While such examples are only selections from the works in which they appear, they do represent the essential simplicity of most literary children's syntax. The short story "Teddy" focuses on the natural wisdom and intuition of children, and Teddy himself is so smart people travel great distances to ask him questions; nevertheless, Teddy's speech is syntactically uncomplicated. Pearl in *The Scarlet Letter* has an uncanny understanding of the adult situations around her, but the actual structures of her utterances are unremarkable. The boys in *Tom Sawyer* are older than Teddy or Pearl, so their sentences are longer, but their speech is still fairly simple and direct. In contrast to the simplicity of the structures, the content of all three of these sample utterances is significant. Since Teddy is about to die, tiredness may be an appropriate foreshadowing of his imminent demise. Without a father and without any direct community ties, Pearl knows herself only in relation to her mother. Huck's discomfort with "civilized" living habits is the cornerstone of his personality.

Hence, age differences among literary children are usually shown by what the children do or what they talk about rather than by how they say things; that is, syntax is not usually altered for different age groups. For instance, while Salinger's Sergeant X and Esme are conversing, Esme's little brother keeps intruding with the same joke, "What did one wall say to the other wall?" and laughing hysterically when he blurts out the punch line, "Meet you at the corner!" ("For Esme—with Love and Squalor" 98). The boy's choice of subjects and his demeanor in interrupting and in repeating the same joke indicate his youth and his frame of mind; the structure of what he says is of minimal importance. As always, exceptions occur; in Hawthorne's "The Snow-Image" syntax is age-graded, for the older child Violet has longer sentences than her little brother Peony, she repeats his phrases as if to reinforce his speech, her talk is strewn with words such as *must* and *ought*, and she frequently qualifies and modifies with phrases that begin with *but*. This gives her speech a didactic overtone characteristic of the approach older children take with younger ones (Lederberg, "A Framework for Research" 52-70).

The general language capacity of retarded or damaged children sometimes receives special treatment in fiction, even if their syntax is not presented distinctively. Benjy, the mental equivalent of a child, has no direct discourse in William Faulkner's *The Sound and the Fury*, expressing himself to others only through moans and cries. The deaf child in Langston Hughes's "Red-Headed Baby" likewise does not speak, though he is only two years old. In John Steinbeck's *Cannery Row*, the retarded and disturbed eleven-year-old Frankie speaks in unusually clipped phrases, but his emotional problems may be more significant than his retardation or his age for his language development. For example, one day Doc asks him why he hangs around the lab:

> Doc asked, "why do you come here?"
> "You don't hit me or give me a nickel," said Frankie.
> "Do they hit you at home?"
> "There's uncles around all the time at home. Some of them hit me and tell me to get out and some of them give me a nickel and tell me to get out."
> "Where's your father?"
> "Dead," said Frankie vaguely.
> "Where's your mother?"
> "With the uncles." [51]

Structurally, the boy's speech in this section is fairly unremarkable, though his sentences are uniformly short, and he does not initiate any topics of conversation. Obviously, he does not understand what is going on around him. So even in the case of special fictional children, what they say or do not say seems to be of greater importance than the structure of their speech.

However, one striking syntactic feature of fictional children's language is constant questioning: "Do many men kill themselves, Daddy?" ("Indian Camp," *In Our Time* 19); "When am I going to be big enough?" (*Call It Sleep* 18); and "What does the letter mean, mother?—and why dost thou wear it?—and why does the minister keep his hand over his heart?" (*The Scarlet Letter* 180). Again, the structures of these questions are not exceptional, but their frequency is notable. Further, these questions and others like them are crucial to the fiction in which they occur, indicating once again that children are important barometers for the subjects and themes of American literature.

While it would be impossible to compare the syntax of all fictional child speech with all fictional adult speech, C.P. Heaton's "Style in *The Old Man and the Sea*" has studied old and young characters' sentence patterns in one novel. Heaton finds that 15 percent of the sentences in Hemingway's book involve dialogue between the old man and the boy. Over 75 percent of those dialogic utterances are simple sentences, 6 percent are compound, 2 percent are complex, and the remaining 17 percent are fragments. Heaton draws the following conclusions about characterization from his data: "The structure of their manner of phraseology when speaking together is probably designed to reflect the simplicity of their characters and the directness of their relationship. The simplicity of the speech of both man and boy symbolizes their likeness as individuals. The boy is but a youthful version of the old man" (20). After the boy leaves, the old man speaks without an audience, and the proportion of sentence types in his monologue is the same as the proportion of sentence types exchanged between the boy and the old man. This indicates that the boy's and the man's speech are structurally similar. Interestingly, each character's speech is simpler than the surrounding expository prose and simpler than the rendering of the old man's thoughts. Even with a writer such as Hemingway, known for the directness, clarity, and simplicity of his style, the syntactic representations of direct speech and unspoken reflection are different, with spoken language (direct discourse) presented more simply.

A similar distinction between the structures of direct discourse and of other prose can be found in Faulkner's fiction. In "The Bear," for example, a notoriously complex style dominates expository passages: "It had already begun on that day when he first wrote his age in two

18 The Voice of the Child

ciphers and his cousin McCaslin brought him for the first time to the camp, the big woods, to earn for himself from the wilderness the name and state of hunter provided he in his turn were humble and enduring enough" (192). But ten-year-old Ike McCaslin speaks simply: "It's Old Ben!" (197) and " 'I didn't see him,' he said. 'I didn't, Sam' " (203). And Sam Fathers, to whom are attributed several childlike characteristics despite his advanced age and mythical wisdom, gives this relatively straightforward advice to the boy: "Be scared. You cant help that. But dont be afraid. Aint nothing in the woods going to hurt you if you dont corner it or it dont smell that you are afraid" (207).

Sam's thoughts, though, are more rambling and more complicated structurally: *And he was glad, he told himself. He was old. He had no children, no people, none of his blood anywhere above earth that he would ever meet again. And even if he were to, he could not have touched it, spoken to it, because for seventy years now he had had to be a negro. It was almost over now and he was glad* (215; italics are Faulkner's). The thoughts of Faulkner's other characters are often expressed in more complex patterns than Sam's. In fact, people's thoughts are sometimes so complex they defy syntactic analysis. Even in the case of Benjy in *The Sound and the Fury*, unspoken thoughts, feelings, and memories fill the character's mind but never receive verbal expression. So, the proportional difference of Faulkner's sentence types between exposition, dialogue, and stream of consciousness may not be too different from Hemingway's, despite other differences in their styles.

In most writers, we might hypothesize, sentence structures attributed to any character could vary according to several factors: the age, personality, and mental complexity of the character; the audience to whom the character is speaking; the style of the author; and all the behind-the-scenes factors that affect an author's style. Evidence indicates, though, that, almost regardless of these other factors, simplicity is the primary syntactic feature of children's speech in American literature.

3. Case Grammar
Role Structures of Child Speech

Most models of language are based on syntax, that is, on grammatical structures. Without linguistic structures that all speakers of a language understand (either at a conscious or an unconscious level), communication between people would be impossible. If, for example, English somehow existed as a language with words but without commonly held syntactic structures, a speaker would have difficulty using words to express even the simplest ideas. To complicate matters even further, a sentence can be syntactically acceptable even if it is not meaningful, as Noam Chomsky has shown with the famous sentence "Colorless green ideas sleep furiously." However, as we can see when a toddler asks for milk or when the President addresses the nation, expressing meaning rather than expressing structure is the reason for communication. In addition, many features of syntax are language-specific; that is, as seen earlier, a fluent speaker of one language cannot become a fluent speaker of another just by learning a new vocabulary. Because of the underlying communicative function of language and because of the differences in syntactic structures among languages, an individual's capacity for language cannot be explained by syntax alone. Therefore, some linguists have found syntax-based grammar unsatisfactory.

Case grammar, which emphasizes the centrality of semantics, that is, of meaning, is one alternative to syntax-based grammar. Its language model focuses on what is referred to as the proposition of a sentence, clause, or phrase. The proposition is composed of the set of relationships between nouns and verbs, and these relationships are described by semantic cases, or, as they are sometimes named, case roles or case frames. Thus, the meaning of ideas and the relationship between ideas are central to case grammar. The semantic cases of case grammar are not to be confused with the syntactic cases, familiar in English mainly to distinguish nominative and accusative pronouns such as *I* and *me*. Whereas syntactic cases are based on surface structure, semantic cases are concerned with the underlying deep-structure relationships between nouns and verbs.

Because case grammar explores below-the-surface meaning relations, it can be used to describe various kinds of languages and perhaps, though this has not been definitively established, to describe all languages. The advantage of case grammar is that it describes the meaning relationships between parts of an utterance, whereas a syntactic description is limited to function rather than meaning. To illustrate the foundations of case grammar and the distinctions between the syntactic cases of traditional analysis and the semantic case frames of case grammar, compare the sentence "Faulkner wrote the novel" with the sentence "Faulkner recognized the plight of the impoverished." In both examples, under traditional analysis, *Faulkner* is the subject of the sentence. However, from a case grammar perspective, in the first example *Faulkner* is the agent of the action described by the word *wrote*, and in the second example *Faulkner* is the experiencer of the process involved in *recognizing* a situation. It makes no difference in case grammar terms that *Faulkner* happens to be what we call the surface subject of both sentences. Case grammar theory involves more than just a delineation of the basic case frames, but the role relationships described by the case frames (see Table 1) are the single most revealing feature of case grammar, and they have drawn the most attention in both theoretical and applied linguistics.

Notions about semantic case are not new, but the first comprehensive presentation of case grammar within contemporary grammatical analysis appears in Charles J. Fillmore's 1968 "The Case for Case." Wallace Chafe's 1970 *Meaning and the Structure of Language* supplies a more detailed system of case grammar. John Anderson's 1971 *The Grammar of Case: Toward a Localistic Theory* sets forth yet another framework for case analysis. Despite the theoretical and practical differences between the systems of Fillmore, Chafe, Anderson, and others, all hold in common a concern for meaning and a similar method of identifying meaning relationships. Reviewing the challenges case grammar has faced in the decades since 1968, Gunter Radden, in "Looking Back at Case Grammar," finds much still worthwhile and appealing about the case approach, especially if it is not

Table 1. A Description of Selected Case Frames

Noun Cases
   Agent. One who performs an action. Example: The *children* ran in the grass.
   Patient. One to whom something happens. Examples: The *boy* was injured by the car. The *girls* grew two inches that summer.
   Experiencer. One who experiences perception, cognition, or feeling. Examples: *Joan* knew her father would not return. *John* felt badly about the accident.
   Beneficiary. One who gains or loses. Examples: Robert built a swing set for his *family*. *Roberta* won five dollars at the races.

Verb Classes
   State. State of being. Example: Jack is *dead*.
   Action. Doing. Example: Jill *drew* a picture.
   Process. A happening. Not an action. Example: Saintly children in literature often *died* after a long illness.
   Action/process. Doing and happening together. Example: The couple *sold* their property.

proclaimed as the solution to all problems involving the relationship between syntax and semantics or between meaning and structure.

This chapter relies primarily on Wallace Chafe's categories of cases, described in Table 1. In *Meaning and the Structure of Language*, Chafe identifies other noun cases and verb classes which are not included in Table 1 because they do not appear in the literary discussions below. Too, other case grammarians have described additional cases or have defined some of the cases in ways different from Chafe.

Research into child language acquisition has provided excellent opportunities for testing case theory. Work by Bowerman ("Structural Relationships") and work by Schlesinger ("Semantic Assimilation") indicate that a type of case system operates in children's initial word combinations. Reliance on semantic roles rather than on parts of speech or syntactic functions can be observed, for example, in such typical and early two-word utterances as "cookie hot" [a patient-state construction] or "doggie run" [an agent-action construction]. In addition, according to Retherford, Schwartz, and Chapman's "Semantic Roles and Residual Grammatical Categories in Mother and Child Speech," children have been found to model the case categories of their speech on the case categories of their mothers' speech, providing additional evidence that case roles may indeed be a fundamental part of language.[1] In an experiment described in Braine and Hardy's "On What Case Categories There Are," four-year-olds demonstrated the

22   The Voice of the Child

ability to distinguish cases by appropriately placing different shapes (triangles, circles, squares, and so on) representing different cases on pictures accompanying a sentence spoken to the children. Despite the symbolization and coordination involved in this experiment, the children performed the task easily. Numerous studies of child language verify that case role relationships have psychological reality (which means that the mind recognizes and utilizes them) and confirms that children use some sort of case grammar system in their acquisition of language.[2] Employing case grammar to analyze child language is, then, an established and acceptable procedure, though it is new here in its application to fictional child speech.

Case grammar has rarely been applied in literary studies. Walter Cook and his students at Georgetown University have examined case roles in Hemingway's *Old Man and the Sea* to characterize Hemingway's style in the novel. William Bivens has developed an interpretation of Yeats's "A Prayer for My Daughter" based on case concepts. In an examination of William Golding's *Inheritors*, M.A.K. Halliday has found that different groups of characters express different world views in the novel through different patterns of role relationships. Traugott and Pratt have explored role structures in Daniel Defoe's *Moll Flanders*, contrasting the roles Moll Flanders uses in her speech with the roles she assumes in actual behavior; this analysis demonstrates that Moll Flanders's character is ironically revealed to the reader through the disparity between the two sets of roles, the linguistic and the behavioral. In "Characterization and Language," I have shown that in Faulkner's *As I Lay Dying* each character produces identifiable and consistent patterns of role relationships which are even used by fellow characters when referring to one another; furthermore, the character-specific patterns of role relationships in Faulkner's novel accurately reflect the characters' personalities. So, although few, the case grammar studies of literature that have been done prove case grammar can be successfully used in literary analysis.

First Impressions, Lasting Images

The first few lines of a novel or short story often set the tone for the entire work. Likewise, a character's first spoken words, whether or not they coincide with the opening lines, establish that character's identity. First impressions create lasting images, and subtle variations in language use greatly influence those first impressions. A striking correlation can be found between the case constructions of first utterances of some literary children and the key features of those characters' personalities. In some instances, the case frames of initial dialogues could even serve as fictional abstracts.

In Nathaniel Hawthorne's "The Gentle Boy," which is set in the 1656 conflict between Quakers and Puritans, a child of "not more than six years" (72) lies weeping at the grave of a recently hanged Quaker. The boy speaks to a Puritan passer-by only in response to the man's direct inquiry about his name and address, "They call me Ilbrahim, and my home is here" (72). Attributing agency and action to others ("They call"), he places himself ("me") in the role of a patient, and he asserts his existence ("my home is here") in a very mild patient-state frame. The way Ilbrahim casts his sentence correctly expresses his condition, for others have acted upon him by executing his father and by leaving the boy to starve, to freeze, or to be eaten by wild animals. Lines which follow continue with the same case frames: ". . . though I be hungry and shivering with cold [patient-state, referring to self], thou wilt not give me food nor lodging [agent-negative action, referring to others]" (72). Moreover, Ilbrahim perceives himself to be like his father in his relationship to the world: ". . . my father was of the people [patient-state, referring to his father] whom all men hate [agent-action/process, referring to others]. They [others as agents] have laid [action/process] him [patient] under this heap of earth" (72). Poetically, the child concludes his speech by repeating his mild claim to existence: ". . . and here is my home [patient-state]" (72). In this story, and historically as well, the Puritan population was the agent of cruel acts against the passive and resigned Quakers. The case frames of the first few lines of Ilbrahim's speech appropriately describe the boy's personal peril at the same time that they accurately reflect the status and relationship of Quakers and Puritans within the story.

In Harper Lee's *To Kill a Mockingbird*, the case frames of the first conversation among children foreshadow what will happen in the rest of the book. Dill, a boy of six who has just arrived in town, introduces himself to Jem, nearly ten, and his sister Scout, almost six:

> "Hey [no proposition, but implies an announcement of self like, 'Notice me, everybody']."
> "Hey yourself [repeats the initial speaker's expression of attention and indicates the speaker may continue]," said Jem pleasantly.
> "I'm Charles Baker Harris [experiencer-state]," he said. "I can read [agent-action]."

"So what? [no proposition, but marks a question of the reason to assert agency, again implying a challenge]" I said.

"I just thought [experiencer-process, referring to self] you'd like to know [experiencer-process, referring to others] I can read [restates agent-action]. You got anything needs readin' [in other words, if you are a patient in need of an agent to perform an action] I can do it [agent-action, referring to self]." [11]

To Kill a Mockingbird is about children learning how to assert their identities, learning how to behave, and learning how to build relationships with others. All three points are introduced through the case frames of this opening dialogue. Dill tentatively asserts his presence with the nonpropositional "Hey." After a noncommittal response ("Hey yourself") by Jem, Dill explicitly expresses his state of being ("I'm Charles Baker Harris"). He does not let Jem and Scout reciprocate by introducing themselves, but instead he rushes ahead to announce his ability to act and to be an agent ("I can read"). Sensitive to the nuances of language and to the abrogation of polite behavior that has just occurred, Scout challenges the need for such an affront, saying, "So what?" Dill then tries to establish an atmosphere of equality by casting himself ("I just thought") and his listeners ("you'd like to know") in the same experiencer-process role relationship. Repeating his agent-action claim ("I can read"), he attempts to justify it by connecting the usefulness of that information to his audience; he suggests he is not boasting about his ability to read, but rather offering his services ("You got anything needs readin' I can do it"). This answer successfully meets the challenge of Scout's "So what?" but also carries the suggestion that Jem and Scout would be his inferiors. So, the challenges continue to be exchanged until Jem and Scout later accept Dill as a child worthy of their friendship. The case frames of the children's speech create the sense of live children talking, they establish the children's characters, and they also suggest, almost subliminally, the themes of *To Kill a Mockingbird*: developing self-identity, learning appropriate social behavior, and building interpersonal relationships.

In both *Tom Sawyer* and *Huckleberry Finn*, the case structures of Tom Sawyer's first few utterances predict his behavior throughout the novels. In the second chapter of *Adventures of Huckleberry Finn*, Tom's first spoken words are: "Now we'll start this band of robbers and call it Tom Sawyer's Gang. Everybody that wants to join has got to take an oath, and write his name in blood" (12). Tom alone has thought up this plan, and the nouns and verbs in the first sentence of his utterance have agent-action relationships, but the agency is to be shared by all the boys. Tom initiates the idea and will have the glory of the gang being named after him, but he asserts that all the boys will share the responsibility for starting and naming the gang. In the second sentence, he directs the boys to take further action, oath-taking and name-writing. Throughout the novel, Tom makes up plans and gets others to act on them. His primary character trait is established within his first statement of the novel and is revealed by the case structures—particularly the shared agency—of that statement.

Likewise, in the first scene of *Tom Sawyer*, Aunt Polly catches Tom eating forbidden jam and asks, "What you been doing in there?" He denies his agency by replying, "Nothing." She then asks what he has on his mouth, and he answers by casting himself as a negative experiencer, "*I* don't know, aunt." She recognizes the jam, however, and is ready to strike him with a switch when he quickly orders her to "Look behind you, aunt!" (40). As she turns to look, Tom flees, his escape made possible by his ability to order agency and action in others. His facility for manipulating other people serves him well, for he manages to obscure his own actions as he gets other children to paint the fence in *Tom Sawyer*, gets Huck and Jim to play his absurd rescue game in *Huck Finn*, and, throughout both novels, gets children and adults alike to do his bidding.

In *The Innocent Eye*, Albert Stone observes that while most of Samuel Clemens's child characters are passive observers and commentators on adult society, "certain of his fictional children are supremely active agents in the world of adults" (271). The larger significance of this "vacillation between assigning active and passive roles to his youthful characters" is, Stone writes, that "representing the child as victim and victor, often in the same character demonstrated unresolvable tensions within Mark Twain's outlook" (272). Though Stone does not have case grammar in mind, he nevertheless employs terminology much like case grammar's to describe the characters' language. To clarify the sense in which Clemens's child characters are agents in their behavior or in their speech, examine the examples above: the children actually achieve their aims by manipulating the actions of other people, especially adults. As David Sewell has pointed out in *Mark Twain's Languages*, Clemens was sensitive to the relationship between language and power and to the dynamics of communication between individuals. Clemens's use of dialogue and character-specific language for Tom Sawyer allows him to demonstrate how an individual, ostensibly powerless because of his age, can wield power by manipulating others.

Langston Hughes's first published novel, *Not Without Laughter*, opens with a cyclone ripping through a small Kansas town where nine-year-old Sandy lives with his parents, his grandmother, and his aunts. The boy's first words, among the first in the novel, are uttered as he and his grandmother fret about the approaching storm clouds; they reflect his concern for his family and his hope for a positive outcome: "I hope [experiencer-state] mama gets home 'fore it rains. . . . Hope she gets home" (4). His other utterances in the first chapter also show his concern for his family's state of being and for his personal feelings: "Where's my grandma?" (9). "Where you been, mama?" (11). "I been waiting [patient-process] for you" (12). "I was afraid [experiencer-state] you'd get blowed away, mama. . . . Let's go home [shared agent-action], mama. I'm glad [experiencer-state] you ain't got blowed away" (12). "Put me down, 'cause I'm awake [patient-state]" (14). Except for the request to go home, which implies a shared agency with his family, Sandy otherwise casts himself exclusively as an experiencer or as a patient in the first chapter.

Throughout the remainder of *Not Without Laughter*, Sandy continues to absorb the life of the town and to react to events in it. He is not passive or inactive, only young. As a black child in a working class household, his opportunities for direct action are limited by society's racial prejudice, by his own family's protectiveness, and by his personal preference for watching and reading rather than doing or playing. Even in the last scene of the novel, which takes place when Sandy is a teenager, the same basic pattern persists. The scene reveals Sandy working in Chicago at his mother's request but longing to return to high school. When his aunt questions him about his desire to go to school, he places himself in experiencer roles: "I want to, Aunt Harrie" (323). His aunt agrees to provide the money necessary for school, and the novel ends with Sandy poised on the brink of a more active and fulfilling life, but mindful of his family and of his hometown roots. As he hears the sound of hymns coming from a nearby church, he remarks appreciatively on his personal state of affairs and on the sounds around him by saying, "It's beautiful!" (324). From the beginning to the end, Sandy's character is consistently concerned with states and experiences, and thus the case frames of his utterances convey his characterization.

Connections between case, character, and theme can also be demonstrated in popular fiction. For instance, in Stephen King's 1980 *Firestarter*, the story of an eight-year-old girl who can ignite people or objects merely by thinking about them, the first lines are those of the girl Charlie herself: "Daddy, I'm tired. . . . Can't we stop?" (1). Her words show concern for her state of being, casting herself ("I'm tired") in an experiencer-state role. As readers quickly discover, her strange existence and the unfolding of her experiences are the focus of the novel. Destructive acts occur throughout, and this, too, seems to be foreshadowed by her early agent-negative action expression ("Can't we stop?"). A book whose first sentence describes a sense of weariness and a desire to stop might not leave itself much room for development, but King still clearly portrays Charlie's states of mind throughout the novel. Perhaps Charlie's characterization comes alive because, as King announces in his afterword, interacting with his own daughter helped him understand how a young girl might think and react.

Overall, literary children place themselves in experiencer-state roles more often than in agent-action roles. This can be partially explained by children's powerlessness to act in terms of physical strength, legal recourse, and so on. Yet even in *Firestarter*, Charlie's ability to start fires imprisons rather than empowers her. However, experiencer roles make sense for children because they are life's ultimate experiencers; to them everything is new and must be sensed and understood for the first time from their own fresh perspectives. Experiencing the fullness of life is a common theme that coexists happily and not coincidentally with the large numbers of young characters in American fiction.

It should be no surprise, then, to find a child character frequently serving as the voice of an author, for artists often concern themselves with the impact of experiences on the individual and with the search to express those experiences. In *Call It Sleep*, David Schearl's first spoken words are a five-year-old's plea, "Mama, I want a drink" (17). More polite than the alternative "Get me a drink," the experiencer-process words ("I want") emphasize the self and how the self feels, an appropriate start for a book presenting an introspective look at the developing consciousness of a sensitive and poetic boy modeled on the author himself. In *Tar*, Sherwood Anderson's representation of his own boyhood, the link between the child and the artist is plainly stated in the introductory passages of the book and can be demonstrated in a line from his boyhood, "I see the man running" (7). From the experience of his childhood ("I see") observing the agency of another ("a man running"), Anderson says he later created the story "The Untold Lie" in *Winesburg, Ohio*. A major theme in *Winesburg* concerns people watching one another's actions.

In *Look Homeward, Angel*, Thomas Wolfe's fictionalized account of his own life, the main character's role as an experiencer begins in the cradle. As Eugene Gant lies in his crib listening to the rest of the family eating Sunday dinner, he dreams of the day when "I shall be in there with them" (38). Wolfe thus credits Gant with the ability to form sentences before he can speak them, and his prespeech thought ("I shall be in there with them") is cast in an experiencer-state frame as it considers the actions of others. This first thought-statement is, ironically for a retrospective book, excited by the possibilities of future events; in *Look Homeward, Angel* an adult artist, the author, looks back on experiences to which the juvenile artist, the character, looks forward.

Examining the case frames of characters' direct discourses need not blind us to other features of their language. For example, the young hero Nat speaks the first line of Louisa May Alcott's *Little Men*, "Please, sir, is this Plumfield?" (1) and a question about location is a reasonable utterance for an orphan who has yet to find his place in the world. But if we look only at the semantic relationship between the nouns and verb, we miss the politeness of the speech which enables Nat to gain acceptance into the school and into the hearts of the people there. In James T. Farrell's *Young Lonigan*, the first words of Studs Lonigan as he contemplates his grammar school graduation are, "Well, I'm kissin' the old dump goodbye tonight" (17). The agent-action/ process basis of the sentence ("I'm kissin'") foreshadows the future course of Studs's life, which is tragically full of action and misguided agency. But, obviously, more is expressed by his initial language use than can be picked up by looking only at the case roles. Equally important to his characterization and to the tone of the book are Studs's slang, his disparaging description of school, and even his pronunciation of "kissin'." Case role analysis cannot tell us everything we as readers need to know about characters and their fictional environments. Still, case roles contain useful and important information, and an examination of the case constructions of literary children's first spoken words provides insight into the children's characters, into their situations, and into the themes of the surrounding work.

Maisie and Lolita: Little Victims?

Most fictional characters face difficulties or complications in their lives, but a few experience outright victimization. Such would seem to be the case in Henry James's *What Maisie Knew* and in Vladimir Nabokov's *Lolita*. Both novels have provoked much critical discussion, but, in the furor over their controversial depictions of society, the question of how the young characters Maisie and Lolita view their circumstances usually goes unnoticed. How do the two girls feel about the ways adults treat them? Do they perceive themselves as victims? The case roles of the girls' speech offer a good starting point for investigating their views, for case role analysis gives us information about a person's or a character's self-presentation. Both James and Nabokov are acknowledged as masters of language and the subtleties of language, so close attention to their characters' speech is warranted. In fact, what Randall Craig has said about *What Maisie Knew* and its "linguistic texture . . . [which] compels readers into increasingly active interpretation" (210) could be a challenge for reading both *Maisie* and *Lolita*: "readers must hermeneutically produce, not romantically consume the text" (212).

What Maisie Knew and *Lolita* both describe children caught up in the affairs of adults. In a shared custody arrangement less shocking today than in James's time, Maisie's divorced parents war with one another by forcing each other to take care of the child. Maisie manages to retain a unique sense of purity and justice, though she is affected by the unconventional lifestyles of her parents and step-parents who use her for their own purposes. James himself calls her a "little victim" (Preface v). In *Lolita*, Humbert Humbert's aesthetic appreciation of the loveliness of young girls he terms "nymphets" (18) has a plainly physical side which he practices, but does not explicitly describe, with Dolores Haze, better known as Lolita. Thus, Humbert finds Lolita to be an object for the fulfillment of his own needs rather than a child with needs of her own.

Lolita's conversations revolve mainly around herself or Humbert, though we should remember that Humbert narrates the story, so her speech has been filtered through his point of view. The chart in Table 2 is based on a case role analysis of all of Lolita's utterances until the time she leaves Humbert. Due to her age, Lolita could no longer be considered a child after she leaves Humbert, and her direct speech is not reported after that point until a final meeting with the older man in a conversation to be examined separately.

A review of the data summarized in Table 2 indicates Lolita sees herself as capable of initiating action, for she casts herself as an agent almost as many times as she does Humbert, and her agency also occurs with a greater frequency than that of most other fictional juveniles. Her percentage of patient roles is exactly the same as Humbert's, suggesting that she does not, on the whole, see herself as a victim of his or of other people's actions. Lolita presents herself and Humbert with the same percentage of beneficiary cases, so, on balance, she does not show either Humbert or herself gaining or losing

Table 2. Case Roles in Lolita's Speech

Lolita refers to herself 100 times. Out of 100 references, she places herself in the following roles:

Case role	Number	Percentage
Agent	43	43
Experiencer	37	37
Patient	18	18
Beneficiary	2	2

Lolita refers to Humbert 83 times. Out of 83 references, she places him in the following roles:

Case role	Number	Percentage
Agent	45	54
Experiencer	21	25
Patient	15	18
Beneficiary	2	2

more than the other. Like the literary children discussed earlier in this chapter, Lolita puts herself in an experiencer role more than she places an adult in that role.

A different picture of Lolita's self-image emerges, however, when we examine her speech in separate sections of the novel. The narrative could be divided into six sections based on important events in Lolita's life. The first section, in which she appears to be innocent of any conscious sexual overtures, lasts until Humbert removes her from summer camp. The second section describes their first trip and their first hotel check-in before the seduction. At this time, Lolita knows nothing of her mother's death but has just been, she later tells Humbert, initiated into sexual relations at the camp. In this section she makes teasing remarks such as, "Say, wouldn't Mother be absolutely mad if she found out that we [shared experiencers] were lovers?" (105).The third section includes Lolita's and Humbert's first overtly sexual act together. The fourth section, in which Lolita willingly remains with Humbert, lasts until he tells Lolita about her mother's death; she then becomes trapped because she has nowhere else to go. The fifth section stretches across their trans-America travels, across Lolita's year at school, and across their return to the road until she leaves Humbert sometime in her fourteenth year. This long fifth section could be subdivided into various parts, but one constant factor uniting the section is that Lolita expresses dissatisfaction with her relationship to Humbert but has no other person to whom she can turn for help. A final section includes their last encounter when Lolita is a married seventeen-year-old whose husband knows nothing of her past; Lolita, of course, would not be considered a child in this section.

A chart detailing all the case frames of Lolita's speech as a child in the first five sections of the book can be found in Table 3. Several observations can be made about the information gathered in Table 3. In the first two sections of the novel, Lolita speaks of Humbert almost as many times (45 references) as she speaks of herself (51 references). She presents both herself and Humbert as agents with a very high rate of frequency, but she casts Humbert as a patient twice as often as herself. So, in the early stages of their relationship, Lolita perceives herself—or Humbert presents her as perceiving herself—in control of her situation, and she also perceives the older man as more vulnerable, that is, more the recipient of action, than herself.

The turning point of their relationship occurs during their first sexual act together. Lolita describes a game she played at camp, but Humbert professes ignorance:

> "You [experiencer] mean," she persisted, now kneeling above me, "you [negative agent] never did it when you [experiencer] were a kid?"
> "Never," I answered quite truthfully.
> "Okay," said Lolita, "here is where we [shared agent] start." [123]

Lolita's only agent structure in this section of the novel is shared here with Humbert in the pronoun *we*. So Lolita seems to be a willing partner and could perhaps even be considered to initiate sex with him. At least, this is the conclusion of Humbert, who tries to rationalize his behavior by providing evidence for his argument that "it was she who seduced me" (122) and that "I was not even her first lover" (125).

Readers have disagreed and will continue to disagree over whether Humbert's evidence about who seduced whom is convincing. For example, in "'My Ultraviolet Darling': The Loss of Lolita's Childhood," Robert Levine argues that Humbert is responsible for ending Lolita's childhood. On the other hand, critics such as Leslie Fiedler *(Love and Death)* and Lionel Trilling ("The Last Lover") tend to accept Humbert's version of the origin and nature of his relationship with Lolita.

What Lolita thinks is not entirely clear. For some time after her first direct sexual encounter with Humbert, few of her remarks are

32   The Voice of the Child

Table 3. Case Frames of Lolita's Speech in Sections of *Lolita*

Section I ends when Humbert removes Lolita from camp. Section II ends when they check into a motel. Section III ends when they leave the motel. Section IV ends when Lolita is told of her mother's death. Section V ends when Lolita leaves Humbert.

Section I

Case	Number	Percentage
Lolita as:		
Agent	4	44
Experiencer	3	33
Patient	1	11
Beneficiary	1	11
Total	9	
Humbert as:		
Agent	5	71
Experiencer	0	0
Patient	2	29
Beneficiary	0	0
Total	7	

Section II

Case	Number	Percentage
Lolita as:		
Agent	23	55
Experiencer	14	33
Patient	5	12
Beneficiary	0	0
Total	42	
Humbert as:		
Agent	18	71
Experiencer	8	0
Patient	11	29
Beneficiary	1	3
Total	38	

Section III

Case	Number	Percentage
Lolita as:		
Agent	1	100

Table 3—Continued

Experiencer	0	0
Patient	0	0
Beneficiary	0	0
Total	1	

Humbert as:

Agent	7	70
Experiencer	3	30
Patient	0	0
Beneficiary	0	0
Total	10	

Section IV

Case	*Number*	*Percentage*
Lolita as:		
Agent	4	36
Experiencer	4	36
Patient	3	27
Beneficiary	0	0
Total	11	
Humbert as:		
Agent	6	67
Experiencer	3	33
Patient	0	0
Beneficiary	0	0
Total	9	

Section V

Case	*Number*	*Percentage*
Lolita as:		
Agent	11	30
Experiencer	16	43
Patient	9	24
Beneficiary	1	3
Total	37	
Humbert as:		
Agent	9	48
Experiencer	7	37
Patient	2	11
Beneficiary	1	5
Total	9	

reported. But later that day when Humbert alludes to the possibility of a tryst in the woods, Lolita is blunt: "You [experiencer] revolting creature. I [experiencer] was a daisy-fresh girl, and look what you've [agent] done to me [patient]" (130). She even threatens to tell the police "you [agent] raped me [patient]" (130). Humbert reports that Lolita smiles as she says this, but that "an ominous hysterical note rang through her silly words" (129). He is uncertain how to interpret her speech, perhaps because it is not consistent with what he wants to believe. It is then that Humbert tells Lolita of her mother's death.

In the first three sections of the novel, Lolita has a low percentage of speech describing herself as a patient (11 percent, 12 percent, and 0 percent), but after she and Humbert become sexual partners, the percentages double (27 percent in the fourth section and 24 percent in the last). The reverse change occurs in her references to Humbert as a patient: 29 percent in the first section, 29 percent in the second, 0 percent in the third, 0 percent again in the fourth, and 11 percent in the fifth. However, the older Lolita gets, the less often she speaks of Humbert. A significant percentage difference also occurs in the decline of Lolita's rate of agency in the fourth and fifth sections of the novel (36 percent and 30 percent) as compared to the earlier sections (44 percent, 55 percent, and 100 percent). And, as Lolita gets older, she casts herself in an experiencer role more frequently until such roles account for 43 percent of her speech in the fifth section.

Although Lolita is not a child at the end of the novel, she does have one last scene in which her speech is directly reported. In Lolita's final meeting with Humbert, she appears as a pregnant seventeen-year-old who refers to herself seventeen times. In nine of those seventeen references, she casts herself as an experiencer, in five as an agent, and in three as a patient. All three patient references are to herself and her husband grouped together under the pronoun us. In addition to these three patient references for herself and her husband, Lolita describes her husband as an agent once and as an experiencer twice. Humbert she casts as a patient once, as an experiencer five times, as an agent six times. Besides the new development of aligning herself with her husband, Lolita's speech in this last section emphasizes her emerging identity as an experiencer rather than an agent or a patient.

All these changes appear in Lolita's language even though the story is told by Humbert and even though her speech has been filtered through his point of view. Taken together, the shifts in Lolita's speech patterns suggest, first, that the child gradually becomes more in touch with the reality of her situation and more in touch with her own feelings and, second, that as time passes she sees herself more as the recipient of action rather than the initiator of action. In her final meeting with Humbert when she is married and pregnant, Lolita bears no obvious ill will toward the older man, but she is nevertheless anxious to let the past remain in the past. She may never feel hostile enough or victimized enough to prosecute him, but she does, after all, leave him as soon as she is able, and her language does show marked changes as the novel progresses.

In *Marvell, Nabokov: Childhood and Arcadia*, Michael Long observes that one of the key themes in Nabokov's fiction is the concept of childhood as an Arcadia doomed to destruction yet always remaining a rich sourcebook for the imagination. This concept of childhood clearly operates in *Lolita*. Quite the opposite concept operates in *What Maisie Knew*; Maisie's prospects improve rather than darken as she leaves childhood behind and as the novel closes. Maisie's girlhood is not viewed by James or any of his characters as an Arcadia, and her youth is not an imaginative sourcebook for Maisie or the adults around her. Maisie's childhood finally ends, but neither she in particular nor childhood in general is destroyed by its conclusion.

Part of the distinction in the plots and themes of the two novels may derive from distinctions in the two girls' experiences. Maisie's exposure to adult sexuality is more subtle than Lolita's. Ruth Yeazell has pointed out in *Language and Knowledge in the Late Novels of Henry James* that in *Maisie* and in James's other novels of the late 1890s, "sexual passion becomes the central mystery, the hidden knowledge which the Jamesian innocent must at last confront" (20). Nevertheless, James does not at any time say that Maisie is directly involved sexually with the adults, though the linguistic dynamics between Maisie and Sir Claude (shared statements of agency, frequent references by her to him, and terms of endearment) have some similarities to the linguistic dynamics of verbal exchanges between Lolita and Humbert.

Beginning at the age of six, Maisie is treated—or mistreated—in an unseemly way by her father's friends: "Some of these gentlemen made her strike matches and light their cigarettes; others, holding her on knees violently jolted, pinched the calves of her legs till she shrieked" (10). But at her mother's, Maisie is so verbally abused by women that she comes to prefer the company of those men (37). Neither parent prepares a suitable home for the child. In *Women: The Longest Revolution*, Juliet Mitchell compares Maisie to a billiard ball shot about by the adult characters, and, using this billiard analogy, Mitchell asks the same question we are investigating, "Is the ball the victim of the game?" (179). To understand Maisie's perspective on her

Table 4. Case Roles in Maisie's Speech

Character referred to by Maisie	Case roles—Number and percentage*			
	Agent	Patient	Experiencer	Beneficiary
Maisie	73 - 26%	67 - 24%	141 - 50%	2 - 1%
Father	14 - 39	8 - 22	13 - 36	1 - 3
Mother	27 - 45	15 - 25	16 - 27	2 - 3
Mrs. Beale	49 - 35	41 - 29	46 - 33	4 - 3
Sir Claude	76 - 39	57 - 30	57 - 30	3 - 2
Mrs. Wix	24 - 39	20 - 33	17 - 28	0 - 0

*Number refers to the total number of times Maisie places herself or another character in a particular case frame. Percentages for each character are based on the number of references Maisie makes to that character.

situation, we can turn to the case roles in her direct discourse references to herself and to the other main characters. Maisie's case role usages are summarized in Table 4. All of Maisie's approximately 500 spontaneous utterances are included in this data; the only exclusions are those quotations such as her first—" 'He said I was to tell you, from him,' she faithfully reported, 'that you're a nasty horrid pig'" (13)—which merely repeat what her elders have instructed her to say.

Throughout the novel Maisie consistently refers to the adults with similar percentages of case roles. Thus, Maisie's speech patterns maintain the "proper symmetry" James said he intended (Preface v) for the relationships between the adult characters. For example, although Maisie never refers to Mrs. Wix as a beneficiary, one who gains or loses, only 2 or 3 percent of her references to the other adults places them as beneficiaries. Likewise, although Maisie's speech casts her mother as an agent in 45 percent of her references to her mother, the other adults are characterized by Maisie as agents almost as often, from 35 to 39 percent of the time. While Maisie places her father in the role of an experiencer in 36 percent of her references to him, she shows the other adults to be experiencers only slightly less often, from 27 percent of the references to her mother to 33 percent of the references to Mrs. Beale. Maisie's references to the adults as patients, recipients of action, are not as balanced as the distributions of her other case references, but her perception of the adults as patients matches the amount of control or lack of control they actually exert in the novel. That is, Mrs. Wix, the adult with the lowest social power, is shown most often as a patient, whereas Maisie's father, arguably the adult who has or should have the most control over his circumstances, appears least often as a patient in Maisie's speech.

Maisie's references to herself, however, differ from her references to the adults. Most noticeably, as well as typically childlike, she places herself in an experiencer role in 50 percent of her self-references, much more often than she places adults in that role. Maisie's speech emphasizes the importance of her experiences, of what she sees and feels and knows. As if to reinforce the title and theme of the book, Maisie repeats the experiencer-process phrase "I know" over and over; it is even her last utterance of the novel (363). Because the child has no formal education, no religious training, no friends, and no outside interests, she has nothing to do except watch the adult behavior and language around her. Also, although Maisie's references to herself as a patient are not that much different from her patient references to the adults, her references to herself as an agent are substantially fewer than her references to any of the adults as agents. Taken together, these two case role representations indicate that though Maisie does not see herself as the recipient of adult actions to an unusual degree, neither does she see herself as able to act very much within the adult world.

Maisie refers to herself as a patient less often than she refers to Mrs. Beale (the lover of her father and later of Sir Claude), Sir Claude (the lover of her mother and later of Mrs. Beale), Mrs. Wix (her caretaker) or Mrs. Farange (her mother) as patients. So, it would seem she does not view herself as a victim of circumstances or as a victim of adult misbehavior. Even, as in Table 5, when we divide the novel into sections based on Maisie's youngest years (Chapters 1-9), her experiences with Sir Claude (Chapters 10-28), and the conversations leading to her decision to stay with Mrs. Wix (Chapters 29-31), we discover that in all three sections, she casts herself in patient roles less than she does any other character. In fact, unlike the changes in Lolita's speech over the course of Nabokov's novel, the changes in Maisie's speech in different parts of James's novel are not dramatic, though some subtle shifts do occur.

The concluding scenes of the novel, the ones in which Maisie must decide what she will do and with whom she will go, should clearly be discussed separately, much as the pivotal early scene at the motel in Lolita deserves to be analyzed individually. Although Maisie's other experiences could be subdivided in various ways, her direct interactions with Sir Claude signal a new phase in her life for two reasons. First, the complications of Sir Claude and Mrs. Beale are then added to those of Ida and Beale Farange, creating an even more complex emotional web for Maisie to struggle against. Second, Sir Claude is the only person in the novel whose attention to Maisie is not solely motivated by a desire to use her for leverage against someone else. Table 5 provides a complete breakdown of Maisie's case roles in these three sections of the novel: her early years, her interactions with Sir Claude, and her time of final decision. (The format of this chart differs from the one of Lolita's speech because Maisie interacts with five adults whereas Lolita interacts mainly with only one.)

The up-and-down shifts in personal relationships and in power positions during the three sections of the novel can be traced through identifiable shifts within Maisie's language. For example, Maisie's father is completely out of the picture by the third section, but before he goes, Maisie reverses the case roles of her references to him; in the first section, Maisie refers to him half of the time as an experiencer and only once as an agent, but in the second section, she refers to him as an agent almost half of the time, while substantially reducing her references to him as an experiencer. In contrast, in the first section, Maisie never refers to her mother as an experiencer, while in the second section, she makes several references to her as an experiencer. Also, in the second section the rate of agency Maisie attributes to her mother increases to nearly 50 percent of her references. So, in some ways, the case frames Maisie uses for her mother and father are almost opposites. Changes in their positions of power are mirrored by changes in Maisie's manner of speaking about her parents. The types of references Maisie makes to Mrs. Beale and to Sir Claude are similar in both their total averages and individual section averages, except that Maisie's language casts Sir Claude as an agent more often in the second section. The emerging dominance of Mrs. Wix also appears in Maisie's language, for Mrs. Wix becomes a prominent agent in the final section, primarily at the expense of her experiencer roles, which are cut dramatically in both their number and their percentage of occurrences.

Maisie's self-references in the three sections also change, though not sharply. The data in Table 5 concerning Maisie's use of patient cases for herself almost lead to the conclusion that Maisie must be operating under a hostage mentality, loving her captors and denying their control over her. Yet, again, Maisie does not use many agent cases for her self-references, either, so if she does not perceive herself as a victim, neither does she perceive herself as having much power to act. She may become more aware of her situation as she gets older, for as the novel progresses, her rate of agency declines while her rate of patient cases increases in self-reference. In addition, she places herself in agent roles much less on average than she places adults in that frame, and many of the agency statements she has are actually nega-

Case Grammar 39

Table 5. Case Frames of Maisie's Speech in Sections I–III of *What Maisie Knew**

	Case roles—Number and percentage**			
Character***	Agent	Patient	Experiencer	Beneficiary
Maisie				
I	4 - 36%	1 - 10%	6 - 55%	0 - 0%
II	40 - 25	31 - 19	89 - 56	0 - 0
III	29 - 32	15 - 16	46 - 50	2 - 2
Total or average	73 - 26	67 - 24	141 - 50	2 - 1
Father				
I	1 - 13	2 - 25	4 - 50	1 - 13
II	13 - 46	6 - 21	9 - 32	0 - 0
III	0 - 0	0 - 0	0 - 0	0 - 0
Total or average	14 - 39	8 - 22	13 - 36	1 - 3
Mother				
I	1 - 25	2 - 50	0 - 0	1 - 25
II	24 - 50	10 - 21	13 - 27	1 - 2
III	2 - 25	3 - 38	3 - 38	0 - 0
Total or average	27 - 45	15 - 25	16 - 27	2 - 3
Mrs. Beale				
I	0 - 0	3 - 38	5 - 63	0 - 0
II	26 - 36	19 - 26	25 - 34	3 - 4
III	23 - 39	19 - 32	16 - 27	1 - 2
Total or average	49 - 35	41 - 29	46 - 33	4 - 3
Sir Claude				
I	0 - 0	3 - 38	5 - 63	0 - 0
II	52 - 48	28 - 26	27 - 25	2 - 2
III	24 - 32	26 - 34	25 - 33	1 - 1
Total or average	76 - 39	57 - 30	57 - 30	3 - 2
Mrs. Wix				
I	0 - 0	1 - 50	1 - 50	0 - 0
II	8 - 26	9 - 29	14 - 45	0 - 0
III	16 - 57	10 - 36	2 - 7	0 - 0
Total or average	24 - 39	20 - 33	17 - 28	0 - 0

*Roman numerals indicate the sections of the book. In Section I (Chapters 1-9), Maisie is tossed from parent to parent. In Section II (Chapters 10-28), the complications of Sir Claude and Mrs. Beale are added to those of Ida and Beale Farange. In Section III (Chapters 29-31), Maisie must choose with whom she will live.

**Number means the number of references Maisie makes to each character in each case. Percentages are based on the number of references per section or per total which Maisie makes to each character.

***Character means the character to whom Maisie refers in her direct quotations.

tives, as, "Well, you know, I'll never [negative agent] tell" (155). When she does cast herself as an agent, Maisie concentrates on her one accomplishment, bringing together Mrs. Beale and Sir Claude. Most of her utterances referring to herself as a positive agent are variations of the often repeated phrase "I brought you together" (340). Maisie's pleasure at having been the operative agent in their meeting weighs heavily in her ultimate decision to go with Mrs. Wix rather than to force Sir Claude to promise what he may not be able to do—give up Mrs. Beale.

Previous literary critics have variously interpreted the novel's controversial conclusion in which Maisie decides to leave with Mrs. Wix.[3] A case grammar analysis of Maisie's speech allows us to develop an interpretation of the ending based on an understanding of Maisie's final choice within the context of the language she exchanges with the adults. In the last chapter Maisie says, "I [experiencer] feel as if I [beneficiary] had lost everything" (353). Whatever she chooses to do, stay with Sir Claude or go with Mrs. Wix, she will lose something or someone; in case grammar terms, she will become a beneficiary. If she goes with Mrs. Wix, she will lose Sir Claude. However, if Maisie should convince Sir Claude to leave Mrs. Beale, Maisie would negate her primary act of positive agency. Looked at in this way from Maisie's point of view as expressed in her direct discourse and read with an appreciation of the importance Maisie places on her successful agency, her decision to leave with the old governess is not so very surprising.

Linguistic signals differentiate the individual situations of Lolita and Maisie. Maisie's few positive statements of agency indicate her powerlessness. Lolita's speech evolves, and her declining agent case roles and her increasing patient case roles in the second half of the novel represent her growing awareness of being less able to act and of being more often the recipient of action. Though readers may view Maisie and Lolita as victims sacrificed at the altar of adult sexuality and may marvel at the lack of overt signs of discontent and anger in the girls' language patterns, their characters might be interpreted as showing the resiliency and adaptability of children. Both Maisie and Lolita, growing up without much knowledge of other families and other possibilities, manage to get along in life by accepting their circumstances until, with childhood at an end, they are old enough to make their own choices. Unfortunately for Maisie and, especially, for Lolita, many factors in their early experiences have limited their range of choices and narrowed their possibilities.

As we have seen in this consideration of the childhood speech of

Maisie, Lolita, Tom, Jem, Scout, Dill, Studs, Sandy, Nat, Eugene, Tar, David, Charlie, and Ilbrahim, case grammar provides us with a methodology useful for discussing various aspects of literary discourse. Through a case grammar analysis of fictional discourse, we can develop text-specific interpretations for characters and their situations. Though there is no universally accepted explanation for the relationship between semantics and syntax—that is, between meaning and structure—case grammar seeks to establish the roots of meaning by integrating syntax with semantics. Case grammar, bridging the gap between ideas and the expression of ideas, allows us to begin identifying the elusive glimmers of meaning that lie just below the conscious surface of language.

4. Functions of Child Speech

Sidestepping the controversial relationship between meaning and structure, some linguists contend that a functional basis for language must be present before either semantics or syntax comes into the picture. M.A.K. Halliday defines speech functions as the "uses of language," adding that the functionalist approach is concerned with "how people use language and . . . how language varies according to its use" (*Explorations in the Functions of Language* 37).[1] In her book *Language and Context: The Acquisition of Pragmatics*, Elizabeth Bates expresses the attitude of those who view pragmatics as the foundation for language: "Recent psycholinguistic research . . . has suggested that syntax might be derived ontogenetically from semantics. We are carrying that suggestion a step farther, proposing that semantics is derived ontogenetically from pragmatics" (354). Here Bates says that syntactic structures develop to express meaning and that practical situations are the basis for the need to express meaning. John W. DuBois, in an essay in *Language*, goes so far as to state that "we should not be surprised if, in the coming years, more and more of the most fundamental aspects of grammar are revealed as shaped by language use" (851).

In his article on "Children's Conversations" in the *Handbook of Discourse Analysis*, John Dore counts functionalism as one of the three major influences on child discourse studies. The functions of child speech invite special interest because in children's conversations functions are more discrete, whereas in adult speech an individual utterance often relates to a multitude of functions simultaneously. Still, numerous factors complicate the examination of children's speech functions. For instance, as Katherine Nelson has illustrated in "Explorations in the Development of a Functional Semantic System" and in "The Syntagmatics and Paradigmatics of Conceptual Development," the cognitive development of the speaker affects the way a child uses language. As Joan Tough has found, a correlation also exists between children's social classes and language use. So the functions of children's speech are affected by factors similar to those influencing adult speech and by factors unique to children. Of course, the more variables one admits as present in speech situations, the wider the topic of functions becomes, and the more difficult formulating a coherent language model becomes.

A number of models have been proposed to code the various functions of language. In his book *Discourse Analysis*, Michael Stubbs follows Dell Hymes's division of speech types into the following seven categories: expressive/emotive; directive/conative/persuasive; poetic; contact (physical or psychological); metalinguistic (focusing on meaning); referential; and contextual/situational (46). M.A.K. Halliday's functional categories in *Explorations in the Functions of Language* are derived from the uses of language he witnessed in his own son. He posits that the same functions are observable in adult speech, but are better regrouped under one of two macrofunctions, which he names ideational speech and interpersonal speech, since adult conversations are usually not motivated by one single goal at a time. Other researchers have proposed other functions, other labels for functions, and other systems of functions.

Discussions in this chapter rely primarily on the coding system developed by Thelma Weeks in *Born to Talk*. Weeks's system incorporates the research of many people, but draws most heavily on M.A.K. Halliday's 1975 *Explorations in the Functions of Language*. Not only does Weeks's system incorporate prior work, but it also attempts to be comprehensive, and it has been further tested on children in an extensive study conducted by Weeks herself. In *Born to Talk* Weeks describes ten communicative functions and seven noncommunicative functions of child speech. These two sets of functions are enumerated in Table 6 and are further discussed in the remainder of this introductory section.

Noncommunicative speech differs from communicative speech in that the noncommunicative variety is not directed at an outside audience. People routinely talk to themselves to plan schedules, to avoid thinking about an unpleasant subject, to congratulate themselves, to practice an anticipated conversation, or to replay mentally a verbal

Table 6. Communicative and Noncommunicative Functions of Child Speech (Adapted from Chapter 1 of *Born to Talk*)

Communicative function	How used
Instrumental	To request personal needs
Regulatory	To control others' behavior
Interactional	To facilitate communication
Personal	To express feelings
Heuristic	To question for learning
Imaginative	To play, to make up stories
Informational	To inform
Poetic	To focus on sounds
Interpretive	To recall, plan, or interpret
Performative	To promise or to bet
Noncommunicative funciton	*How Used*
Language Play	To amuse and to create
Metalingual	To practice language
Concept Formation	To develop ideas
Self-directing	To direct one's behavior
Self-image Formation	To define roles
Avoidance	To avoid something else
Magical	To imbue words with power

exchange that has already occurred. Adults generally do not talk to themselves aloud, but children frequently do. Weeks, like Piaget, observes a strong tendency toward noncommunicative speech in young children, yet writers rarely portray children in literature using speech which is not part of a conversation with another individual or group.

The labels and short explanations for the noncommunicative functions in Table 6 are self-explanatory, although the magical function may merit a special note since the magical power of words is widely accepted by primitive cultures or, as Walter Ong has termed them, oral peoples. The belief that words have magical powers may even explain such cross-cultural phenomena as cursing. Young children often think of language as having magical properties and, as Vygotsky and others have found, are especially prone to identify an object with its name. Very young children may not perceive the symbolic nature of language in the same way that adults do, and children may use language in a creatively magical way more than most adults.

The labels for the communicative functions of child language, listed in Table 6 in the general order in which children most often acquire them, require some additional clarification.

Instrumental speech conveys needs or protests such as "I want some juice" or "No!" The first reported child speech in Henry Roth's *Call It Sleep* illustrates the instrumental function: "Mama, I want a drink" (17).

The regulatory function, which can sometimes overlap with the requests of instrumental speech, aims to control the behavior of others, usually with demands such as "Watch me." It is used in *The Scarlet Letter*, for instance, when Pearl tries to get her mother to tell her a story. Regulatory speech is not necessarily dishonorable, but naughty children in literature frequently try to manipulate others in obvious and transparent ways by using regulatory language. This happens, for example, in Faulkner's "That Evening Sun" when Jason, always selfish and sneaky, says he will behave properly only if Dilsey bakes a chocolate cake.

The ways we manage to get other people to do something for us through regulatory language have been intensely studied. Brown and Levinson have formulated a model of such strategies organized by levels of politeness in adult speech, and Susan Ervin-Tripp has made a similar analysis of child speech. Ervin-Tripp ("Wait for Me, Roller Skate" 165) says that up to half of child speech is regulatory, that both form and content of children's directives change as children get older, and that children learn to alter their regulatory speech to fit the social circumstances of an exchange. Likewise, in "Pragmatics of Directive Choice Among Children," Claudia Mitchell-Kernan and Keith T. Kernan conclude that children's regulatory speech is very much like adults' and that, sensitive to the rank and status of their audience, older children gear the forms of their demands to suit their listeners and to maximize their chances for getting what they want.

Interactional speech covers greetings and departures as well as phrases used to open or connect conversations. "Know what?" or "Let's talk about . . ." or "That's true, but . . ." are examples of interactional language. In Faulkner's *The Sound and the Fury*, Caddy uses interactional speech with Benjy when she encounters him on her way home from school: "'Hello Benjy.' Caddy said. She opened the gate and came in and stooped down. Caddy smelled like leaves. 'Did you come in to meet me.' she said. 'Did you come to meet Caddy'" (5).

The personal function includes expressions of feelings such as, "I think you're beautiful," "I'm tired," or "That's hard for me to do." In the opening scene of E.B. White's *Charlotte's Web*, the girl Fern prevents her father from killing the runt of a pig litter, so her father gives the helpless pig to Fern to raise. Delighted, Fern cannot take her eyes off the pig and gushes, "He's absolutely perfect" (4). Another example of personal speech occurs in Carson McCullers's *The Member of the*

Wedding when Frankie says of her cousin John Henry, with whom she has spent the day talking and playing, "I'm sick and tired of him" (7).

Heuristic language is used by a child exploring the environment or trying to learn about something. Typically, it takes the form of questions, often *why* questions. Heuristic speech is used, for example, by Pecola in Toni Morrison's *The Bluest Eye* in a conversation among young girls discussing where babies come from. Pecola asks, "Well, if the belly buttons are to grow like-lines to give the baby blood, and only girls have babies, how come boys have belly buttons?" (59). More simply, in Steven Millhauser's *Edwin Mullhouse*, the narrator informs the reader that Edwin's "favorite word between the ages of two and three was 'Wussat?' accompanied by a pointing finger" (38). Not all questions are heuristic, though. Depending on context, "Know what I'm thinking about?" might be interactional, while "Would you get me a drink?" could be regulatory. Sharon James and Martha Seebach ("The Pragmatic Function of Children's Questions") find that while all children use questioning language to gain knowledge, younger children use it primarily for that purpose, while older children produce questions with various intents.

Story-telling, fantasy play, and games require imaginative speech. This form of children's language does not appear in literature as often as in life, but instances of it can be found, for example, in Sylvia Wilkinson's *Bone of My Bones*; interspersed among sections of narrative and dialogue in this novel are stories, fantasies, and dreams created by the main character, the child Ella Ruth Higgins.

The poetic function under Weeks's coding system is different from the imaginative function and mainly involves the manipulation of sounds, as in singing or making up new words. In pointing out that poetic speech is not restricted to reciting or inventing poetry, Weeks notes (15) that the poetic function's focus on sounds is crucial in advertising slogans. Indeed, commercial jingles are among many children's first complete phrases, but children can be inventive as well as imitative in poetic speech. A literary example of a child's poetic language which is also imaginative—not to mention symbolically significant in its context—appears in *Moby-Dick* when Pip says, "I look, you look, he looks; we look, ye look, they look.... And I, you, and he; and we, ye, and they, are all bats; and I'm a crow, especially when I stand a'top of this pine tree here. Caw! caw! caw! caw! caw!" (362). Due to Pip's young age and his psychological wounds, he does not understand his own utterance beyond the level of sound play.

Declarative sentences conveying information usually fill an informative function. For example, when Seymour Glass in J.D. Salinger's

"A Perfect Day for Bananafish" (11) asks the little girl on the beach, "What's new?" she provides the informative fact: "My daddy's coming tomorrow on a nairiplane" (11).

Interpretive speech, on the other hand, involves more reasoning and more abstract thinking, as in solving problems recalling experiences, or interpreting the meaning of events. This manner of speaking is demonstrated in Betty Smith's *A Tree Grows in Brooklyn* when the girl Francie reflects on the way pregnant women of different ethnic backgrounds behave, remembering her mother's comment that Jews still await the Messiah:

> "I guess that's why the Jews have so many babies. . . . And why they aren't ashamed the way they are fat. Each one thinks that she might be making the real little Jesus. That's why they walk so proud when they're that way. Now the Irish women always look so ashamed. They know that they can never make a Jesus. It will just be another Mick. When I grow up and know that I am going to have a baby, I will remember to walk proud and slow even though I am not a Jew." [9]

Francie takes a statement made by her mother, adds to it her own observations, thinks about the world around her, and then produces interpretive language.

Performatives are promises or bets. A literary example of a performative with regulatory overtones occurs in Langston Hughes's *Not Without Laughter* when a group of boys taunt each other, and one promises to fight back if attacked. His performative also makes a play on the words *match* and *strike*: "And the short boy replied: 'I'm your match, long skinny! Strike me an' see if you don't get burnt up!'" (123). Here the boy threatens to take action, and his threat constitutes a performative.

This discussion of functions documents that the uses of language described in linguists' analyses of children's natural speech can also be discerned in children's literary speech. Now we can examine in fuller detail and more specific situations how children in literature are shown to use language.

Language of Three Possessed Children

The figure of the demonic child holds a place of striking prominence in American literature. Special demands are placed on writers who wish to portray children associated with extreme evil, demonism, or diabolical possession. Chief among these challenges is the need to create dialogue which will reflect not only the juvenile characters' ages, but also their bizarre circumstances. Henry James's "The Turn of the Screw" and William Peter Blatty's The Exorcist are classics in fiction about demonic children. One, aided by the attention its popular movie version received, is the bestseller of its type, while the subtleties of the other have attracted discriminating readers for nearly a century. Both describe the possession of children by evil spirits, and both advocate employing extreme measures to preserve or regain childhood innocence. Despite these similarities, however, James and Blatty manage their stories so differently that the two works of fiction are opposites in their presentations of demonic children's language. A linguistic analysis of child speech in the two fictions reveals much about the two authors, their writing styles, and their approaches to their subjects.

The Exorcist is the straightforward story of an eleven-year-old girl, Regan, whose personality and physical appearance are overtaken by a demon capable of assuming many distinct personae. In this ugly condition, Regan says and does dreadful things, and her mother eventually turns to the Jesuits of Georgetown University for an exorcism. During the procedure, the primary exorcist dies, and his assistant, an athletic priest-psychiatrist, ends the ordeal by inviting the demon into his own body and then leaping to his death from the child's window. Regan returns to her normal self, apparently without any remorse for the destruction she has caused and without any curiosity over her experiences. As Benjamin Beit-Hallahmi has written, "we must proclaim her deficient, boring, possibly retarded in her development" (299). In spite of, or possibly because of, the popular attention received by The Exorcist, the novel has attracted minimal critical consideration.

In contrast, the two children in "The Turn of the Screw" are extraordinary, their tale is anything but straightforward, and the story has been subjected to a veritable mountain of criticism. Orphans left to the custody of an uncle absorbed in his own affairs, the children in "The Turn" have been cared for by servants at the uncle's country house. As the plot unfolds, a new governess arrives for eight-year-old Flora and ten-year-old Miles. At first delighted by her beautiful charges, the woman soon faces conflicts when Miles is expelled from school for an unnamed wickedness, and the children engage in strange activities such as outdoor strolls at midnight. Two deceased employees, Peter Quint and Miss Jessel, appear to the new governess and, she is convinced, to the young pair. She determines to save the lives and souls of the children, whom, we might infer, the deceased couple have exposed to depravity and debauchery. After confrontation, Flora demands to be removed and is taken to London, where, presumably, she will be free of the evil influences. Miles, however, dies in the arms of the governess in an ambiguous finale.

Interpretations of James's story have been as numerous as its readers. Some, such as Peter Coveney in *The Image of Childhood*, believe that the only threatening element in the story is the governess, viewed by these critics as deranged. Howard Faulkner's "Text as Pretext in *The Turn of the Screw*" contends that the governess is psychotic and that the ghost story is real only in her imagination. Muriel Shine remains fairly neutral on the subject in her comprehensive *The Fictional Children of Henry James*, as does Robert Pattison in *The Child Figure in English Literature*. Most recent opinions, such as those in Eliot M. Schrero's 1981 "Exposure in *The Turn of the Screw*" or in Peter Beidler's 1985 "The Governess and the Ghosts," tend to accept the governess as good, the danger as real, and the children as evil, or, at least, overtaken by evil spirits.[2] Although James's own commentary on "The Turn of the Screw" perpetuates the novella's ambiguities, one passage from his *Notebooks* clearly states, "The servants, wicked and depraved, corrupt and deprave the children: the children are bad, full of evil, to a sinister degree" (178).

Regardless of one's view on the reality of the ghosts or the goodness of the governess in James's story, it is indisputable that both *The Exorcist* and "The Turn of the Screw" are about evil. In *The Exorcist*, evil is a force outside human nature which strikes at innocent, helpless victims. By the novel's end, evil is banished, the characters are exonerated, and the essential goodness of humankind is affirmed. In "The Turn of the Screw," the children seem to be at least partially responsible for the evil around them; Miles, for instance, consciously demonstrates his capacity for wrongdoing and then initiates conversations about this badness. No one in this story escapes implication, as the uncle did not take care of his wards, the servants may have been perverted, the housekeeper kept quiet, the schoolmasters ignored Miles's underlying problem, and the governess sought no assistance from her community, her family, or her church. Ironically, the darker and more complex story is established in a less serious setting than the one in which evil and good are marked like black and white, for *The Exorcist* opens with references to Cosa Nostra tortures and Nazi death camps, while "The Turn" starts out as an after-dinner story.

The distinction between evil invading from without and evil arising from within appears in differences in the children's language.

That is, in James's tale the children's surface-level speech patterns remain constant, but in Blatty's novel Regan's speech changes when the devil possesses her and then returns to normal after Father Karras dies. Language use here also cues readers to differences in the sensibilities of the two authors and their audiences. In *The Exorcist*, curses, vulgarities, and obscenities spew from the possessed child's mouth. In "The Turn," all "horrors," as the housekeeper refers to such talk, are uttered offstage and are not repeated for the reader.

Both works exhibit an unusual concern for language. Blatty takes pains to distinguish the speech of Regan from the speech of the demon within her, as we can see from the following passages juxtaposed in the novel. The first excerpt shows Regan preparing a tape recording to send to her father: "'Hello, Daddy? This is me. Ummm . . .' Giggling; then a whispered aside: 'I can't tell what to say!'. . . . 'Umm, Daddy . . . Well, ya see . . . I mean, I hope you can *hear* me okay, and, umm—well, now, let's see. Umm, well, first we're—No, wait, now. . . . See, first we're in Washington, Daddy, ya know? I mean, that's where the President lives, and this house—ya know, Daddy?—it's—No, wait, now; I better start over. See, Daddy, there's . . .'" (271). Convinced that the child who taped this is not the creature he has just visited, Father Karras returns to Regan's house to tape the possessed Regan:

> "Oh, yes, hullo hullo hullo. What's up?" it said happily. "Are we going to record something, Padre? How fun! Oh, I *do* love to playact, you know! Oh, immensely!"
>
> "I'm Damien Karras," said the priest as he worked. "And who are you?"
>
> "Are you asking for my credits, now, ducks? Damned cheeky of you, wouldn't you say?" [279]

After a few more inconsequential exchanges and obscenities, another voice appears:

> "And what are we doing now, Karras? Recording our little discussion?"
>
> Karras straightened. Stared. Then he pulled up a chair beside the bed and sat down. "Do you mind?" he responded.
>
> "Not at all," croaked the demon. "I have always rather liked infernal engines." [280]

At least superficially, these before-and-after language samples are worlds apart, particularly in features such as tone and vocabulary.

However, the deeper qualities of the language do not contrast so drastically. That is, there are few significant differences in language functions, and the primary functional distinctions which do appear complement each other. For example, the percentages of Regan's normal and possessed regulatory and interactional language throughout the novel are nearly mirror images of each other. In her normal state she uses 6 percent regulatory language compared with 13 percent when possessed. Interestingly, her interactional speech comprises 13 percent of her utterances in a normal state and 7 percent when possessed. (A complete breakdown of functions in the speech of Regan, Flora, and Miles can be found in Tables 7 and 8). While regulatory and interactional functions are not exactly opposites, their usage indicates dissimilar priorities and personalities: regulatory speech represents efforts to control the behavior of other people through one's language, and interactional speech represents attempts to support and smooth conversations. In her normal state, Regan uses regulatory speech, which attempts to control others, only half as much as she uses interactional speech, which tries to make connections with others. In her possessed state, on the contrary, the girl uses regulatory speech twice as often as interactional. Regan's biform functional patterns could represent two sides of one Jeckyll-and-Hyde person, or they could be interpreted as the patterns of two unlike people, meaning Regan is truly possessed. The force of the novel depends on the latter choice, but while Regan's possessed and normal patterns of functions are different, they are not otherwise so radically different as the surface facets of her language.

Representations of child speech in the two novels are quite distinct. Blatty's Regan has a limited vocabulary, and the structures of her sentences are simple. Typical utterances include the following: "I enjoyed my dinner, Mom" (31); "I dunno" (41); and "Oh, okay" (399). Miles and, to a lesser extent, Flora, discuss more complicated ideas, draw upon a more extensive vocabulary, and express their thoughts in more sophisticated ways, even though they are untutored orphans from the country and are younger than Regan. Here are some typical excerpts from their conversations: "Oh, *you* know what a boy wants!" (Miles, 103); "I'll tell you anything you like. You'll stay on with me, and we shall both be all right and I *will* tell you—I *will*. But not now" (Miles, 132); "You naughty: where *have* you been?" (Flora, 72); and "I don't know what you mean. I see nobody. I see nothing. I never *have*. I think you're cruel. I don't like you!" (Flora, 116). All of the above are plausible utterances for children, but their credibility is not at stake. The point is that the cumulative effects of the two sets of examples illustrate distinctive styles, qualities, and techniques of writing, as well as distinctive attitudes toward children.

The occurrences and percentages of all the speech functions in all the children's direct discourse in the two novels are listed in Tables 7 and 8. The functional categories named are those presented in Table 6 and discussed in the first section of this chapter. The functional counts reflect the overall import of a single quoted block of material, that is, an indented paragraph in the text, whether that block happens to be a phrase, a sentence, or a string of sentences.[3] The functions used by Flora and Regan, especially in her normal state, are easily classified; for example, Regan's "*I want Mom*" (144) plainly serves an instrumental function. Miles's use of speech or sometimes Regan's possessed language can be more difficult to index. When Miles asks about his sister's departure, saying, "Did Bly disagree with her so terribly suddenly?" (128), his utterance could be variously interpreted and achieves several conversational purposes; due to its context, in this study it was counted as filling an interpretive function because it contributes to Miles's reflection on his sister's condition and his governess's handling of the crisis. So, the individual decisions involved in compiling Tables 7 and 8 depended on the contexts in which the utterances occurred.

Some scenes showing the affected children alone and talking to themselves might have enhanced their characterizations, but few noncommunicative functions are represented in these three children's speech, and those that are, the last four entries on Tables 7 and 8, form a minor percentage of the total functional range. Of course, everything known about the children in "The Turn of the Screw" comes from the governess's letter; she could not be responsible for knowing what happened when the children were not in her presence. In fact, the four instances of Miles using his speech as avoidance (to avoid something worse) have some communicative function, since they occur in conversation with the governess and since what he wishes to avoid are the more serious topics of his school expulsion and the evil which infects him. Because it is audience-directed, this speech might be classified as personal, but classifying it as avoidance makes more sense since that term best describes how language is being used. Neither Flora nor Regan in her normal state uses noncommunicative language, but the demon in Regan does. Again, a communicative intent actually underlies some of the demon's noncommunicative speech, since some of it is uttered to taunt listeners. The demon's avoidance, like that of Miles, is directed at an audience with whom conversation is not desired. In addition, the utterance "Nowonmai," repeated by the demon-pos-

Table 7. Functional Categories in the Speech of Miles and Flora in "The Turn of the Screw"

	Miles		Flora	
Function	Number	Percentage	Number	Percentage*
Instrumental	4	3	0	0
Regulatory	3	3	1	6
Interactional	9	8	2	13
Personal	7	6	3	19
Heuristic	16	13	3	19
Imaginative	0	0	0	0
Informational	30	25	4	25
Poetic	0	0	0	0
Interpretive	42	35	3	19
Performative	4	3	0	0
Self-image	0	0	0	0
Avoidance	4	3	0	0
Magical	0	0	0	0
Self-directing	0	0	0	0
Total utterances:	119		16	

*Number indicates the number of utterances in each category; percentage indicates the percentage of each character's speech that falls into that category.

sessed Regan several times in response to nothing, might be interpreted as the real Regan's effort to communicate since, written backwards, it means "I am no one." Again, this emphasizes that the evil is external, that Regan is no more, and that the devil occupies only the shell of her body. The absence of noncommunicative speech, while perhaps necessary in "The Turn" because of James's narrative technique, creates a void in both fictions that, if filled, would have provided greater insight into the children's characters.

Another surprising omission in the children's speech is in the imaginative-poetic-magical functions. Despite the emotional and supernatural elements of the stories, the characters respond with mostly calm and rational speech. Other practitioners of the horror genre, such as, for example, Edgar Allan Poe in "The Murders in the Rue Morgue," have also heightened terror by contrasting the rational and the irrational, the extraordinary and the mundane. Yet children are especially apt to use speech in imaginative or freshly poetic ways and, at least at a certain stage, attribute magical properties to language. Perhaps Regan is too dull for such creativity, and perhaps Miles and Flora, described by the governess as old beyond their years (111), have lost some of

Table 8. Functional Categories in the Speech of Regan in *The Exorcist*

Function	normal Number - %	possessed Number - %	total Number - %*
Instrumental	11 - 8	6 - 3	17 - 5
Regulatory	8 - 6	29 - 13	37 - 10
Interactional	17 - 13	16 - 7	33 - 9
Personal	13 - 10	22 - 10	35 - 10
Heuristic	10 - 8	0 - 0	10 - 3
Imaginative	0 - 0	20 - 9	20 - 6
Informational	61 - 47	63 - 29	124 - 35
Poetic	0 - 0	5 - 2	5 - 1
Interpretive	8 - 6	30 - 13	38 - 11
Performative	0 - 0	9 - 4	9 - 3
Self-image	0 - 0	2 - 1	2 - 1
Avoidance	0 - 0	10 - 4	10 - 3
Magical	0 - 0	16 - 7	16 - 4
Self-directing	0 - 0	2 - 1	2 - 1
Total utterances:	130	228	358

*Number indicates the number of utterances in each category; percentage indicates the percentage of each character's speech that falls into that category.

their childlike traits. In both stories, though, activities such as shrieking, howling, laughing, and piano playing provide outlets for noncommunicative vocables and imaginative expression.

Major differences exist between the two fictions in their characters' operations in informational and interpretive modes, the two functions most used by all three children. For both Miles and Flora, utterances designed to give information comprise 25 percent of their total speech. In contrast, informational speech accounts for 47 percent of Regan's discourse, nearly twice that of James's characters. This reinforces Regan's characterization as literal-minded. Her possessed speech also relies on informational exchanges to an absurd degree, as when the demon tries to prove its omniscience by reciting facts like the name of the largest lake in South America.

About 6 percent of Regan's normal utterances and 13 percent of her possessed utterances are interpretive. However, 19 percent of Flora's language and 35 percent of Miles's involves the reasoning and abstract thinking that comprise the interpretive function. Interpretive speech requires sophisticated thought patterns and mature intellectual powers, so it is odd Regan's demonic language has so little of it. Perhaps Blatty meant to convey the demon's power through its efforts to control other people, as 13 percent of its speech is regulatory, or through its lack of questions, for it uses no heuristic speech. (Regan's normal talk is only 8 percent heuristic, whereas Miles [13 percent heuristic] and Flora [19 percent heuristic] are more inquisitive.) Miles's language reaches unusual levels for a ten-year-old, not only in his interpretive speech (35 percent), but also in the connectedness of his discourse and in his ability to sustain conversations. His language grows increasingly complex at the end of the story, and his final conversation with the governess incorporates the entire range of communicative functions into most utterances, with interpretive speech predominating. After Miles's speech becomes almost entirely interpretive, he dies. Perhaps excessive interpretation can drain the life from any subject. In any case, Miles's dense and suggestive speech is unusual even for a Jamesian juvenile, drawing attention to the precocity and uncanniness which suggest his evil connection.

Two similarities in the speech of Flora and Regan hint at a gender-based link. First, both rarely use language to manipulate the behavior of others; specifically, regulatory speech amounts to 6 percent of each one's total language function. Second, interactional speech accounts for 13 percent of each girl's linguistic output, more than either Miles's (8 percent interactional) or the demon's (7 percent interactional). As we will see in the chapter on gender differences, girls tend toward less assertive and less overtly manipulative speech and are generally more sensitive to the nuances of verbal interaction, usually bearing the burden of keeping conversations alive and moving. The speech behavior of Flora and Regan conforms to these patterns.

Functionally, Regan's possessed speech has a more masculine aura because it is less interactional (7 percent) and more regulatory (13 percent) than her normal talk. It also contains some performatives (promises and bets) and numerous curses, both absent from her unpossessed speech.[4] Although Miles's discourse is the least regulatory of the children's—or perhaps he is just more subtle in his manipulations—it does have two gender-based connections to the male persona in Regan's possessed speech: a low proportion of interactional language (8 percent interactional for Miles, 7 percent interactional for the possessed Regan) and a similar use of performatives (4 percent performative for Miles and 4 percent perormative for the possessed voice of Regan), whereas Flora and the normal Regan utter no performatives. A character's gender influences how a writer portrays his or her speech, and gender apparently can supercede other factors in language characterization. Here, despite differences in the styles of Blatty and James and despite differences in the approaches they take toward their topic of children possessed by evil, similar language patterns mark Regan and Flora as female and Miles and the demon as male. The masculine characterization of Regan's possessed speech also reinforces the conclusion that evil in The Exorcist is completely external to the child it attacks.

In both The Exorcist and "The Turn of the Screw" child characters have individualized language, and examining the functions of that child language assists us in understanding the themes, characterizations, and styles of the fictions. Despite some similarities between The Exorcist and "The Turn of the Screw," the subject of possessed children receives dissimilar treatments by the two authors, and the two fictions create dissimilar effects in their readers. One is easier and more obvious. The other is richer and more shaded. One explains everything, while the other explains nothing. One is accessible to a mass audience, the other to a select audience. Both are frightening, but one neatly disposes with the terror in its conclusion, while the other allows nothing, especially not the cause of the terror, to be explained at the end. In one the child character, though almost a teenager, has limited verbal skills, while in the other the children are verbally talented. In one the evil causes the child to alter her speech behavior, while in the other the pervasive evil is not so easily expressed. In one the child's speech functions emphasize facts and information, while in the other the children's speech functions underline the importance of analysis and interpretation. In many ways, the two fictions and their presentations of child speech represent opposite responses to a similar literary impulse.

Speech Functions and Other Artistic Considerations

Various pressures shape an author's portrayal of speaking child characters. The individual personalities of the children determine much about the presentation of their speech. Also important are the children's relative status, that is, whether they are primary or secondary characters and what relationship they have to others in the fiction. The impact of personality and social status on fictional child language can be illustrated in an examination of the functions of child speech in Harriet Beecher Stowe's Uncle Tom's Cabin.

Though the message, style, and characterizations in Uncle Tom's Cabin have been harshly criticized, its memorable story nevertheless endures. The abundance of dialogue and the ease with which Stowe reveals her characters through their speech contribute to the novel's force and attractiveness. One of its most familiar scenes details the

Table 9. Children's Speech Functions in Chapters 25 and 26 of *Uncle Tom's Cabin*

	Topsy		Eva	
Function	Number	Percentage	Number	Percentage*
Instrumental	0 -	0	3 -	3
Regulatory	0 -	0	17 -	17
Interactional	2 -	12	18 -	18
Personal	3 -	18	10 -	10
Heuristic	0 -	0	10 -	10
Imaginative	0 -	0	0 -	0
Informational	7 -	41	15 -	15
Poetic	2 -	12	1 -	1
Interpretive	2 -	12	15 -	15
Performative	1 -	6	11 -	11
Total utterances:	17		100	

*The Number column indicates the number of utterances in each category; percentage indicates the percentage of each character's speech that falls into that category.

death of Eva, a much loved white child from a well-to-do family. Eva's purity, sweetness, and beauty are set up in opposition to the traits of Topsy, a black slave child described by white adults as troublesome and unattractive. The data in Table 9 show the contrasts between the speech functions of Eva and Topsy in Chapters 25 and 26, which depict the demise of Eva and her parting words to her parents, Topsy, and the other slaves.

Topsy's functional range in these two chapters reflects her status as a slave: she never expresses her own needs, she never gives orders to others, she never asks questions, and her only performative is a promise to Eva that she will try to behave better. Many of her statements are fact-oriented because adults constantly ask her what she is doing. Eva, on the other hand, utilizes a broad range of functions in her conversations because she is a privileged child, a lovely girl with high social status. She has a good deal of interactional speech, indicating her concern for building bridges of communication with other people. Her percentage of regulatory speech is also high, especially for a female child, and no doubt is possible only because she is a member of the ruling class and because she is speaking from her deathbed. However, Eva never issues obnoxious orders or cruel commands, but rather she exhorts her listeners to follow Christ and love each other. The two distinctive speech patterns of Eva and of Topsy reflect two different personalities and two different sets of social relationships.

The interpretation of these two different characters is influenced, in other words, by how their language is formed as well as by the content of what they say.

Of course, individual personalities and relative social status cannot by themselves account for distinctive patterns of fictional characters' speech. In literature and in life, children, as well as adults, speak differently in different situations, so setting or context also affects the portrayal of characters' language. This truth can be illustrated in the fiction of Stephen Crane. In Crane's *Whilomville Stories*, the boy Jimmie Trescott and his cohorts in the town of Whilomville share a variety of adventures, and, basically, the same group of children appear throughout the collection of stories. The boys' patterns of speech are tailored, however, to the situations they encounter. A comparison of "A Little Pilgrimage" with "The City Urchin and the Chaste Villagers" reveals that the same characters speak differently depending on the setting of the story.

In "A Little Pilgrimage," Jimmie convinces his father to let him switch from the Presbyterian to the Big Progressive Sunday school. Jimmie wants the change because of the Presbyterians' decision to forgo a Christmas tree and to use their tree money in support of the victims of the Charleston earthquake; naturally, however, Jimmie invents other arguments to persuade his father that Big Progressive is better. Most of the remaining dialogue in this story shows Jimmie talking to the children and their teacher at the new Sunday school. (In a twist of plot, the Progressives also decide to deny themselves the pleasure of a Christmas tree.) In "The City Urchin and the Chaste Villagers" the boys of Whilomville jockey for position by demonstrations of brute strength, and the boy who can beat up the others is understood to be the leader. The story describes a series of street fights and ends when the best fighter, Johnnie Hedge, is cornered and retrieved by his fierce mother. The functional patterns of the children's speech in these two stories are described in Table 10.

The appearance of certain functions remains fairly constant in both stories. The proportions of the boys' greetings (interactional function), their expressions of personal feelings (personal), their questions (heuristic), and their levels of analysis (interpretive) are similar, as they should be since the same characters are drawn by the same author at about the same time. However, the boys fighting in the street express their needs (instrumental), issue orders and commands (regulatory), and make bets and promises (performatives), none of which the boys in church dare do. The Sunday school episode does prompt some imaginative discourse, including Jimmie's discussion with his

Table 10. Children's Speech Functions in Two *Whilomville Stories*

Function	"Pilgrimage" Number	Percentage	"City Urchin" Number	Percentage*
Instrumental	0 -	0	3 -	10
Regulatory	0 -	0	4 -	13
Interactional	4 -	21	6 -	20
Personal	1 -	5	2 -	7
Heuristic	2 -	10	2 -	7
Imaginative	2 -	10	0 -	0
Informational	8 -	42	6 -	20
Poetic	0 -	0	0 -	0
Interpretive	2 -	10	3 -	10
Performative	0 -	0	4 -	13
Total utterances:	19		30	

*Number indicates the number of utterances in each category; percentage indicates the percentage of each character's speech that falls into that category.

father on the deficiencies of Presbyterians and, later, another boy's interpretation, made with "a grand pomposity born of a sense of hopeless ignorance" (767), of a particular passage of Scripture. Too, the boys at church are more directed toward information because their teacher tests their knowledge by asking them questions of fact. In sum, the two different situations require and receive different uses of language from the same set of children.

Crane's ability to convey children's responses to setting through below-the-surface aspects of language such as functional category contrasts with Blatty's handling of speech differences in *The Exorcist*. In Blatty's novel, the possessed Regan appears to have a very different pattern of speech than she normally exhibits, but, in fact, most of the distinctions are obvious ones, as in tone and vocabulary, and the functional patterns, though somewhat different, are not nearly as different as the surface distinctions would lead us to expect. In these two stories by Crane, however, the functional patterns of the child characters are significantly different, though, on the surface, the characters' speech is very similar. Surface similarities include the presence of nonstandard grammatical usages such as "No, I ain't, either, but you're a liar" (761), colloquialisms such as "I am goin' to tan the hide off'n you!" (759), and variant pronunciations rendered orthographically (such as "an'" for *and* or "'im" for *him*). Thus, Crane portrays differences in children's speech with skill and subtlety.

Various factors such as setting and a character's personality, gender, age, or relationship to other characters might influence an author's presentation of fictional dialogue. Although an analysis of speech functions aids the development of text-specific and author-specific conclusions, the many variables influencing the presentation of a particular character make it difficult to draw broad generalizations about the functions of literary children's speech. Nevertheless, at least two general conclusions can be made based on data presented in this chapter.

First, literary children have low rates of poetic speech and have virtually no noncommunicative language. This surprising conclusion defies easy explanation. Since the functions of *all* literary child language have not been reviewed here, it is possible that data in this chapter might not represent the whole corpus of child language in American fiction, though the selections scrutinized offer a sizable amount of evidence and reflect a wide range of literature. Including poetic-imaginative or noncommunicative speech would perhaps divert attention from the main plots and themes in digressions which American writers usually avoid, regardless of the contributions such departures may have made in Shakespeare's plays or in Dickens's novels. Too, most fictional children are beyond the age, at least as Piaget described the periods of development (*Language and Thought of the Child* 14), when creative and magical speech play a large role in language acquisition, though these functions are never totally outgrown. In addition, according to Thelma Weeks (112), emotionally stressed or anxious children do not play with language, and literature typically presents characters struggling with problems. When child characters are free from stress, as Pearl is, for example, at the beginning of the forest scene of *The Scarlet Letter*, they do engage in some language play. In addition, there are no complete studies of naturally occurring child language to tell us exactly what the proportions of speech functions are in living children's utterances. That is, children may not actually operate in imaginative, poetic, or magical modes of speech to any great degree; adults may just focus on such usages because they sound so fresh and innovative to grown-up ears.

A second generalization about the functions of fictional child speech is that literary children, like their living counterparts, ask questions constantly. The propensity of children to ask questions is noticeable throughout American fiction, and, except in unusual circumstances such as Topsy's enslavement, heuristic speech seems to dominate fictional children's linguistic output. To test this generalization, let us review five more fictional works reflecting a broad spectrum of American literature: Nathaniel Hawthorne's *The Scarlet Letter*

(Chapters 6, 7, 16, 19, 21, and 22, those focusing on Pearl), Sarah Orne Jewett's "The Dulham Ladies," James Weldon Johnson's *The Autobiography of an Ex-Coloured Man* (Chapter 1, detailing his character's childhood), Ernest Hemingway's *In Our Time* (the "Indian Camp" segment, describing a childhood experience), and J.D. Salinger's "A Perfect Day for Bananafish." This group includes short stories and novels, nineteenth-century and twentieth-century works, different philosophical perspectives (what might be referred to as romanticism, realism, and so on), and male and female, black and white, parent and non-parent authors. Two features link these disparate selections: all can be classified as American literature and all contain child characters. The functions of each child's speech in these five literary works are displayed in Table 11.

A review of the data in Table 11 reveals that an overall average of 65 percent of the children's speech in these five fictional works is heuristic. The average percentage of heuristic speech in all fictional child language discussed in this chapter is 33 percent. (This latter figure represents the average of individual heuristic speech in the language of Miles, Flora, Regan, Topsy, Eva, the Whilomville boys, and the five child characters represented in Table 11.) For Pearl in *The Scarlet Letter*, 27 of 78 utterances, 35 percent of her speech, are heuristic questions, and the older she gets as the novel progresses, the more questions she asks. In "The Dulham Ladies" a child speaks once, asking one question. In *The Autobiography of an Ex-Coloured Man* the child asks five questions, representing 83 percent of his direct discourse. In the "Indian Camp" chapter of *In Our Time*, the boy asks ten questions, which, of 14 total utterances, represent 71 percent of his language. In "Bananafish" 14 of 42 utterances, or 34 percent of the child's speech, are questions.

American literary children plainly ask many questions. Even more importantly, those questions are piercing, challenging, problematic, penetrating, and often unanswerable. They touch at the very heart of the concerns in the fiction. Here are some examples of these children's questions: "Doth he [Dimmesdale] love us? . . . Will he go back with us, hand in hand, we three together, into the town?" (*Scarlet Letter* 212); "Do Miss Dobinses wear them great caps because their heads is cold?" ("Dulham Ladies," 76; the story is about the absurdities of two spinsters, but only this once are their habits openly addressed); "Tell me, mother, am I a nigger?" (*Autobiography of an Ex-Colored Man*, 18); "Is dying hard, Daddy?" ("Indian Camp" in *In Our Time*, 19); and "Why?" ("A Perfect Day for Bananafish," 16).

Children ask questions for a variety of reasons, but their queries

Table 11. Functions of Child Speech in Five Works

Function	In The Scarlet Letter* No.	%	In "The Dulham Ladies" No.	%	In Chapter 1 of Autobiography of an Ex-Coloured Man No.	%	In "In Indian Camp" segment of In Our Time No.	%	In "A Perfect Day for Bananafish" No.	%
Instrumental					1	17			1	2
Regulatory	8	10							3	7
Interactional	6	8							3	7
Personal	3	4					2	14		
Heuristic	27	35	1	100	5	83	10	71	14	34
Imaginative	7	10								
Informative	10	13					2	14	19	45
Poetic	7	9							2	5
Interpretive	6	8								
Performative	4	5								

*Chapters 6, 7, 16, 19, 21, and 22, those that focus on Pearl.
Number indicates the number of utterances in each category; percentage indicates the percentage of each character's speech that falls into that category.

are often voiced to obtain information and facilitate learning. The last line of Sherwood Anderson's short story "I Want to Know Why" expresses in indirect discourse the main character's central question and the eternal question of any child: "I want to know why." This "Why?" underlies most children's questions and provides the stimulus for much of our literature. American writers frequently present but rarely answer the "Why?" of a young voice. This is the case in the literature discussed in this chapter and in other fiction as well, from Samuel Clemens's "Little Bessie Would Assist Providence," which recounts a mother's efforts to meet her three-year-old daughter's queries about the Virgin Mary and the foundations for religious belief, to William Faulkner's *Absalom, Absalom!*, which attempts to resolve Quentin's inquiries into the Sutpen tragedies and the entire Southern experience.

American writers who have chosen to portray child characters have, in most cases, been sensitive to the forms of actual child language and have shaped their young characters' speech to suit the authors' fictional goals without violating the major linguistic patterns found in living children's language. The emphasis in literary children's discourse on questioning speech, for example, not only reflects the child's natural use of language as a tool for discovering and exploring reality, but this emphasis also draws our attention to major issues in our literature and to authors' techniques for presenting those issues. The questions and conversations of children are at the very core of American literature.

5. Parent-Child Discourse

Generalizing about parent-child language is risky because new studies constantly question the motivations, assumptions, methodologies, and interpretations of earlier work. Most language specialists would, however, agree with Catherine Snow that parent-to-child speech is universally simple, well-formed, redundant, and semantically concrete ("Conversations with Children"). Most linguists would, furthermore, concur that these features of adult-to-child speech are mirrored in the language of children. That is, as Catherine Snow has shown in her exploration of patterning ("Saying It Again"), children imitate adult speech, although imitation alone cannot account for children's development of language. Elza Stella-Prorok ("Mother-Child Language in the Natural Environment") has demonstrated that distinctive patterns emerge in the speech between a particular mother and a particular child, so that a mother becomes extremely sensitive to alterations in the patterns, silences, and other nuances of language behavior her child may exhibit. Wilkinson and Rembold ("The Communicative Context of Early-Language Development") report that the utterances of parental speech are shorter when addressing young children, the vocabulary of parental speech is less diverse than it is in other contexts, and parents typically ask their children many questions. Durkin, Rutter, and Tucker ("Social Interaction and Language Acquisition") have also found that parents call children by name more often than adults otherwise invoke proper names in conversations.

Some of these findings come from studies dealing exclusively with mothers' speech. This raises the question of whether language used by mothers is a unique type of adult-to-child language. Are fathers' conversational styles different from mothers'? Do caretakers other than parents have identifiable speech patterns in verbal exchanges with children? Opinions vary. Amy Lederberg ("A Framework for Research on Preschool Children's Speech Modifications") details how even older children modify their speech for younger ones in similar ways to mothers' modifications. Also, Catherine Snow ("Mothers' Speech to Young Children Learning Language") has shown that women who are not mothers make adjustments similar to mothers' when talking to young children. Regarding men's speech, Weintraub ("Parents' Speech to Children") has observed fathers using more complex vocabulary to children than mothers use. Giattino and Hogan ("Analysis of a Father's Speech") have determined that the father in their study rarely repeated his utterances or expanded his child's utterances. Gleason and Greif ("Men's Speech to Young Children") have found that while fathers at home use fewer polite forms and more imperatives than mothers, male day-care teachers' speech is more like the speech of female day-care teachers and mothers than that of fathers at home. This has led Gleason and Greif to conclude that when men "occupy a nurturant role they become increasingly sensitive to the needs and intentions of the children" (145). This mixture of evidence could support the hypothesis that individual situations vary and that factors such as emotional attachment, level of responsibility for child care, or familiarity with a specific child may be paramount in determining how an adult will speak to a child, but that gender or gender-related cultural roles may influence some aspects of parent-child communication.

This leads us to another important component in parent-child discourse, cultural roles and cultural norms. Not all cultures value children in the same manner, not all treat children in the same way, and not all talk to children with the same type of language. Ervin-Tripp and Strage ("Parent-Child Discourse") describe four different approaches that parents around the world take in their language to their children: some parents ignore their children's language, some challenge their children, some help them speak with a special style of speech, and some assist them with prompts and questions. The last approach seems to be the one selected by most middle-class Americans, though as Ervin-Tripp and Strage remark, not all cultures within America are the same, with most differences occurring between small town, urban, and rural environments, between various ethnic groups, and between different economic classes within those subdivisions. Not much analysis has been done comparing parental speech styles in different American communities, but studies such as Viola King's "Dialect Awareness in Preschoolers" indicate that children themselves may be conscious of differences in language varieties.

Hawthorne's Pearl

Because our language and customs today differ from those of the Puritans and from those of nineteenth-century New Englanders, Nathaniel Hawthorne's *The Scarlet Letter* poses some problems for a review of its parent-child discourse. As David Leverenz points out in *The Language of Puritan Feeling*, child-rearing practices varied among Puritan settlements and among generations of Puritans, though Leverenz notes that in contrast to practices in England and Europe at the same time, in Puritan New England, "broadly speaking, mothers were more tender to infants, since nearly every woman breast-fed her own children, and fathers were more patriarchal throughout, while the social frame induced security and restriction rather than uncertainty and change" (158). In *The Scarlet Letter* Pearl's mother is tender to her (and is, in fact, described as nursing her baby), and the security and restriction of the culture surrounding Hester and Pearl create the characters' conflicts, so Leverenz's observations and Hawthorne's fictional situation agree on this point of history. Read in terms of Hawthorne's own day, the novel, according to Bernard Wishy in *The Child and the Republic*, is a judgment on Jacksonian America. Wishy also claims that *The Scarlet Letter* illustrates "some of the classic problems of child and parents in American culture" (6). So, the novel holds historical interest for the time in which it is set, the time in which it was written, and the time in which each new reader discovers it. Thus, while we must acknowledge some complications for twentieth-century readers studying the language of a seventeenth-century story written by a nineteenth-century author, these complications need not deter us from examining the language of a literary work hailed for its timeless insights.

Some critics have had difficulty accepting Pearl as a believable child portrait, perhaps because she is a very young, female child. Most fictional children, at least those with speaking roles, are older than Pearl, who is shown as an infant, a three-year-old, and a seven-year-old. Richard Fogle (*Hawthorne's Fiction: The Light and the Dark*), for instance, says Pearl is pure symbol. Robert Emmet Whelan ("Hester Prynne's Little Pearl") declares that Pearl's "sole reality is that of an allegorical mirror" (489). John Andola ("Pearl: Symbolic Link Between Two Worlds") claims that "one cannot effectively argue that Pearl is believable" (72). F.O. Matthiessen adds in *American Renaissance* that Pearl is a one-dimensional Spenserian allegory who is "worth murdering" (278). Even Randall Stewart, whose explorations into *The American Notebooks* trace the parallels between Pearl and Hawthorne's daughter Una, has said that Pearl's real characteristics are subordinated to symbolism.

To be sure, others disagree. Frederick Crews (*The Sins of the Fathers*) deplores the trend of seeing Hawthorne only in light of symbolization. The *Literary History of the United States* (edited by Robert E. Spiller, et al.) describes Pearl as "a living child, not an animated monograph on the nature of Puritan children" (1: 425). When women have written about Pearl, they have been more likely than their male colleagues to accept her as an authentic child portrait. For example, Anne Marie McNamara says in "The Character of Flame: The Function of Pearl in *The Scarlet Letter*" that Pearl is both real and more than real. The differing approaches to Pearl can be seen, in part, to reflect various American attitudes toward children, but the controversy bears discussion because how we interpret Pearl's character informs our understanding of the novel as a whole.

Hawthorne actively participated in fatherhood and involved himself in the lives of his own children. Even before he became a father, his short stories included child characters such as the Quaker lad in "The Gentle Boy." His early child characters are more wooden in speech and behavior than are his later creations, particularly those developed after his own fatherhood commenced. Hawthorne's letters of the late 1830s and early 1840s document his desire to write a book for children, and, in 1851, he finally completed *A Wonder-Book for Girls and Boys*. Hawthorne's journals amply document his fascination with his own three children: Una, born in 1844, Julian, born in 1846, and Rose, born in 1851. So, whatever symbolism Hawthorne intended for the character of Pearl, he was well suited in 1849 and 1850 to fashion a realistic female child for his masterpiece.

Language in *The Scarlet Letter* is conceived as such a powerful entity that Hester in the first scaffold scene is admonished to "Speak; and give your child a father!"—as if the very act of speaking could create a male parent for the baby. This is not, though, a story which rests on the conversations of its characters; the plot moves more by narrative than by dialogue. Still, conversations appear throughout, and exchanges between the characters occur at turning points in the story, making them ideal points of focus. Observing the book's emphasis on the power of written and spoken language, John Dolis

("Hawthorne's Letter") discusses the explicit connections Hawthorne makes between discourse and authority, concluding that the subject of the novel is language. Roy Male notes the importance of language in *The Scarlet Letter* by saying that "The book's structure is fearless symmetry; distilling its language patterns of utterance and vision, its themes of origin and relationship, it ends in the one word that fuses the Letter of Scarlet with the Tongue of Flame. 'Gules' in its heraldic context or relationship means 'scarlet,' but its origin is the Latin *gula*, meaning 'throat.' This is the perfect capstone for a book that capitalizes upon the guilty heart's native language" (*Hawthorne's Tragic Vision* 90). We might add that while the last word in the book is *gules*, etymologically related to the Latin word for *throat*, the first verb in "The Custom House," Hawthorne's introductory to *The Scarlet Letter*, is *talk*.

Pearl's initial appearance in the book is marked by her sounds, for when Hester Prynne, taking her punishment by standing on the scaffold, clutches Pearl too tightly, the infant cries. Toward the end of the day, as Hester's public ordeal wears on, Pearl begins to wail and scream. The first act of Roger Chillingworth, who arrives in town just as Hester and Pearl are displayed on the scaffold, is to administer a soothing medicinal draught to the baby. As a physician and as a human being and as Pearl's legal father since he is married to the babe's mother, Chillingworth responds to the needs made clear by little Pearl's crying, her only means of communication.

Chillingworth's behavior contrasts with that of Arthur Dimmesdale, Pearl's biological father. Dimmesdale never knows how to respond appropriately to the child's crying or talking. For instance, in the momentous forest scene, Reverend Dimmesdale pleads with Hester Prynne to pacify the cranky girl, admitting that only the wrath of an old witch could disturb him more than the shrieking of a child. The differences illustrated in Dimmesdale's and Chillingworth's reactions to Pearl mirror their final legacies to her. That is, just before he dies Dimmesdale publicly but ambiguously acknowledges he should have stood on the scaffold with Hester and Pearl seven years earlier; his admission may redeem his soul, but it produces no particular benefit for Pearl or her mother. Chillingworth, on the other hand, makes no public announcement of his relationship to Hester and Pearl, yet upon his decease he bequeaths his considerable fortune to his wife's daughter.

Throughout the novel, Hester Prynne's language and behavior demonstrate her love for Pearl. She articulates her motherly love, for example, with impassioned pleas to the Governor that she be allowed to keep her child. She speaks affectionately to her daughter, and Hawthorne even alludes to Hester using baby talk: "How soon—with what strange rapidity, indeed!—did Pearl arrive at an age that was capable of social intercourse, beyond the mother's ever-ready smile and nonsense-words!" (93).

The first reported direct discourse between the two has all the markings of a mother-child ritual. Here Hester's speech contains repetitions, expansions, and questions; it features naming, syntactic simplicity, and dialogue modeling; and it also takes a motherly didactic turn:

> "Child, what art thou?" cried the mother.
> "Oh, I am your little Pearl!" answered the child. . . .
> "Art thou my child in very truth?" asked Hester. . . .
> "Yes; I am little Pearl!" repeated the child, continuing her antics.
> "Thou art not my child! Thou art no Pearl of mine!" said the mother, half playfully; for it was often the case that a sportive impulse came over her, in the midst of deepest suffering. "Tell me, then, what thou art, and who sent thee hither?"
> "Tell me, mother!" said the child, seriously, coming up to Hester, and pressing herself close to her knees. "Do thou tell me!"
> "Thy Heavenly Father sent thee!" answered Hester Prynne. . . .
> "He did not send me!" cried she, positively. "I have no Heavenly Father!"
> "Hush, Pearl, hush! Thou must not talk so!" answered the mother, suppressing a groan. [97-98]

This conversation begins with Hester engaging her daughter in an identity-building exchange, prompting her to state her name and relationship to her mother, but it ends with Pearl rejecting the idea of a Heavenly Father, perhaps because, as D.H. Lawrence has said in *Studies in Classic American Literature*, she finds the idea of an earthly father to be so fraudulent.

Even with the presence of elements typical of mother-child discourse (repetitions, expansions, questions, simplicity, naming, and modeling), this conversation has some unusual twists. Of course, the characters' situation is unusual, for they are social outcasts, isolated from other mothers and children. The distinctive flavor of the dialogue also comes from the contrary directions of their moods; Hester starts seriously but becomes playful, while Pearl begins playfully but grows serious. Furthermore, Hester invites trouble by asking her daughter "what thou art and who sent thee hither." Such questions were directed at very young children in Puritan times, as we know from sources such as Cotton Mather's diaries, but they lack the concrete, here-and-now focus that characterize most mother-to-young-child conversations described in current linguistic studies.[1] Pearl's verbal skills are advanced to the point of precocity, but perhaps she inherited some of Arthur Dimmesdale's language abilities, for he is reputed to be one of New England's most effective speakers.

As if to reassure readers that Pearl is concerned with the realities inquisitive youngsters normally face and that, in addition, she is an intelligent little being aware of the distortions of her situation, her very next spoken remarks ask her mother about the strange reflections their images have in the polished armor at the Governor's mansion. This scene has a symbolic overlay, for the reflections emphasize and enlarge the scarlet A on Hester's bosom. Other scenes, whatever allegorical significance they may have, also ground the story in realities of childhood. For instance, like all children, Pearl demands that her mother tell her a story, she begs and cries to be given something that catches her fancy (a rose, for example), and she screams when her mother denies her requests.

The close relationship between mother and daughter in this novel is also shown by the way Pearl anticipates her mother's thoughts. When Pearl fashions the letter A out of seaweed while playing by the water, she asks herself (178), "I wonder if mother will ask me what it means!" Immediately, Hester does notice her daughter's creation: "'My little Pearl,' said Hester, after a moment's silence, 'the green letter, and on thy childish bosom, has no purport. But dost thou know, my child, what this letter means which thy mother is doomed to wear?'" (178). Here again, Hester emphasizes Pearl's name, speaks simply, and asks a leading question. After Pearl responds with reference to the concrete meaning of A, saying, "It is the great letter A. Thou hast taught it me in the hornbook," Hester repeats and expands her question, "Dost thou know, child, wherefore thy mother wears this letter?" Pearl's insightful answer astounds her mother: "It is for the same reason that the minister keeps his hand over his heart!" Thus Pearl demonstrates through her language her advancing capacity for logical thought. Though Hester tries to facilitate Pearl's education by asking her questions, Pearl manipulates her mother into talking about the A, a subject that obsesses the child. The speech of both characters at this point is still structurally simple, but their utterances are longer than at the first part of the novel, as they should be since several years have elapsed.

Soon after this waterside scene with Pearl, Hester meets Dimmesdale in the forest, and her interaction with him can be contrasted with her approach to her child. Most obviously, her utterances directed at Dimmesdale are longer and more complex than those directed at Pearl. Also, while Dimmesdale invokes Hester's name at almost every one of his conversational turns in this climactic forest meeting, Hester seldom uses his name, whereas she almost always calls Pearl's name or a name substitute such as "my child" when talking to her. Furthermore, Hester does not repeat herself when she speaks to the adult man, though she does sometimes expand on what he says. She also asks him many questions, though that may be appropriate, since the text implies they have not met alone since before Pearl's birth. Interestingly, however, man-to-man exchanges in the text, as between Dimmesdale and Chillingworth or between Governor Bellingham and the Reverend Mr. Wilson, contain noticeably fewer questions than does either this conversation or those that occur between Hester and Pearl. In short, the style and content of Hester's speech differs when she is talking to an adult rather than to her child.

Although Dimmesdale's fate is tied to Pearl, he does not know how to respond to her, offers little or no fatherly language to her, and admits that children in general "are not readily won to be familiar to me. They will not climb my knee, nor prattle in my ear, nor answer to my smile; but stand apart, and eye me strangely" (207). Perhaps this is because he does not, judging from his approach to Pearl, treat children as children. Whenever he speaks to his daughter, as when he first ascends the scaffold with her and her mother in the dark of night, he talks to her more as if she were an adult. That night on the scaffold when Dimmesdale questions the identity of Chillingworth, Pearl claims to know who he is, and Dimmesdale immediately bends over so that she might whisper her information into his ear. Rejecting this response from a man she seems to recognize intuitively as her father, "Pearl mumbled something into his ear, that sounded, indeed, like human language, but was only such gibberish as children may be heard amusing themselves with, by the hour together" (156).

In the forest scene, Hester undertakes to unite Pearl with her father. She explains to Dimmesdale, "Thou has seen her,—yes, I know it!—but thou wilt see her now with other eyes" (203). But no special fatherly insight dawns on Dimmesdale, and he is unable to speak to his child at this momentous reintroduction by Hester. Pearl instantly recognizes Dimmesdale as a rival for her mother's affection, and she

72 The Voice of the Child

Table 12. Functions of Adult Speech to Pearl in *The Scarlet Letter**

Type of speech: Speaker:	Heuristic	Regulatory	Interpretive/ informative
Hester Prynne: (47)	40%	30%	30%
Arthur Dimmesdale: (6)	50	17	33
Shipmaster: (3)	67	0	33
Mistress Hibbins: (3)	33	33	33
Governor: (2)	100	0	0
(For Contrast:) Functions of Pearl's Speech**			
Pearl:	35%	10%	22%

*Percentages are based on the number of utterances to Pearl (listed in parentheses). All of the minor characters' speech to Pearl is represented in the figures above, but a few utterances by Hester Prynne and Arthur Dimmesdale to Pearl have not been tabulated since not all their speech fits into the selected functional categories.
**See Table 11 and the subsequent discussion in Chapter Four for more information about Pearl's speech functions.

throws a tantrum when she sees that her mother has been paying attention to someone other than herself and has removed her scarlet A. Dimmesdale entreats Hester to quiet the raving girl, complaining, as we have already observed, that except for the wrath of an old witch, nothing could upset him more than "this passion in a child" (210). From then on Dimmesdale does not speak to Pearl until the final episode when he calls Hester and Pearl to join him on the scaffold in public acknowledgment of their sin. The novel might have taken a different course if Dimmesdale and Pearl had been able to speak to each other, particularly at that critical juncture in the forest.

Most of Pearl's speech occurs in conversation with her mother. She has some direct discourse with her father and some with three other characters: the governor, Mistress Hibbins, and a shipmaster. With the functional categories introduced in the previous chapter, we can analyze most of the adult speech to Pearl as belonging to one of the three following functions: heuristic (questioning), regulatory (ordering, commanding, controlling), and informational-interpretive (giving instructions, making comments, or discussing). Information about the adult language directed toward Pearl is summarized in Table 12.

As the information in Table 12 establishes, Pearl's relatively powerless status as a child is shown by her low rate of regulatory speech compared to the higher incidence of commands, orders, and requests issued to her by her mother. Interestingly, the two adult females, Hester Prynne and Mistress Hibbins, have similar patterns of speech toward the child. Surprisingly, two of the male characters, the shipmaster and the governor, give Pearl no commands, and Dimmesdale's rate of regulatory speech is much lower than Hester's. No doubt Hester's parental role as disciplinarian and primary caretaker of Pearl necessitates her regulatory speech, though studies of fatherly language, such as that done by Gleason and Greif, indicate that men typically send many direct orders to female children. The short supply of regulatory language from male characters underscores Pearl's fatherless condition and emphasizes Hester's motherly responsibilities.

While the three functional categories presented in Table 12 cover all the speech to Pearl by the governor, the shipmaster, and Mistress Hibbins, nearly all of Dimmesdale's speech to Pearl, and most of her mother's speech to Pearl, it accounts for only about two-thirds of Pearl's discourse. The remainder of her speech falls into expressive, imaginative, and poetic categories, elements almost entirely absent from the reported direct discourse of the adults to her. This suggests a loss of creativity and freedom in the mature characters, probably because their adult cares do not permit such talk and because the restrictions of their Puritan culture do not encourage it.

Nearly half of both her mother's and her father's speech to Pearl involves questioning, and one-third of Mistress Hibbins' speech, two-thirds of the shipmaster's speech, and all of the governor's speech to Pearl are composed of questions. In the previous chapter, we observed the frequency of Pearl's questioning language; here we also note a great frequency of questions in the adult talk of the novel. Some of the adult questions have as an ulterior motive a distant regulatory aim, as when the shipmaster's inquiries lead to Pearl carrying a message from him to her mother. Nonetheless, Pearl, like most children, models her behavior, including her questioning, on patterns she observes in adults.

Randall Stewart's second chapter ("The Adaptation of Material from the American Notebooks in Hawthorne's Tales and Novels") of commentary in his edition of *The American Notebooks* traces parallels between Una in her father's journals and Pearl in *The Scarlet Letter*. Specifically, Stewart states that entries about Una from July 1849 are reflected in *The Scarlet Letter*, which Hawthorne was writing in the summer of 1849. However, Hawthorne's personal observations from the entire year preceding his start on *The Scarlet Letter* are directly influential, and his journal entries as far back as June 1847 may be relevant. For example, compare some of Pearl's fictional demands to Una's real one from the previous winter:

74 The Voice of the Child

> Pearl, looking at this bright wonder of a house, began to caper and dance, and imperatively required that the whole breadth of sunshine should be stripped off its front, and given to her to play with. [*Scarlet Letter* 103]
>
> "Come, my child!" said Hester, looking about her from the spot where Pearl had stood still in the sunshine. "We will sit down a little way within the wood, and rest ourselves."
> "I am not aweary, mother," replied the little girl. "But you may sit down, if you will tell me a story meanwhile." [184]
>
> Today Una is exceedingly ungracious in her mode of asking, or rather demanding favors. For instance, wishing to have a story read to her, she has just said, 'Now I'm going to have some reading'; and she always seems to adopt the imperative mood, in this manner. She uses it to me, I think, more than to her mother, and from what I observe of some of her collateral predecessors, I believe it to be an hereditary trait to assume the government of her father. [Sunday, 28 Jan. 1849; *American Notebooks*, Centenary Ed., 414]

In Hawthorne's descriptions of Una, we find elements of Pearl's speech and manner of talking, the roots of Pearl's approach to her parents, and a reference to inherited traits, one of the great themes in *The Scarlet Letter*. In creating Pearl's language, Hawthorne clearly drew on his specific observations of his own daughter's speech.

While symbolism surrounds Pearl's presentation, lifelike details of her characterization grew out of Hawthorne's personal interactions with living children. Furthermore, a sensitivity to childhood permeates the entire book, not just a few paragraphs which parallel Hawthorne's journals. Generational lines are highlighted constantly; the Custom House section contains references to forefathers and grandchildren, and the conclusion hints that Pearl later bears a child of her own. Children generally provide a softening influence within the story: the woman holding a child has the kindest remarks about Hester as she is first led out of prison, and the responsibility of caring for Pearl keeps Hester from various temptations throughout the book. Yet the darker side of children and family ties are also represented, as when some of the Puritan children behave cruelly or when Hawthorne notes that "out of the whole human family" (64) it would be hard to find a group of people less capable of passing judgment on Hester than those who actually do. Thus, the human race is said to be a "family," the town is described as "natal soil" (31), and the narrator speaks of his "filial duty" in telling the tale (33).

Family imagery pervades *The Scarlet Letter*, and the relationship between parents and children in the novel is crucial, both literally in the case of Pearl, Hester Prynne, and Arthur Dimmesdale, and metaphorically in the American concern of dealing with the heritage left by our Puritan predecessors. Language either connects or fails to connect the generations, from the narrator telling the story of his town's ancestors, to Hester's patient and motherly exchanges with Pearl, to Dimmesdale's inability to talk to his daughter, to Pearl's overseas letters to her mother. The success or failure of parent-child communication is vital for *The Scarlet Letter* in both its literal and symbolic contexts.

Fathers and Sons

In *The Scarlet Letter* Pearl suffers from her illegitimate status and isolated condition, but at least she is affiliated with a single group of people who are in control of their particular environment and whose cultural boundaries are clear. In contrast, Jerzy Kosinski's *The Painted Bird* illustrates the powerful ties between cultural conflicts and linguistic tensions. In this novel, a child who is brutalized because of his ethnic and religious identification responds to his grotesque treatment by becoming mute. In refusing to talk, he embodies, literally and figuratively, the total collapse of intercultural communication. Multicultural settings do not automatically create linguistic problems, but when children are placed in situations in which different backgrounds clash, language difficulties can result. When parent-child language must deal with multicultural conflicts as well as with the ordinary difficulties associated with growing up and developing a relationship with one's parents, such burdens can cause a deterioration in parent-child discourse.

Fathers and sons seem particularly susceptible to upsets in communication. Some linguists assert that father-to-child language must be recognized as different from mother-to-child language but that the notion of "different" does not entail the notion of "inferior" or "harmful." In fact, Gleason and Greif conclude their study, "Men's Speech to Young Children," by saying that fathers' different speech style is useful since children must learn to communicate with people who are "not tuned in to them in the warm, sensitive ways their mothers are" (149). Nevertheless, in many multicultural literary situations, fathers' language behaviors betray antagonism toward their sons. The conflicts and inappropriate language observed in these literary situations may not represent what really happens between most fathers and sons, and father-son language in multicultural settings has been given little, if any, attention in linguistic studies. On the other hand, father-son relationships and the conflicts of the surrounding culture as they impinge on the family are at the heart of much American fiction.[2] The following four novels and short stories illustrate the problems of father-son communication in multicultural settings: William Faulkner's *Light in August*, Henry Roth's *Call It Sleep*, Langston Hughes's "Father and Son," and Flannery O'Connor's "The Lame Shall Enter First."

In *Light in August* Joe Christmas spends the first five years of his life in an orphanage where he is constantly referred to by derogatory epithets. Though his grandfather works at the orphanage, in five years they have "not spoken a hundred words" (129). When unsubstantiated rumors surface that Joe has black blood, the agency hastily places him in an adoptive home. The only portion of the adoptive interview Joe later remembers is that McEachern, the man who takes him, remarks on his name, saying, "Christmas. A heathenish name. Sacrilege. I will change that," adding, "He will eat my bread and he will observe my religion.... Why should he not bear my name?" (135-36). Thus, the man who would be Joe's father begins by trying to eliminate the boy's only possession, his name.

The first exchange of words between the man and the boy is prophetically incomplete. Mr. McEachern tells the boy they have arrived at the McEachern residence, and then, when he gets no response, he repeats the information: "'I said, there is your home.' Still the child didn't answer. He had never seen a home, so there was nothing for him to say about it. And he was not old enough to talk and say nothing at the same time" (135). Even thereafter Joe has little to say to this man, for his tone and words do not invite discussion. As Faulkner writes, "His voice was not unkind. It was not human, personal, at all. It was just cold, implacable, like written or printed words" (139). McEachern completely dominates his wife, and for the first three years of Joe's stay in her home, Mrs. McEachern is reported as saying to the young boy only his name, "Joe." Cleanth Brooks includes *Light in August* in his study of "Faulkner's 'Motherless' Children," and it is true that Joe is motherless because his biological mother is dead and his adoptive mother is ineffectual. Yet, while Joe's motherless condition influences the development of his character, the presence of the fathers and grandfathers seems just as significant as the absence of the mothers.

From various childhood events, Joe learns to despise religion, to despise women, to despise men, and, above all, to despise himself. Both his biological grandfather and his adoptive father prove unwilling or unable to talk to him or love him, and the inability to talk and to love seem closely related. To his grandfather he represents a racial problem, and to McEachern he represents a religious problem. Their racial and religious intolerances and their failures as father figures help mold Joe Christmas into a warped adult who leads a destructive, unhappy life until he is finally killed by a mob.

Flannery O'Connor's "The Lame Shall Enter First" comes to a less grisly end than the climax of *Light in August* only because the violence is confined to one family, though the family is a microcosm of the larger society. Shepard, the father in "The Lame Shall Enter First," does not appreciate the good qualities of his ten-year-old son Norton and instead dwells on the boy's materialistic tendencies:

> "Norton," Shepard said, "do you have any idea what it means to share?"
> A flicker of attention. "Some of it's yours," Norton said.
> "Some of it's *his*," Shepard said heavily.
> It was hopeless. Almost any fault would have been preferable to selfishness—a violent temper, even a tendency to lie. [317-72]

When Shepard sees his son eating chocolate cake for breakfast, it does not occur to him that he ought to be giving the child a nutritious meal. Rather, he is reminded of a boy he saw digging in a garbage can for food, and he chastises his son:

> "When I saw him yesterday, he was skin and bones. He hasn't been eating cake with peanut butter on it for breakfast."
> The child paused. "It's stale," he said. "That's why I have to put stuff on it." [372]

The cake is stale, and so is the father-son relationship, which is why the boy is driven to "put stuff on it" by hoarding coins and eating cake and entering contests. The father's failure to recognize his son's needs is shown by his lecturing and his verbal coldness not unlike McEachern's. Moreover, the man is unwilling to address the one issue close to the child's heart, the death of his mother:

> "You have a healthy body," Shepard said, "a good home. You've never been taught anything but the truth. Your daddy

gives you everything you need and want. You don't have a grandfather who beats you. And your mother is not in the penitentiary...."

"If she was in the penitentiary," he began in a kind of racking bellow, "I could go seeeeee her...."

Shepard sat helpless and miserable, like a man lashed by some elemental force of nature. This was not normal grief. It was all part of his selfishness. She had been dead for over a year and a child's grief should not last so long. "You're going on eleven years old," he said reproachfully.

"If you stop thinking about yourself and think what you can do for somebody else," Shepard said, "then you'll stop missing your mother." [373]

Norton suffers from a double loss; in this story, as in Faulkner's, the child's mother has died, and his father is incapable of helping him cope with his loss. The man's advice does not help his son and only illustrates Shepard's weaknesses as a father. Shepard's behavior is made more reprehensible by the fact that, professionally, he is a youth counselor.

The garbage-eating child held up to shame Norton is Rufus Johnson, a black fourteen-year-old juvenile offender raised by a religiously fanatical grandfather. Impressed by Johnson's high IQ score, Shepard, who is white, invites him into his home. When Rufus Johnson's grandfather takes his Bible into the hills to await the end of the world, Johnson moves into the Shepard house, where Norton is forced to share everything with him, and where Shepard tries to father him. Of course, Shepard could not be a father to his own son and is certainly no more adept at communicating with Johnson across race and class lines, and what Norton needs is more attention, not a rival for his father's limited affection. Johnson recognizes Shepard's foolishness and the friction between the father and son, and he uses situation to his own advantage.

Johnson, who believes his evil is due to Satan and who is resigned to damnation, teaches Norton about the Bible. Shepard, a nonbeliever, does not explain his feelings or the process that lead him to disbelief to his son. Therefore, Norton receives Johnson's explanation of Christianity with great joy, for it offers him the hope of seeing his dead mother in heaven. Johnson's continued problems with police, his insolent response to what Shepard mistakenly believes is untainted goodwill, and his biblical instructions to Norton prove too much for Shepard. When Johnson is finally taken away in handcuffs, Shepard realizes he must go to Norton, "to kiss him, to tell him that he loved him, and that he would never fail him again" (404). But it is too late for any physical or verbal display of love. The boy has hung himself to join his mother. Once again, fathers and grandfathers have failed to communicate with their sons and grandsons, have failed to nurture them, and, against a backdrop of religious and racial confusion, have set themselves and their descendants on a fatal course.

"Father and Son," the final selection in Langston Hughes's *The Ways of White Folks*, also finds death and destruction a natural outcome of failed father-son communication. *The Ways of White Folks* contains many variations on the theme of white fathers with biracial sons. In this case, Colonel Thomas Norwood is a white Southern planter and his son Bert is the product of Norwood's long-term relationship with his black servant. The father provides an education for the son and takes some interest in him, while the son emulates his father and insists on being around him until he is sent away to school. Still, because no words ever express the father-son connection, bitter rancor builds.

In an early, life-shaping event, the boy is severely beaten for referring to the Colonel as his father:

> Young Bert sassed the Colonel, too, just as though he were colored. And somehow, he had acquired that way of referring to Norwood as papa. The Colonel told him, sternly and seriously, "Boy, don't *you* use that word to me." But still, forgetful little devil that he was, he had come running up to the Colonel that day in the stables yelling, "Papa, dinner's ready."
>
> The slap that he received made him see stars and darkness, Bert remembered. As though he were brushing a fly out of the way, the Colonel had knocked him down under the feet of the horses, and went on talking to his guests. After the guests had gone, he switched Bert mercilessly. [215-16]

Bert grows up desperate to be acknowledged as the Colonel's son and determined not to be treated according to the social limits placed on his race. When he returns from school one summer, a handsome, strong, and stubborn man much like his father, the conflicts that might be natural between a father and a son with similar temperaments are increased by the racial barrier between them and multiplied by the years of unspoken hostility. Their final interview, held at gunpoint, is sparked by Bert's refusal to work in the fields or to behave subserviently:

"Oh, but I'm not a nigger, Colonel Norwood," Bert said, "I'm your son."

The old man frowned at the boy in front of him. "Cora's son," he said.

"Fatherless?" Bert asked.

"Bastard," the old man said.... "You black bastard," he said.

"I've heard that before." Bert just stood there. "You're talking about my mother." [233]

The Colonel could not talk to Bert as his son when Bert was a boy, and the Colonel is even less able to talk to him as a man. Bert understands the Colonel's predicament but refuses to accept it: "'I'm not a nigger,' Bert said. 'Ain't you my father? And a hell of a father you are, too, holding a gun on me'" (233). The Colonel cannot bring himself to fire at Bert; they struggle, and the younger man accidentally kills the older one. He is hunted down but shoots himself before he is captured, so the pursuing mob, cheated of its prey, avenges itself on Bert's brother Willie. The next day's newspaper reports the murder of the Colonel and the lynching of his two "field hands," stating that "the dead man left no heirs" (248).

A different kind of ending appears in Henry Roth's *Call It Sleep*, a story in which the problems of Jewish immigrants take center stage. Written mostly from the perspective of David Schearl when he is between five and seven years old, this novel layers the native languages of many immigrant groups, the broken English of newly naturalized citizens, and the distinctive dialects of New York. The book also contrasts the relationships between the boy and his parents as those relationships are expressed through their language. From the beginning, the mother is loving and protective toward the boy, while the father is angry and suspicious. Though the facts of the case do not emerge until novel's end, the father, who has a violent temper anyway, has long harbored a grudge against his wife and David because he thinks, mistakenly, that she married him while pregnant with a gentile's child. The father also believes his in-laws rushed him off to America to avoid the scandal brewing over his own mother's implications that he had killed his father or at least permitted him to die in an avoidable accident. This family has a history of father-son violence.

The contrast between the treatment David receives from his mother and his father is set up in the first two chapters of the book. In the first, his mother, who knows little English and has explored only the block or two around her apartment, is shown patiently and kindly

Parent-Child Discourse 81

explaining things to her son. Interrupting her housework, David asks for his calendar:

> He held back. "Show me where my birthday is."
> "Woe is me!" she exclaimed with an impatient chuckle. "I've shown it to you every day for weeks now."
> "Show me again."
> She rumpled the pad, lifted a thin plaque of leaves. "July—" she murmured, "July 12th . . . There!" She found it. "July 12th, 1911. You'll be six then."
> David regarded the strange figures gravely. "Lots of pages still," he informed her.
> "Yes."
> "And a black day too."
> "On the calendar," she laughed, "only on the calendar. Now do come down." [19]

In the second chapter, his father is impatient and hateful, resenting the necessity of explaining things to his young son. In this scene, which David reports as the first time he and his father had ever been alone, the father, having been dismissed from the premises for attacking another worker with a hammer, sends his son into his former workplace. Albert Schearl instructs David to retrieve his clothes and his final pay:

> "Do you see that door?" He shook him into attention. "In the grey house. See? That man just came out of there."
> "Yes, Papa."
> "Now you go in there and . . . say this: I'm Albert Schearl's son. He wants you to give me the clothes in his locker and the money that's coming to him. Do you understand? When they've given it to you bring it down here. I'll be waiting for you. Now what will you say?" he demanded abruptly.
> David began to repeat his instructions in Yiddish.
> "Say it in English, you fool!" [24-25]

While the mother and child can talk back and forth, exchanging words as they might exchange kisses, the boy is reserved with his father and does not dare ask questions or make demands. For his part, the father can only command and question his son. He even refers to him in roundabout ways, as when he introduces his family to a new friend: "'This is my wife. This is Joe Luter, my countryman. And that over there,' he pointed to David, 'is what will pray for me after my death'" (29). To his father, David is not a *who*, but a *what*, and so he speaks not with him, but to him and, more commonly, at him.

David, the brightest boy in his cheder, is intrigued by the rabbi's account of the angel purifying Isaiah's lips with a burning coal. In the novel's poetically appropriate conclusion, which links David to other American literary children such as Hawthorne's Pearl for whom fire imagery and the power of speech are connected, David is burnt by an electrical current in the train yard. Various plots and themes have converged in an open family fight over David's paternity, causing the boy to flee his home. When David makes contact with the electrical current, an interruption in the power supply surprises nearby residents. Traffic lights flicker and trolley cars stop. People's activities and conversations come to a halt. Thus, David's problems are shown to affect the entire neighborhood. Knocked unconscious but not seriously injured, David is carried home by a doctor and a policeman. Back at the apartment, his parents seem to have resolved their quarrel, and when the father realizes the son is hurt, "His eyes bulged, his jaw dropped, he blanched" (434). David does not understand he has purified the atmosphere in his family by causing a cleansing and clarifying discussion about the issue that has poisoned his father's attitude toward him and his mother, but he is pleased his injury could have such an effect on his father. Though Albert Schearl does not speak to his son after David's near-electrocution, he addresses his wife with unaccustomed civility.

Like the characters in *Light in August*, "Father and Son," and "The Lame Shall Enter First," the characters in *Call It Sleep* struggle against ethnic and religious prejudices while cultural pressures exacerbate hostilities between father and son. In *Call It Sleep*, the situation is mitigated by a measure of solidarity among the Jewish immigrants, the essential hope they have for a future in America, and their sense of significance in history. Yet, in the end, the possibility for normalization of father-child relations exists because family members have begun to verbalize their fears and talk about their problems. Their future seems to depend on whether the parents will maintain lines of communication and on whether the father and son can open a direct communication.

Mothers and Daughters

In her study of "Mother-Daughter Identification in *The Scarlet Letter*," Lois A. Cuddy observes that Hawthorne's picture of Pearl and his description of the mother-daughter relationship between Hester Prynne and Pearl "remain in literature unsurpassed for their psychological validity and integrity" (101). As the discussion earlier in this chapter has established, Pearl's language and the communication between mother and daughter are likewise remarkable for their linguistic validity and integrity. Most presentations of language between literary mothers and daughters have, at least until recently, lacked the vitality and verisimilitude found in Hawthorne's romance. Fiction from the traditional American canon has not tapped the rich topic of mother-daughter struggles in the way it has seized upon father-son tensions. The intensity and significance of conversations between mothers and daughters in multicultural settings have been captured in only a few novels. Betty Smith's 1943 *A Tree Grows in Brooklyn*, Paule Marshall's 1959 *Brown Girl, Brownstones*, Toni Morrison's 1970 *The Bluest Eye*, and Sylvia Wilkinson's 1983 *Bone of My Bones* are among the first and best to explore mother-daughter relationships in multicultural contexts.

Women have been identified as mothers or daughters throughout American fiction, but—except in *The Scarlet Letter* and in some recent novels—their familial roles have rarely been demonstrated by conversations with female parents or children. In much American literature, motherliness has been reduced to stereotype.[3] For example, black women have usually appeared in traditional American fiction only as mammies; while the mammy figure is often a strong and sympathetic character, as Dilsey is in *The Sound and the Fury*, this accentuates rather than fills the blank space created by the absence of women, particularly black women, as mothers in literature. As Susan Fraiman says, "The mammy marks gender as well as race. To the extent she is excluded implies the exclusion not only of blacks from a white society, but also of mothers from a patriarchal one. Her blackness encodes the invisibility of all mothers" (448).

Changes can be felt in the literary climate, however, and the silence has been broken concerning the problems of mothers and daughters in multicultural situations. In "Warrior Women: Immigrant Mothers in the Works of their Daughters," Helen M. Bannan emphasizes the significance of mothers and motherhood in writings by second-generation American women. King-Kok Cheung further traces a movement from silence to articulation in women's writing: "Both Alice Walker's *Color Purple* and Maxine Hong Kingston's *Woman Warrior* open with parental warnings against speech. Celie's stepfather threatens, 'You better not never tell nobody but God. It'd kill your mammy' (11). Maxine's mother admonishes her daughter, 'You must not tell anyone . . . what I am about to tell you' (3). Despite these explicit prohibitions, both the black and the Chinese American protagonists proceed to tell all—on paper" (162). As Barbara Christian writes in *Black Feminist Criticism: Perspectives on Black Women Writers*, "The primacy of motherhood for women is the one value that societies, whatever their differences, share" (212), so it should not surprise us that "Motherhood is a major theme in contemporary women's literature, the 'unwritten story' just beginning to be told" (212).[4]

The story of motherhood and daughterhood varies from culture to culture and even from family to family. Discussing "The Truths of Our Mothers' Lives: Mother-Daughter Relationships in Black Women's Fiction," Gloria Wade-Gayles has said that "Black women are not a monolithic group with the same needs, and same strengths, the same weaknesses, and the same dreams. They are variegated flowers in the garden of humanity" (11). All women and all mothers, regardless of race or ethnic background, are different. On both personal and cultural levels, individuals can be proud of their differences at the same time that they dread being singled out for those differences. In *Brown Girl, Brownstones*, for example, Selina Boyce is humiliated when the mother of an Anglo acquaintance draws attention to Selina's racial and ethnic identity, imploring her to say something in "that delightful West Indian accent" (289). In *The Bluest Eye*, Pauline Breedlove, a black woman from the South, feels shame when Northern black women snicker at her pronunciation of "chil'ren" (94). Literary portrayals of women in multicultural situations often center on the tension between individuality and conformity. The tensions may be related to economic, religious, racial, ethnic, social, sexual, or other pressures, but they inevitably affect the relationships between the mothers and daughters.

Of the four novels considered here, Toni Morrison's *The Bluest Eye* presents the bleakest picture of family life. The novel opens by contrasting the use of language by children and adults. The narrator, reflecting on the time when she was a girl of nine or ten, describes how adults speak, saying, "Adults do not talk to us—they give us directions. They issue orders without providing information" (12). In the first dialogue of the novel, the author then demonstrates the principle just described, showing the narrator's mother addressing her daughter: "When, on a day after a trip to collect coal, I cough once, loudly, through bronchial tubes already packed tight with phlegm, my mother frowns, 'Great Jesus. Get on in that bed. How many times do I have to tell you to wear something on your head? You must be the biggest fool in town. Frieda? Get some rags and stuff that window'" (13). Overworked and overburdened, the mother becomes further incensed when her daughter vomits on the bed she has been ordered to occupy. Unfortunately, this is the most positive example of mother-daughter interaction in the novel.

The Bluest Eye tells the story of a young black girl named Pecola Breedlove who is placed in foster care and so comes to live temporarily with the narrator, Claudia, her older sister Frieda, and their mother and father. Though Claudia's family is poor, Pecola's family is sometimes homeless. At one point, they take up residence in an abandoned storefront, and the narrator states that "They lived there because they were poor and black, and they stayed there because they believed they were ugly" (34). Holding on only to a wish for blue eyes, her personal symbol of prettiness, Pecola is abused by her classmates, ignored and disliked by her mother, and ultimately raped and impregnated by her father. The novel ends after Pecola's baby has died and Pecola has become insane.

Although the book does not feature a great deal of dialogue, Pecola and her mother are shown in direct communication only once. In this climactic scene, Mrs. Breedlove rejects her daughter while embracing the doll-like white child of her employers. The sequence begins when Claudia and Frieda accompany Pecola to the house where Mrs. Breedlove is a housekeeper. Mrs. Breedlove, the name by which even her own daughter addresses her, asks Pecola one question ("Pecola, who are these children?" [85]) and gives the three girls two orders ("Come on in while I get the wash" [85] and "You all stand stock still right there and don't mess up nothing" [86]). As the three stand in the kitchen, a little white girl enters and asks, "Where's Polly?" (86). The narrator Claudia reports a feeling of violence surging within her at the sound of this child using Mrs. Breedlove's first name. Just then the girls notice a fresh berry pie cooling on a counter, and Pecola accidentally knocks the pie onto the floor where it crashes, burning Pecola's legs and splashing sauce all over the freshly cleaned kitchen. Mrs. Breedlove runs in, slaps Pecola, and, incoherent with anger, screams at her daughter:

> "Crazy fool . . . my floor, mess . . . look what you . . . work . . . get on out . . . now that . . . crazy . . . my floor, my floor . . . my floor. . . . Pick up that wash and get out of here, so I can get this mess cleaned up!" [87]

In contrast, Mrs. Breedlove comforts the white girl with soothing words: "Hush, baby, hush. Come here. Oh Lord, look at your dress.

Don't cry no more. Polly will change it" (87). The anger and disgust which the mother feels for her daughter—a reflection of the anger and disgust Mrs. Breedlove undoubtedly feels for herself—are highlighted by the facts that this is the only direct communication shown between them in the novel and that obviously the white child is the sole object of Mrs. Breedlove's gentler feelings.

Thereafter, Pecola, acutely aware that everyone, including her mother, thinks she is unattractive, says little to anyone, even to her peers. She spends time in the company of three neighborhood prostitutes who serve in many respects as substitutes for her mother, providing some adult female companionship and conversation. Her father, also starved for attention and love, eventually rapes her while he is drunk. Both of Pecola's parents are described as having grown up without nurturing parents, and all the novel's descriptions of parents show both mothers and fathers to be flawed. The conclusion of this problem is death for Pecola's baby and madness for the baby's mother. Even so, the novel presents parents more as the victims of a failed society than as the producers of social failure.

Brown Girl, Brownstones shows a different outcome of the conflicts faced by mothers and daughters. Critics have praised *Brown Girl, Brownstones*, Paule Marshall's first book, as one of the earliest American novels to describe an interior life for black women and to portray relationships between black women in a realistic manner, not stereotyping them positively or negatively. Published in 1959, *Brown Girl, Brownstones* draws on many of Paule Marshall's own experiences growing up in Brooklyn during the 1930s and 1940s as the child of West Indian immigrants. Though it shows unvarnished bitterness between mother and daughter, the book bears its author's dedication "To My Mother." *Brown Girl, Brownstones* takes Selina Boyce from her childhood to her college years as she struggles to assert her personality and independence. Keenly conscious of their Barbadian roots, the adults, particularly the mother Silla Boyce, look askance at Selina's contacts with blacks from the American South, with whites, and with other ethnic groups, but the family embraces and pursues the American dream of financial success and achievement.

For Silla Boyce, success means "owning house." Silla and Deighton Boyce both have jobs, they have ample food, they live in a comfortable rented brownstone with elegant furnishings left behind by previous owners, and they have a network of friends. In comparison with the characters in *The Bluest Eye*, they are incredibly well-to-do, but Silla is aware of the imminent pressures of poverty and racism, and she is determined to become a property owner at any cost. She sells her husband's land in Barbados without his knowledge, she has her husband deported, she nearly kills an elderly, nonpaying tenant, and she drives away another tenant who is one of Selina's few friends. At least on the surface, Selina is appalled by her mother's behavior.

The book begins with ten-year-old Selina complaining to her father about her mother's rules while her father tells her "to heed yuh mother. . . . Yuh mother know best" (9). Though "the mother"—the term often used by the omniscient narrator and always used when representing Selina's consciousness—overshadows everything in the opening passages, her first conversation with Selina does not occur until the older sister tattles that Selina and her father have been making plans about building a house on his island land. In this passage, the mother is aggressive, defensive, and angry. She utters commands and questions and mild insults such as the following: "Get in the house. . . . What you two was talking today? . . . Don play ignorant. . . . The plans 'bout the piece of ground. . . . Oh, your womanishness gon do for you, soul" (44-45). When Silla describes to her daughter the hardships in Barbados that prevent her from wanting to return, Selina responds to her mother evasively, for she loves her father and admires his dreams. They argue, and Silla suddenly remembers her son who died of heart problems. At that point they are both angry:

> "I keep telling you I'm not him. I'm me. Selina. And there's nothing wrong with my heart." For a moment the words hung between them, then Selina darted around her and strode from the kitchen.
> Stunned, Silla could only stare. . . . "Look how I has gone and brought something into this world to whip me." [47]

This conversation includes the expression of conflicting points of view, an anger tempered by respect, and a moment of pregnant silence.

Silla can be respectful to her daughter, as when she gives permission for Selina to go to the movies without her older sister: "What you need Ina for any more? You's more woman now than she'll ever be, soul. G'long" (53). But Silla usually approaches her daughter from a superior position of strength and anger. For example, when Selina overhears her mother's plans to sell her father's land, Silla threatens to kill her if she tells: "I gon kill you even though you's my child. . . . Oh, I know. I know I isn't to do a thing against your beautiful-ugly father. He's Christ to you. But wait. Wait till I finish with him. He gon be Christ crucified" (76-77). Selina reacts to such language with feelings of fear and awe. When she wants tenderness from an adult woman, she seeks out the company of Miss Thompson, an understanding hairdresser from the South, or Suggie Skeetes, the Barbadian tenant whom Silla later evicts for alleged prostitution. These women add other dimensions to the meaning of womanhood for Selina.

Most of the conversations between Silla and Selina turn into confrontations. The end of Selina's childhood is signalled in the most bitter confrontation of all after Silla sells Deighton's land and turns him in as an illegal alien. Selina calls out the name "Hitler" over and over, hitting her mother with each vocalization. She stops only when she finally falls asleep in exhaustion. Selina looks down at her daughter "with a strange awe and respect" and begins to touch her with "a frightening possessiveness": "Each caress declared that she was touching something which was finally hers alone" (185). Silla's sense of victory comes from generating in her daughter the kind of anger and frustration which will allow her to speak and act defiantly and which will spur her on to successful living.

After Deighton Boyce dies during deportation, Silla buys her house, and Selina goes through a period of rejecting her mother's values. Despite much unhappiness between them, Selina finally admits she admires her mother. When she announces her intention to leave Brooklyn for Barbados, Selina explains: "Because you see I'm truly your child. Remember how you used to talk about how you left home and came here alone as a girl of eighteen and was your own woman? I used to love hearing that. And that's what I want" (307). In this speech, not only does Selina admit her respect, but she even ties her feelings to earlier conversations she had with her mother. For her part, Silla gives a sort of blessing to her daughter's leaving: "G'long! You was always too much woman for me anyway, soul. And my own mother did say two head-bulls can't reign in a flock. G'long!" (307). Recalling her own mother's language, Silla approves her daughter's plan. Although much has been left unsaid between the two over the years and although they have often spoken harshly to each other, at least Silla and Selina have continued to communicate. Silla has been a model of linguistic and behavioral strength, refusing to submit her will to anyone's. While her methods of preparing her daughter for womanhood have been rough, the mother has ultimately achieved her goal of getting her daughter to be independent, active, and assertive. Furthermore, the novel shows cultural conflicts to be at least partly responsible for requiring women to be strong if they are to survive.

Betty Smith's *A Tree Grows in Brooklyn*, which begins with events in 1912, also shows how the stresses of being different from the dominant culture can affect family life and require women to behave assertively. This novel shares some important similarities with *Brown Girl, Brownstones*. Both are set in Brooklyn and focus on a young girl growing up in a family proud of its immigrant roots. Both also show the mother-daughter relationship as the central factor in the daughter's development.

Francie Nolan's family is oppressed because they are immigrants, Catholics, uneducated, and poor. Francie and her brother are the first in their family to graduate from grammar school. They survive on the economic fringes of life, often having a place to live only when their mother can clean an apartment building in exchange for rooms. They eat mostly leftovers their father brings home from parties where he sings for a little money, food, and drink. Describing the women in Francie's mother's family, the narrator says they were made "of thin invisible steel" (62) and then compares the maternal and paternal lines: "The Rommelys ran to women of strong personalities. The Nolans ran to weak and talented men" (63). Still, the mother and father in this story genuinely love each other, and both love their children.

The language Katie Nolan uses with her daughter Francie is, like that in *Brown Girl, Brownstones*, aimed at building survival skills in the daughter. Their conversations are never sweet, but they are not marked by the overt bitterness and anger shown in Silla and Selina's exchanges, possibly because the mother in this story, though poorer, is more secure about herself and has a happier relationship with the father. Here, too, the characters have a clear spiritual and familial framework from which they operate, and they do not define themselves on the basis of economic achievement. They are not driven toward materialism, but they believe in the American system. Katie Nolan is acutely aware of her own mother's reasons for immigrating to America, and so instills in her children the desire to do better than their parents or grandparents. To give them a sturdy foundation in the English language and in cultural concepts, she insists that each night they read one page from the King James Bible and one page from Shakespeare's works.

Katie Nolan does not pamper her daughter. In their earliest conversations, Mrs. Nolan gives Francie numerous instructions in a firm and neutral tone: "Take eight cents from the cracked cup and get a quarter loaf of Jew rye bread and see that it's fresh. Then take a nickel, go to Sauerwein's and ask for the end-of-the-tongue for a nickel" (10). And later, "Stop being so foolish. If there's one thing certain, it's that we all have to get old someday. So get used to the idea as quickly as you can" (37). For her part, Francie always obeys her mother, but even from the beginning she challenges her commands in mild ways: "Oh, Mama, it's *Saturday*. All week long you said we could have dessert on Saturday" (10). Because Katie Nolan is never cruel and because Francie is never defiant, the two get along well. No threats or strong challenges are issued on either side, but neither is there much playful language. Their impoverished circumstances and constant work keep them from having the luxury of playful interaction, though Francie has some fanciful conversations with her father, and she engages in imaginative thinking on her own.

Strong bonds between mother and daughter are nevertheless clear. When Francie has to get her shots to enter school, the doctor and nurse insensitively comment on her dirty arm. Francie, thinking that all women would be reasonable and kind like her mother and her aunts is especially shocked by the nurse's words. When she relates the experience to her mother, though, her mother turns bad into good:

> "Why, Mama, why? Why do they have to . . . to . . . say things and then stick a needle in your arm."
> "Vaccination," said Mama firmly, now that it was all over, "is a very good thing. It makes you tell your left hand from your right. You have to write with your right hand when you go to school and that sore will be there to say, uh-uh, not this hand. Use the other hand."
> . . . After mama explained about vaccination, Francie began to think that maybe it was a wonderful thing. It was a small price to pay if it simplified such a great problem and let you know which hand was which. [132]

Affectionate feelings are rarely expressed, but kindness underlies most of the family's conversations. When Francie and Neely's father dies, the narrator says that their mother

> did something very unusual. It was unusual because she was not a demonstrative woman. She held the children close to her and kissed them good night.
> "From now on," she said, "I am your mother and your father." [269]

So, Francie's childhood ends quite early, for she experiences a (thwarted) sexual attack and lives through her father's death before she graduates from grade school. Though she and her mother have conflicts developing in part from their cultural circumstances—Francie is not permitted to continue on in school, for example, due to their acute financial need—the solid foundation the mother and daughter have established enables them to keep open lines of communication.

Just as *A Tree Grows in Brooklyn* is idealized even though it includes some unpleasant and painful details, *Bone of My Bones* is romanticized even though it contains some ugly and grotesque ones. *Bone of My Bones* is an emotional, almost spiritual, account of a girl who lives in a lower class environment but who by intelligence and talent is far above her surroundings.

The book begins with the main character, Ella Ruth Higgins, writing a narrative for her time capsule and composing short stories:

> My name is Ella Ruth Higgins and it is 1950 the year I will be ten years old. I live in Summit, North Carolina and at the time I am burying this time capsule, the country is called the United States of America. We do not have much money (money is what you buy things with—the two round metal things in here) so there isn't much I can put in this box....
>
> The real reason I am writing this is to tell you the story of Little Star. She is a Croatan Indian, and the white people are very cruel to her. [13-14]

What Ella Ruth knows about Indians she probably learned in books, for she herself is neither an Indian nor a member of any racial or ethnic minority. However, Ella Ruth and her family inhabit a socioeconomic niche at odds with the dominant culture.

Recounting her earliest memories, Ella Ruth presents her mother as her salvation from all disasters. She remembers that after going out on her father's orders to announce that the President had died, she was slapped by a neighbor and then ran home to her mother's arms:

> "She hit me, Mama."
> "What? That old fool hit you? Maynard, that damned old fool hit Ella Ruth. Why did she hit you honey? I'll break her scrawny old neck." [16]

After comforting her daughter, Mama then tries to explain to Ella that they have had nothing to do with the President's death: "You never killed one living thing. He was just an old beat up cripply man had no business still trying to be President. And he died, that's all" (17). When Ella Ruth's father explains his view of Hitler's mistake ("He should have put them Jews to work like we did the niggers. Too much trouble to kill them all" [19]) and begins to rant that ignoring the principle of survival of the fittest will ruin the human race, Mama pointedly asks, "Didn't you have rheumatic fever as a child, Maynard?" (20). When Ella Ruth's pet duck is killed by other ducks, Mama consoles her by saying, "Don't worry, Ella Ruth, honey. Come Easter and I'll get you a brand new pretty little yeller duck" (21). Throughout the book, the mother is extraordinarily gentle and tender to her daughter.

Because of the sensitivity of the mother, it is somewhat surprising when Ella Ruth provides a physical description of her: "I never knew Mama pretty. Her chin had enough white bristles to be on an old man. Her features were lost in too much flesh, her nose much too tiny for her face. Her plucked brows were loose hairs, grown together across her forehead. . . . Only her eyeballs, clear blue and round as marbles had kept their shape. I never knew Mama thin, either. Big as a barrel, Daddy called her" (30). Mama's manners are likewise rough and crude, and she is not very smart. She fumbles in any conversation, whether the topic is how babies get made, what happened in Bible adventures, or who Chester A. Arthur was. Still, she is a good woman, and her feelings are easily hurt.

Ella Ruth's father treats her mother badly. When Mama's stomach bothers her, he suggests she eat Drano to clear out the grease and garbage she has been stuffing down her pipes. He spends most of their money in saloons, so Ella Ruth and her mother have many conspiratorial conversations about hiding the money they earn from selling produce and baked goods. Other people also treat Mama so unfeelingly that she never leaves her house except for a rare emergency visit to the doctor. She is a wonderful cook, and affluent people buy the products of her kitchen but will have nothing else to do with her. Even her son, Ella Ruth's older and illegitimate half-brother, snubs her. But Mama means the world to Ella Ruth, who appreciates the good qualities beneath Mama's startling exterior. As Ella Ruth grows older, she shields her mother as her mother once shielded her, screening information she thinks might injure her mother's fragile feelings. In a psychologically interesting turn of events, Ella Ruth and her mother eventually switch roles, with the daughter protecting her mother. It is not a simple reversal, however, since Ella Ruth can express, either through her speech or through her creative writing, what Mama has never been able to say.

Ella Ruth's mother dies half-way through the novel, but the things she has taught her daughter stay with her forever. Though Mama was peculiarly inarticulate, she taught Ella Ruth to recognize the good and overlook the bad. Shortly before she became ill, she was even able to express this sentiment: "'Ella, Ella Ruth, honey,' she puffed. 'Find some peace and don't look on things so hard. There is only peace out there'" (147). Death does not diminish Mama's role in Ella Ruth's life, for the daughter continues to remember what her mother taught her. The novel closes with the protagonist's recognition that "Daddy is at home, snoring in his bed, but Mama goes with me" (272). Even the last words of the book are Mama's ("Ella Ruth, all you have to do is cut off the light" [272]) as Ella Ruth remembers what her mother used to say; the mother-daughter conversations continue even after the mother has gone.

In these four novels, *Bone of My Bones*, *A Tree Grows in Brooklyn*, *Brown Girl, Brownstones*, and *The Bluest Eye*, mother-daughter relationships are crucial in the daughters' developments. The ways in which the mothers speak or do not speak to their daughters shape their female children's lives. These four novels, all written by women, portray mother-daughter struggles having different results from the father-son struggles. Whereas the father-son relationships discussed here end mostly in tragedy, the mother-daughter relationships end mostly in victory. Even Pecola Breedlove achieves a tragic kind of victory by escaping into madness.

In the eight fictional works examined here, the sons are generally incapable of moving beyond the confines of their cultural and filial circumstances. *Call It Sleep* might present an exception to this generalization, but the protagonist in that novel adopts the kind of survival pattern used by the daughters in the four novels considered here. That is, the daughters seek out someone to love them and to talk to them (if not their mothers, then a mother substitute), and they deal creatively with their feelings toward their mothers. By writing (as in *Bone of My Bones* and *A Tree Grows in Brooklyn*), by dancing (as in *Brown Girl, Brownstones*), or by delving into madness (as in *The Bluest Eye*), the daughters find outlets through which they can vent the frustrations of their multicultural mother-daughter circumstances. All of the daughters reject parts of their mothers' models for living, but most retain the survival strategies their mothers have demonstrated. In general, the daughters are not shown becoming mothers themselves (Pecola's baby dies), and they do not move toward a traditional marriage-and-family lifestyle. However, except for Pecola, the daughters ultimately integrate their mothers' experiences into their own lives and come to understand and accept their relationships with their mothers.

Like father-son relationships, mother-daughter relationships can be extremely complex. Sometimes mothering behavior can be found in women who are not mothers. Too, the speech a mother directs toward her daughter can be as rough as that which a father directs toward his son, although sometimes, as in *Brown Girl, Brownstones*, stern language can be beneficial when it arises from love. Love can be displayed and expressed in various ways, and the different kinds of language exchanged between mothers and daughters reflect the different types of parenting and living. Of course, when there is virtually no positive language interaction, as in *The Bluest Eye*, a total breakdown in the relationship is signalled, and all the people involved suffer. The styles of language used by mothers and daughters reveal their personalities and characters and the dynamics of their relationships.

Examining fictional discourse in multicultural settings leads beyond the bounds of pure linguistics and into the realm of sociolinguistics. What has been discovered is that no one pattern of coping with cultural conflicts emerges in fictional characters' speech. In fact, the correspondence of cultural conflict and language use is difficult to establish. In the cases of mother-daughter language, for instance, the cultural situations shape the environment but do not necessarily shape the direction of the mother-daughter relationship or the mother-daughter speech. A lack of money or a lack of position in the dominant culture do not necessarily harm interpersonal relations within a family. If the individuals maintain pride in their cultural groups or—and this is true especially if they reject the values of the subcultures in which they are raised—if they maintain pride in themselves, they manage cultural clashes more successfully.

Much of the energy in modern American fiction derives from the presence of multicultural and multi-ethnic situations. In fact, issues of culture, language, and family have long influenced American literature. In the fiction examined here, as well as in other American literature, communication between cultures and between generations is a matter of great importance; the implications of the success or failure of parent-child discourse reach far beyond the literal confines of the literary situations. The authors examined in this discussion represent diverse religions, races, heritages, and genders, but they all emphasize the importance of parent-child relations, the need for loving and understanding language in families, and the dire consequences that can result when communication fails between parents and children.

6. Children's Narratives

Although storytelling is an ancient art, narratology is a relatively new area of academic inquiry.[1] In his book *Narratology: The Form and Function of Narrative*, Gerald Prince identifies the formal study of narratives as an emerging field important to many disciplines, including psychology, anthropology, history, aesthetics, literary criticism, and linguistics. Prince defines narrative as "the representation of at least two real or fictive events or situations in a time sequence, neither of which presupposes or entails the other" (4). William Labov defines narrative as "one method of recapitulating past experience by matching a verbal sequence of clauses to the sequence of events which (it is inferred) actually occurred" (*Language in the Inner City* 359-60). As a working definition here, we may think of narrative simply as storytelling, with the story generally unfolding in the same order the events had or might have had.

William Labov and his colleagues have collected and analyzed hundreds of narratives spoken in natural conversations by people of all ages and circumstances, with some emphasis on narratives by inner-city black teenagers. A universal pattern in natural narratives has been described by Labov and Joshua Waletsky in "Narrative Analysis" and by Labov in *Language in the Inner City*. Though complex chaining and embedding of narrative features can occur, Labov believes that fully formed narratives are commonly organized into the following elements in the following order: (1) an abstract; (2) an orientation; (3) a description of the complicating action; (4) an evaluation; (5) a resolution; and (6) a coda (*Language in the Inner City* 368). The abstract summarizes the whole story in a short statement. The orientation identifies the time, place, persons, and situation of the story. The complicating action section tells what happened. In the evaluation, the speaker indicates the point or the meaning of the narrative to avoid the possibility of a listener saying, "So what?" The result or resolution tells what finally happened, how it all turned out. The coda signals the narrative is over, often returning the story to present time, and announces someone else may have a turn to speak.

Here is one of Labov's examples of a natural narrative:

[ABSTRACT] (What was the most important fight that you remember, one that sticks in your mind . . .)
a   Well, one (I think) was with a girl.
b   [ORIENTATION] Like I was a kid, you know,
c   And she was the baddest girl, *the baddest girl in the neighborhood.*
d   If you didn't bring her candy to school, she would punch you in the mouth;
e   And you had to kiss her when she'd tell you.
f   This girl was only about 12 years old, man,
g   but she was a killer.
h   She didn't take no junk;
i   She whupped all her brothers.
j   [COMPLICATING ACTION] And I came to school one day
k   and I didn't have no money.
l   My ma wouldn't give me no money.
m   And I played hookies one day.
n   (She) put something on me.
o   I played hookies, man,
p   so I said, you know, I'm not gonna play hookies no more 'cause I don't wanna get a whupping.
q   So I go to school
r   and this girl says, "Where's the candy?"
s   I said, "I don't have it."
t   She says, powww!
u   [EVALUATION] So I says to myself, "There's gonna be times my mother won't give me money because (we're) a poor family
v   And I can't take this all, you know, every time she don't give me any money."
w   So I say, "Well, I just gotta fight this girl.

x She gonna hafta whup me.
y I hope she don' whup me."
z [RESOLUTION] And I hit the girl: powwww!
aa and I put something on it.
bb I win the fight.
cc [CODA] That was one of the most important.
[*Language in the Inner City* 358-59; labels added at the points when structural elements first begin to appear]

This narrative contains all the structural elements described by Labov as composing the basic narrative framework. Not all narratives necessarily contain all of the elements, but fully elaborated stories contain these basic elements which naturally fall into the organizational pattern described above.

Structure is not the only aspect of narrative which has been examined. One interesting line of study concerns the power relationship existing between speakers and listeners when a narrative is underway. Livia Polanyi has determined that while a narrator has certain conventional responsibilities, the recipient of a conversational story also operates under certain constraints, namely to

1. Agree to hear a story if it is proposed or present a reason why it should not be told.
2. Refrain from taking a turn except to make remarks demonstrating that the story is being followed and understood or asking questions that relate directly to what is being told about the storyworld.
3. At the end of telling, demonstrate understanding by making comments. . . .

["Conversational Storytelling" 200]

The relationship between speaker and hearer affects the literary interpretation of fictional narratives, particularly when children's narratives are involved, because the forms and functions of children's discourse are frequently restricted by the nature of their audience and their relationship to that audience. Issues of power have a particularly significant impact on the ways in which children speak.

One area of speech act theory relevant for narrative study concerns the criteria necessary for communication to occur. Three fundamental principles of communication common to most discussions of speech acts might be paraphrased as: (1) A speaker should refer to real things or ideas (the Reality Principle). (2) A speaker should try to coordinate speech with the listener (the Cooperative Principle). (3) A speaker should make an utterance in an appropriate context for the listener to understand (the Congruence Principle). In "Logic and Conversation" H. Paul Grice writes that to observe the cooperative principle a speaker must satisfy four maxims: (1) the maxim of quantity—give neither too much nor too little information; (2) the maxim of quality—be truthful; (3) the maxim of relation—be relevant; and (4) the maxim of manner—be clear, concise, orderly, and unambiguous. These concepts inherent in speech act theory help us understand and define the responsibilities of a narrator.

In a further development of narrative studies, Mary Louise Pratt shows in *Toward a Speech Act Theory of Literary Discourse* that Labov's analysis of structures in natural narrative corresponds to the organization of narrative literature. Pratt argues that "literary and natural narratives are formally and functionally very much alike" (66). She further insists that "all the problems of coherence, chronology, causality, foregrounding, plausibility, selection of detail, tense, point of view, and emotional intensity exist for the natural narrator just as they do for the novelist, and they are confronted and solved (with greater or lesser success) by speakers of the language every day" (66-67). The role of characters' narratives within the narrative framework of fiction has been given little attention, but the expression of natural narratives by characters within fiction supports Pratt's thesis that there should be no distinction between poetic and nonpoetic language.

The significance of narratives for children and child language has long been recognized. Iona and Peter Opie's 1959 *The Lore and Language of Schoolchildren* documents the degree to which children love to hear and tell stories. Barbara Hernstein Smith (*On the Margins of Discourse: The Relation of Literature to Language*) observes that as a result of children's natural pleasure in storytelling, the conventions of fictive discourse are absorbed very early. Philip Rossi points out in "Moral Imagination and the Narrative Modes of Moral Discourse" that narratives enhance moral learning through their concrete and imaginative formats. As in *Bone of My Bones* and in *A Tree Grows in Brooklyn*, storytelling can serve as an escape or as a survival strategy for children. Starting with Piaget, psycholinguists have measured children's cognitive development on the basis of how they tell and understand stories. In 1963, for example, Evelyn Pitcher and Ernst Prelinger published an extensive study of children's stories which they had collected to evaluate the emotional development of young children.

Susan Beck identifies three stages in the development of narrative. She says that at about age three children are mainly interested in the sounds of stories and in the feelings they evoke, that young school age children become obsessed with the content of stories, insisting that they make sense, and that older children are concerned with the psychological reality of stories, drawing sharp lines between real and pretend. In "Semantic and Expressive Elaboration in Children's Narratives" Keith T. Kernan states that younger children focus on the plain facts of a narrative and that older children like to elaborate on the event, often wandering into external factors and developing the essential narrative with more complex constructions such as relative clauses and temporal markers. These findings support and are supported by delineations of the stages in children's emotional and moral evolution; such divisions in children's development are described, for example, in Robert Kegan's *The Evolving Self.* In "The Development of Structural Complexity in Children's Fantasy Narratives," Gilbert Botvin and Brian Sutton-Smith argue that there may be direct linkage between the development of narrative skills and the evolution of other linguistic abilities.

The importance of temporal order in children's narratives is not well established. Piaget has said that before the age of seven, children are generally unable to reconstruct a series of events in their original sequence. Other investigators, though, have criticized Piaget for introducing into his experiments difficult concepts having nothing to do with temporal order. Recent evidence on this is mixed. At least in their younger years, children seem to have a different grasp of time and order than do adults, but after a certain point children have usually been found competent to understand and express temporal sequence in personal narratives.

In an extensive study of children's narratives, Carole Peterson and Allyssa McCabe have reviewed about thirteen hundred narratives by approximately one hundred children ranging in age from three-and-a-half to nine-and-a-half. Peterson and McCabe subjected child narratives to various types of analyses, finding children of all ages capable of telling coherent and sophisticated stories. Though the authors note differences in narratives which could be related to children's ages, they observe no differences between the narratives of girls and boys. Peterson and McCabe ultimately conclude that no one system or even combination of systems can adequately deal with all the forms and features of children's stories. Indeed, they end their study of *Developmental Psycholinguistics* by stating that the way a narrative is told is so personal that "three ways, even 1300 ways, of looking at children's narratives are not enough to exhaust all there is to be learned from them" (217). Their final observation also applies to the narratives of fictional children, and literary children's narratives are further complicated by the webs of narrative strategies which surround them in the larger works of fiction.

Absence of Narratives in Selected Fiction

Children's narratives do not appear in some American literature. Ironically, this absence occurs even in the writings of authors whose fame rests on their personal storytelling capacity and whose fiction features child characters. In some fictional situations, circumstances of plot render the children incapable of telling narratives. For example, in Stephen Crane's "The Angel Child," Jimmie Trescott's well-to-do cousin Cora, visiting one summer from New York, spends her birthday money on the Whilomville children in riotous mischief, ordering ice cream, candy, and, to the horror of all mothers who cherish precious curls, haircuts for all. In the midst of the tumultuous reaction to these haircuts, Dr. Trescott demands an explanation from his son: "'How did this—how did this happen?' said Trescott. Now Jimmie could have explained how had happened anything which had happened, but he did not know what had happened, so he said, 'I-I-nothin'" (563). Partially shocked by a morning full of sweet treats and partially confused by the maternal outcry around him, Jimmie is unable to trace the events contributing to the debacle. His father, drawing on some of Jimmie's apparently disjointed speech not included in the text, must impose an adult order on the events which have transpired: "In the meantime Trescott was patiently unravelling some skeins of Jimmie's tangled intellect. 'And then you went to this barber's on the hill. Yes. And where did you get the money? Yes. I see. And who besides you and Cora.'" (563). In this instance, Jimmie is unable to articulate cause-and-effect relationships in a coherent narrative.

Sometimes, thematic reasons can be found for the absence of children's narratives in fiction. Such is the case, for example, in Eudora Welty's *The Golden Apples*. This novel describes important events in the lives of several female children—Virgie Rainey, Cassie Morrison, Missie Spights, Jinny Love Stark, and some of Miss Eckhart's other piano pupils—but not one of these girls relates a complete narrative. Nor, for that matter, do any of their mothers except in indirect discourse when, as in the case of Mrs. Rainey in "The Shower of Gold" chapter, one of their voices serves as the narrator of a section. By weaving together several female narratives in indirect discourse, Welty expresses a feminine perspective on a culture which, though it restricts women's actions and bars their public speech, cannot keep women from watching, listening, thinking, and imagining.

In *The Golden Apples* Welty contrasts the absence of female direct discourse narratives with the evocative richness of feminine narratives in indirect discourse. Two examples can illustrate the differences. This indirect discourse excerpt is taken from Mrs. Rainey's chapter: "I believe he's been to California. Don't ask me why. But I picture him there. I see King in the West, out where it's gold and all that. Everybody to their own visioning" (11). The second example, which includes direct discourse, shows Miss Mayo's inability to complete a public narrative: "Miss Perdita Mayo, who had got into the bedroom and formed a circle, was telling a story. 'Sister couldn't get her new shoes back on after that funeral, because while she was in the cemetery—' Suddenly Miss Perdita appeared backing out of the room, thinking herself still telling her story, but mistaken" (252). When their points of view are expressed in indirect discourse, the women seem insightful, but when they attempt to convey narratives in direct discourse, their efforts are incomplete and unsuccessful. In writing this novel Welty creates women narrators, thus breaking, literally and symbolically, some of the chains which have traditionally imprisoned women's voices. Still, the female narrators, all of whom are adults, have difficulty communicating in direct discourse.

Most unsettling in the book is that members of the younger generation do not assume active speaking roles. As they grow older, the girls are, if anything, more mute than their mothers. Whatever verbal skills peek around from behind the curtain of childhood as the girls argue with their brothers or talk back to their teachers, when this novel's younger females move into adulthood they are unable to communicate their stories. The narrative styles of the two generations of females in *The Golden Apples* may be related to what Patricia Meyer Spacks, writing about Welty's *Losing Battles* in *The Female Imagination*, refers to as Welty's emphasis on extinct society. The break seen between the older and younger generations' manners of speaking points to a social shift, and the older styles of living and talking may be moving toward extinction. It is not clear what will replace the older style of indirect discourse expression, but the intersection of language and gender exerts a powerful force on all the characters in the novel.

Similar problems with voice and gender also affect Frankie Addams's ability to formulate narratives in Carson McCullers's *The Member of the Wedding. In this novel, F. Jasmine (Frankie) Addams, a motherless twelve-year-old girl trying to assimilate the facts of life, is cared for by her father's housekeeper, Berenice Sadie Brown, a consummate storyteller. One evening, for instance, the impending wedding of Frankie's older brother leads Berenice to tell about strange matches:

> "I have heard of many a queer thing. . . . I have knew womens to love veritable Satans and thank Jesus when they put their split hooves over the threshold. I have knew boys to take it into their heads to fall in love with other boys. You know Lily Mae Jenkins?"
> F. Jasmine thought a minute and then answered: "I'm not sure."
> "Well, you either know him or you don't know him. He prisses around with a pink satin blouse and one arm akimbo. Now this Lily Mae fell in love with a man name Juney Jones. A man, mind you. And Lily Mae turned into a girl. He changed his nature and his sex and turned into a girl."
> "Honest?" F. Jasmine asked. "Did he really?"
> "He did," said Berenice. "To all intents and purposes."
> [75-76]

Berenice's story, which fascinates Frankie and her younger cousin John Henry, fits Labov's classic pattern of natural narrative with an abstract, an orientation, a description of the complication, a brief evaluation and resolution, and a coda following her listener's question.

Despite countless narratives modeled for her by Berenice, Frankie's preadolescent confusion and insecurity cause her to hide her personal narratives. Earlier during the same day in which Berenice tells of strange couples she has known, Frankie has gotten into conversation with a soldier who buys her a beer and makes a date with her. After Berenice finishes her story about odd couples, she returns to the present time, a common technique in narrative discourse, and advises Frankie to find a beau. This provides Frankie with a perfect opportunity to tell about her adventure with the soldier, but she does not: "F. Jasmine wanted to tell Berenice about the soldier, the hotel, and the invitation for the evening date. But something checked her, and she hinted around the edges of the subject" (78). Barbara White, discussing The Member of the Wedding in her book Growing Up Female, emphasizes that Frankie's attitudes toward gender and sex affect her general behavior. Applying White's ideas here, we can see that Frankie's ambivalence and confusion about growing up are symbolized by, or demonstrated in, the fact that she has not yet discovered her own narrative voice. Her difficulties in expressing herself and in describing her feelings persist to the end of the novel, indicating that she may be, as White says, "crippled" by the process of growing up female (107).

In *Adventures of Huckleberry Finn* it is the novel's complex narrative frame rather than constraints of plot or theme which creates a dearth of child narratives in the text. The whole of *Huckleberry Finn* could be viewed as one narrative or series of narratives by a boy, but not many of those narratives are in direct discourse. As Janet McKay notes in *Narration and Discourse in American Realistic Fiction* (145), Huck's style of casually addressing the reader includes many features of direct discourse. Still, there are distinctions in the novel between direct and indirect passages, and Clemens did choose to set off certain dialogues in quotation marks.

In the direct discourse narratives of the novel, Huck rarely features himself as the primary speaker. More often, the narratives are spoken by someone else, with Huck as the audience. Well aware that the success of a narrative depends on the give and take between speaker and listener, Clemens makes Huck an active and discriminating audience. For instance, when Tom Sawyer tells the other boys the stories he has read in romance tales, Huck refuses to play along, saying, "I reckoned he believed in the A-rabs and the elephants, but as for me I think different. It had all the marks of a Sunday school" (17). But, when Huck discovers Jim hiding on the island, he convinces Jim to tell the story behind his escape—a real-life adventure as opposed to remote Sunday school stories—by assuring Jim of his reliability as a confidential listener: "Well, I did. I said I wouldn't [tell], and I'll stick to it. Honest injun I will. People would call me a low down Ablitionist and despise me for keeping mum—but that don't make no difference. I ain't agoing to tell, and I ain't agoing back there anyways. So now, le's know all about it" (39). Throughout the novel Huck wields power by facilitating or hindering the narratives of others.

When Huck is the narrator of a tale in direct discourse, he makes himself appear to be a very poor storyteller. For instance, early in the novel Huck and Jim are set upon by two men looking for runaway slaves. Jim hides inside the raft, and Huck claims the only man aboard is his father, but the slavehunters announce they will see for themselves, so Huck must talk his way out of their investigation. He haltingly and hesitantly speaks to them:

"I wish you would," says I, "because it's pap that's there, and maybe you'd help me tow the raft ashore where the light is. He's sick—an so is mam and Mary Ann. . . ."

"Pap'll be mighty much obleeged to you, I can tell you. Everybody goes away when I want them to help me tow the raft ashore, and I can't do it myself."

". . . Say, boy, what's the matter with your father?"

"It' the-a-the-well, it ain't anything, much." [75]

Surmising from Huck's intentionally incomplete narrative that the raft carries smallpox victims, the slave hunters toss Huck some gold pieces and flee. Jim and Huck are thus saved by Huck's feigned lack of narrative skill.

Sometimes in the novel Huck's stories nearly falter through weakness in content, and, in rescuing himself, Huck shows his true narrative abilities. During the Wilkeses episode when Huck is forced by two con men to pose as their English valet, Huck is questioned about life in his home country and informs the reader that "The hare-lip she got to pumping me about England, and blest if I didn't think the ice was getting mighty thin, sometimes" (137). Only through quick thinking and clever talking does Huck manage to cover the blunders he makes in telling about English customs.

Huck's narrative persona resembles Mark Twain, the persona of Samuel Clemens. Clemens, though a master storyteller, often let his persona Twain feign naivete, stupidity, or indifference in relating stories in which other characters are the principal narrators telling the words and deeds of yet other characters. So, in "The Celebrated Jumping Frog of Calaveras County" Clemens's persona Mark Twain, responding to the request of a friend from the East, seeks out Simon Wheeler to ask about the friend's friend Leonidas W. Smiley, but Wheeler instead launches into a narrative about Jim Smiley and his horse-racing, dog-fighting, and frog-jumping adventures. Each involved party, from Clemens to Twain to Wheeler to Smiley, has his own point of view and his own narrative voice.

Such intricate narrative layering is even more pronounced in *Huckleberry Finn*. The humor, irony, and ambiguity of the novel grow out of the multiple points of view: Samuel Clemens developed the persona Mark Twain, who wrote *Adventures of Huckleberry Finn*, which is told in first person by Huck Finn, who describes adventures in which he sometimes assumes other roles (a girl, George Jackson, a valet, Tom Sawyer, and so on) and in which he meets other groups of characters, some of whom also tell stories about still other characters (as when Jim describes Miss Watson's plans to sell him), often while themselves operating under a double identity (as when the King and the Duke claim to be the Wilkeses' uncles). Each frame and each level is remarkable within itself. That the entire story hangs together and rests on the indirect discourse, narrative voice of a preteen boy shows Clemens's true narrative skills.

Child Narratives Crucial to Plot and Theme

Children's direct discourse narratives can play a crucial role in the development of both plot and theme. Their significance can be seen, for example, in Harper Lee's *To Kill a Mockingbird* and John Steinbeck's *Grapes of Wrath*.

In *The Grapes of Wrath*, a cruel pecking order rules every social situation: migrants whose camps have toilets have higher status than those living without bathroom facilities, women who have bacon to cook with their potatoes feel superior to those who do not, and children not from the Ozarks make fun of those who are. The Joad children, at the bottom of the social heap in almost every encounter, seize any opportunity to give rather than receive social torment. When Ruthie gets a box of Cracker Jack, she taunts other children with it until a fight breaks out and she resorts to threatening the other children with her older brother. This incident supplies her younger brother, ten-year-old Winfield, with his only moment in the spotlight, as he gives to his mother a complete narrative of what Ruthie has said and done:

> "Ma—Ruthie tol'. . . ."
> "She—didn' eat all her Cracker Jack. She kep' some, an' she et jus' one piece at a time, slow, like she always done, an' she says, 'Bet you wisht you had some lef'.". . .
> "Well, some kids come aroun', an' 'course they tried to get some, but Ruthie, she jus' nibbled an' nibbled, an' wouldn' give 'em none. So they got mad. An' one kid grabbed her Cracker Jack box."
> "Winfiel', you tell quick about the other."
> "I am," he said. "So Ruthie got mad an' chased 'em, an' she fit one, an' then she fit another, an' then one big girl up an' licked her. Hit 'er a good one. So then Ruthie cried, an' she said she'd git her big brother, an' he'd kill that big girl. An' that big girl said, Oh, yeah? Well, she got a big brother too. . . . An' then—an' then, Ruthie said our brother already kil't two

fellas. An'—an'—that big girl said, 'Oh, yeah! You're jus' a little smarty liar.' An' Ruthie said, 'Oh yeah? Well, our brother's a-hiding right now from killin' a fella,' an' he can kill that big girl's brother too. An' then they called names an' Ruthie throwed a rock, an' that big girl chased her, an' I come home." [455-56]

Ma Joad in her nervousness tries to prod Winfield into hurrying his story, but the boy tells his narrative fully and slowly, adhering to the organizational structure Labov describes in natural narrative. The dashes within the text suggest natural pauses in speaking, and the temporal markers such as "An' then" indicate shifts in focus. Like any speaker of natural narrative, especially a child, Winfield takes his listener on side trips with somewhat irrelevant details about munching the Cracker Jack, but the story is efficient and concise enough for use in fiction. The diction and cadence of the passage fit the age and character of the speaker.

Within the dialogue, Winfield resists his mother's efforts to place her own sense of time, importance, and order on his story, but within the context of the entire novel, his narrative is subordinated to adult concerns. The older bother Tom at first brushes off the incident, saying, "That's jus' kid talk, Ma" (460), but he soon realizes that such kid talk can have serious implications. In this case, Ruthie's story and Winfield's descriptive narrative of her story result in the dissolution of the family unit, as Tom must go away to avoid detection and arrest for murder. Thus, Winfield's narrative contributes to the action of the novel, by forcing the family's break-up, and to the theme of the novel, by showing how the social system applies even to children.

In *To Kill a Mockingbird*, a child's narrative provides the details behind the novel's final drama, a climactic Halloween attack on Atticus Finch's two children. After the children are nearly killed by their assailant, who turns out to be their father's courtroom opponent Bob Ewell, the town sheriff must interview them to determine the facts of the crime. Since Jem remains unconscious, eight-year-old Scout must describe the attack by herself. She does not fully understand what has happened, but as she tells her story, the sheriff and her father aid her with prompts and questions. Scout gives several pages of narrative testimony full of factual details (such as, "I said Jem, I've forgot m'shoes" [270] and logical reasoning (for example, she knows they were under a tree because "I was barefooted, and Jem says the ground's always cooler under a tree" [272]). Her long and complex narrative is made believable by the help her father and the sheriff give her in keeping her story on track. Scout's narrative voice in the novel's climax is consistent with her speech in earlier parts of the novel, and it is also a believable representation of a precocious child's storytelling.

In sorting through the evidence of her narrative, Scout and the two men realize that she and her brother were rescued by their reclusive neighbor, Boo Radley, who must have stabbed and killed Ewell while struggling to protect the children. They also realize that because of Radley's delicate nature, they must not publicize his role in the attack and must instead agree to say that Ewell died by falling on his own knife. Despite her young age, Scout understands the morality of their choice. Throughout the book the children are taught to make moral choices; for instance, when Mr. Finch gives his children air rifles, he instructs them to shoot at cans rather than at birds, adding, "It's a sin to kill a mockingbird" (94). When she realizes that they must not publicize the full account of Boo Radley's involvement in their rescue, Scout recalls her father's earlier words and, emphasizing the novel's title, she says in the evaluation section of her narrative: "Well, it'd be sort of like shootin' a mockingbird, wouldn't it?" (279).

Concluding her narrative with the mockingbird analogy, Scout understands that bringing Boo Radley into the public eye would, like killing a mockingbird, only bring harm to an innocent creature. Her narrative ends one of the main plot lines of the novel, the Ewell affair, and it also ties in with the major themes of the book: the need for sensitivity toward other people, the importance of kindness to all living creatures, and the difficulty of making moral decisions. In an interesting narrative technique, the last paragraph of the novel merges the voice of the child character Scout with the voice of the book's narrator, Scout as an adult woman. Thus, the last paragraph serves a dual function because it closes the child's narrative at the same time that it ends the woman's story, economically and artfully functioning as a coda for both the narrative and the book.

Purposes Behind Children's Narratives

All direct discourse fictional narratives are, by definition, framed at least once by their quotation marks, and, as discussed regarding *Huckleberry Finn*, narrative framing can become quite elaborate. In *Huckleberry Finn* the frames remain relatively transparent; not until the reader consciously reflects on Clemens's technique will he or she become aware of the intricate levels of frames. In some fiction, though, child narratives, even if not highly framed, stand out as separate from the rest of the text. The appearance and use of child narratives in fiction—both *why* and *how* they are used—depend upon more than just the number and type of framing devices employed by the author.

The fundamental differences in the uses of children's narratives arise from a distinction in the role of the child in the fiction, on whether the author is recreating a child's perspective on life or whether the author is elaborating an adult point of view by contrasting it with a child's. A combination of both aims may be present in any fictional narrative, but one generally dominates the other. For example, in *Huckleberry Finn* Clemens's primary goal is to establish Huck's world view and Huck's perspective on life, but he cannot achieve his aim without contrasting Huck's point of view with that of the adults he encounters. Quite the reverse is true in *Grapes of Wrath*, where Steinbeck uses Winfield's narrative to illustrate a larger observation about society, though he could not accomplish this end without making Winfield's narrative plausible and appropriate.

Differences in the applications and interpretations of children and their narratives can be illustrated by comparing Henry Roth's *Call It Sleep* with Richard Brautigan's *Trout Fishing in America*. In *Call It Sleep* child narratives are an integral part of the novel and vividly illustrate the point of view of children growing up in an urban immigrant environment. In *Trout Fishing in America* childhood experiences merit significance only in terms of adult sensibility and have only the meaning that the book's adult narrator gives them, though the authorial voice of the book values a childlike imagination that can create its own reality from the sordid and dull elements of modern life.

Within the first few pages of *Trout Fishing in America*, Brautigan (or his authorial persona) brings the reader's attention to the importance of narrative, recalling the stories of his stepfather which changed his childhood and influenced his whole development: "The old drunk told me about trout fishing. When he could talk, he had a way of describing trout as if they were a precious and intelligent metal" (3). Next, the authorial voice turns to an episode from his own childhood which begins with this orientation:

> One spring afternoon as a child in the strange town of Portland, I walked down to a different street corner, and saw a row of old houses, huddled together like seals on a rock. . . . At a distance I saw a waterfall come pouring down off the hill. It was long and white and I could almost feel its cold spray.
>
> There must be a creek there, I thought, and it probably has trout in it. [4]

As the story unfolds, the long waterfall turns out to be a flight of stairs, and the child, becoming his own trout, eats the slice of bread he intended for bait. The story is begun by the adult, then moves to the child's point of view, but finally at the end is retaken by the adult.

A few chapters thereafter, the author again recounts an episode from childhood. This time there is dialogue among children, but still the adult author orders and interprets the experience, as we see in both its abstract ("When I was a child I had a friend who became a Kool-Aid wino as the result of a rupture" [8]) and its later evaluation ("He created his own Kool-Aid reality and was able to illuminate himself by it" [10]). These two sections of the narrative are told by the adult, but, once again, the center of the narrative represents the child's perspective.

About midway through *Trout Fishing in America*, still another chapter is given over to a narrative from the authorial persona's childhood. Its abstract ("One April morning in the sixth grade, we became, first by accident and then by premeditation, trout fishing in America terrorists" [37]) is further explained in its orientation ("One April morning we were standing around in the play yard, acting as if it were a huge open-air poolhall with the first-graders coming and going like pool balls. We were all bored with the prospect of another day's school, studying Cuba" [37]). The complicating action of this story emerges out of direct dialogue between the children as the older students write "Trout fishing in America" on the backs of the younger ones. The evaluation comes through the words of the principal, who finds all the sixth-graders guilty and points out that it would be absurd if he called the teachers into his office and wrote "Trout fishing in America" on their backs. The principal also controls the result of the narrative ("'All right,' he said. 'I'll consider trout fishing in America to have come to an end. Agreed?'" [40]), but the book's narrator writes the coda: "But it wasn't completely over, for it took a while to get trout fishing in America off the clothes of the first-graders. . . . But after a few more days trout fishing in America disappeared altogether as it was destined to from its very beginning, and a kind of autumn fell over the first grade" (40). In all of these narratives, Brautigan's method of operation is to describe a childhood experience, but to tell the story with an adult's understanding.

One might argue that Brautigan's technique does not actually utilize child narrative at all. However, while the controlling voice in *Trout Fishing in America* is an adult's, Brautigan intersperses the direct speech and the indirect thoughts of children within individual segments of narrative, giving whole narratives the flavor of childhood.

110   The Voice of the Child

In truth, Brautigan's method of handling experiences of childhood in *Trout Fishing in America* is only a step removed from Steinbeck's in *The Grapes of Wrath*. In Winfield's narrative in *Grapes of Wrath* the words of a child tell the story, but after the story is told, the controlling voice in the novel overtly traces the effects and parallels of the child's speech on or in the adult characters, the plot, and the theme of the surrounding fiction. Brautigan and Steinbeck show an interest in the experiences of childhood but are mainly concerned with how those childhood episodes are responded to and interpreted by adults.

In *Call It Sleep* Henry Roth lets his child characters tell their own stories, and he also lets the significance of those stories emerge within the course of the novel without making direct comments on them. *Call It Sleep* contains numerous narratives of immigrant children. Here is an early one about killing a rat, told by a young neighbor of the protagonist David Schearl:

> "Dey uz zuh big fat rat inna house, yuh could hear him at night, so my fodder bought dis, an' my mudder put in schmaltz f'om de meat, and nuh rat comes in, an' inna mawingk, I look unner by de woshtob, an'ooh—he wuz dere, runnin' dis way like dot." Yussie waved the cage about excitedly, "An I calls my fodder an' he gets op f'om de bed an' he fills op de woshtob and eeh! duh rat giz all aroun' in it, in nuh watuh giz all aroun'. An' nen he stops. An nen my fodder takes it out and he put it in nuh bag and trew it out f'om de winner. Boof! he fell inna guttah. Ooh wotta rat he wuz. My mudder wuz runnin' aroun', and after, my fodder kept on spittin' in nuh sink. Kcha!" [49]

In this story we are first confronted with the child's dialect, but then we hear the excitement of the event and recognize his incomplete understanding of what happened ("duh rat giz all aroun' in it, in nuh watuh giz all aroun'. An' nen he stops"). When words fail, Yussie uses body language to tell his story, waving his arms and demonstrating the trap, and he also uses creative sound expressions ("eeh" and "Boof") to enliven his tale. Perhaps guilty of some childish hyperbole, Yussie enlarges the rat to epic size ("Ooh wotta rat he wuz"), much to David's disgust. The author, though, refrains from commenting about rats or tenements or any other features of the story, and only through the reaction of David is there any commentary on the implications of the narrative.

In all of the narratives of *Call It Sleep* an awareness of audience motivates and directs storytellers. The boys in the street, for instance, tell stories to enhance their status within the group as well as to entertain themselves. Thus, Izzy brags about getting a pair of shoes for less than the asking price in this short narrative: "'I went wid my modder.' Izzy basked in their gaze. 'An' we bought shoes—best kind onnuh Eas' Side. Waid'll yuh see 'em. Wid buttons 'n' flat toes—for kickin' a foodball. He wanned t'ree dollehs, bod my modder tol' me I shull say, Peeuh! Wod lousy shoes! So we god 'em fuh two'" (291). This story prompts a dispute about what shoes are best, but Izzy stays on top of the conversation.

Then Kushy, the leader of the group, proceeds to tell a story about how he spent his morning. Kushy's timing is professional, and, forcing the six-year-olds away (the story is racy), he allows only those interruptions and questions that will augment his listeners' suspense, as we see in this excerpt:

"We seen a kinerry." A select few snickered as if at a veiled jest.
"W'a kinerry?"
"G'wan tell 'im," someone urged. . . .
"So Sadie Salmonowitz came running downstairs 'n' hollerin', My modder's kinerry, my modder's kinerry flied away! I'll give a rewuhd!"
"Yuh god a rewuhd?" Izzy asked eagerly. "How moch?"
"Waid a second. An' den we seen 'im on sebn-fawdy-six, across de stritt an' ziz! He gives a fly back an' zip! op to duh roof—" [292-93]

The story boils down to this: while chasing the canary, the boys climb to a roof where they spy a woman bathing, a woman whose body Kushy describes with great relish, to David's horror, for the woman is his mother. The general effect of the story on the boys makes Kushy a hero, so he repeats his punch line several times, "Wod a kinerry we seen!" (294), each time receiving lewd guffaws and applause from his listeners.

David's efforts to tell stories in *Call It Sleep* usually fail because he is insecure among his contemporaries on the street and overpowered by his parents at home. When he does attempt narration, as when he fabricates a story for the rabbi about his mother being dead, he needs an adult interpreter and questioner to elicit the necessary parts of the narrative. Despite the falseness and confusion in the story he tells the rabbi, the effect on his immediate audience supplies comic relief, for the rabbis infer from his responses that his father must be a gentile:

> "Then think! Think. What was he, a tailor, a butcher, a peddler, what?"
> "No. He was—He was—He played—"
> "Played? A musician? Played what?"
> "A—A—Like a piano. A—A organ!" He blurted out.
> "An organ? An organ! Reb Schulim, do you see land?"
> "I think I see what is seen first, Reb Yidel. The spire."
> [369]

Despite its amusing sections, the story leads to a terrible family fight over David's paternity and almost results in David's death. Unlike Steinbeck, who immediately returns to the adult world after Winfield's fateful narrative, and Brautigan, who sandwiches childhood stories between adult commentary, Roth keeps the focus on the child's point of view, letting the story's impact on the adult world emerge slowly and naturally. In other words, Roth shows us what happens, while Brautigan and Steinbeck tend to tell us what happens.

Most American writers have chosen to distance fictional children's narratives by funneling them through an adult's point of view. Some, such as Brautigan in *Trout Fishing in America*, have used an adult voice to impose order on a narrative while letting child speakers participate in sections of the narrative. Others, such as Dos Passos in *U.S.A.*, have presented childhood episodes through indirect discourse. On the whole, children's direct discourse narratives are relatively rare in American fiction. Though various reasons can be found for the sparsity of child narratives in literature, their absence is partly caused by the difficulties involved in letting child speakers tell their own stories. Narratives told by children can be loose, rambling, and inefficient, while prose fiction requires dialogue that is tight, focused, and efficient. Psychological difficulties must be considered as well, for, emotionally and experientially, children think and behave differently at various ages. It is less difficult to write shorter sections of dialogue for children or to portray children's thoughts in indirect discourse than to write long passages of narrative for child speakers.

Narrative voices in fiction reverberate against each other; the voice of the author rings separately from that of the narrator, who is to be distinguished from the voices of speaking characters. Whether voices in a single piece of fiction work in harmony, in contrast, or in irony, for instance, depends largely on the vision of the author who created those voices and on the cultural and literary forces that shaped that author's vision. Thus, for example, Eudora Welty's concept of the cultural context of narrative speech is not the same as Henry Roth's, whose view is different from John Steinbeck's, whose approach is distinct from Samuel Clemens's. A general interpretation of the uses of children's narratives in fiction is not possible, although children's fictional narratives clearly fulfill text-specific purposes within various novels and short stories.

7. Gender and Fictional Children's Language

The origins of sex-linked differences in language can be found both in biology and in culture, though neither factor is completely understood with respect to language or to any other human behavior. Biologically, some aspects of brain function may be different for males and for females. A physiological connection between language and gender is suggested, for example, by the fact that males are more prone to dyslexia, a condition characterized by reading difficulties caused by the brain's reversal of letters. Biological distinctions related to hormone levels may also affect language; for instance, the presence of testosterone in the amniotic fluid of in utero males is theorized to be responsible for certain male patterns of neurological development which are reflected in language acquisition.[1] Culturally, all the economic, political, legal, and other influences which create social expectations for female and male behaviors may affect language styles.[2] The present discussion cannot, of course, sort out all the social and physiological causes of gender differences in language, but at least it can stress that the reasons for those differences are myriad.

Problems plague attempts to set forth clear sexual differences in language. First, since many differences are cultural, they are relative. Also, power and status more than gender alone may affect the ways men and women use language; studies by Pamela Fishman and by Zimmerman and West suggest, for example, that the rate at which one's speech is interrupted and the frequency with which one asks questions are similar for women and children, perhaps because both groups are often in similarly inferior power positions. Women's language has traditionally been regarded as containing a number of distinctive features, including more hedges (such as *sort of* or *kind of*), more polite forms, more tag questions (as in "It's hot in here, *isn't it?*"), more intensifiers (such as *so* and *very*), more "empty" adjectives (such as *lovely* or *divine*), more hypercorrect pronunciation and grammar, less humor, and more questions or questioning intonation. However, various research, such as the study of courtroom language by William O'Barr and Bowman Atkins, indicates that these features are characteristic of powerless speech, not necessarily of women's speech.

Perhaps the greatest obstacle in sorting out gender differences in language is the confusion created by folk beliefs, stereotypes, and prejudices. Although it is not always clear whether the stereotypes are incorrect, some have been found to be erroneous. In "Women's Speech: Separate but Unequal?" Cheris Kramer identifies at least fourteen unsubstantiated beliefs about female speech. For instance, women are commonly thought to talk longer and and louder than men, but studies show that, in fact, the reverse is true; Kramer speculates that women may be perceived as more talkative because they are *expected* to be silent. Sometimes, though, research supports folk beliefs about language. For example, in Peter Trudgill's urban dialect survey of Norwich, England, women showed more concern for prestige forms of language, whereas men showed less concern for standard grammar (89-96). Whether accurate or not, stereotypes can create powerful expectations about gender-related behaviors, and expectations can be as significant as actualities.

Research has established that children recognize gender differences in language. Using puppets, Elaine Anderson has found children as young as three differentiating father and mother talk, with fathers portrayed as forceful and straightforward and mothers as polite and hesitating. Children's notions are often stereotypic, and Carole Edelsky has discovered stronger stereotypes about male and female language in sixth-grade children than in adults. It is not clear whether the same gender differences seen in adults' conversations are also found in children's. Modeling from adult patterns may make children's language similar to adults', but whether these patterns extend universally to gender styles is uncertain. Experiments by Jacqueline Sachs have shown that adults can often identify the sex of a child merely by hearing the child speak. Perhaps some sexual difference exists in the sound of the voice even before puberty, but cues to a child's sex are more likely to come from masculine or feminine patterns of speech learned early in childhood.

Various claims have been advanced about the manifestations of gender in children's speech. Daniel and Agnes Ling assert that factors such as age or birth order suppress sexual distinctions in child speech. Other people, such as Jean Berko Gleason in "Sex Differences in the Language of Children and Parents," emphasize parental input, noting that parents often speak differently to boys than to girls and that mothers and fathers have different linguistic expectations for sons and daughters. According to Marjorie Harness Goodwin, boys issue more direct commands, contradict each other more, brag more, and usurp others' conversational turns, whereas girls talk more about appearances and relationships. According to Helen C. Dawe, boys quarrel more and use more threats, whereas girls cry more. In *Language and Woman's Place* Robin Lakoff has stated that children of both sexes initially learn a form of speech Lakoff calls "women's language" and then later, between, the ages of five and ten, boys break away from feminine speech, going through a stage of rough talk and finally adopting a male pattern of speech. Many of these findings are open to challenge, however, and few comprehensive analyses of gender and language research related to children have been conducted.[3]

In "A Cultural Approach to Male-Female Miscommunication" Daniel N. Maltz and Ruth A. Borker have reexamined a variety of studies (mainly of adults) to formulate a framework for examining gender differences in speech. Maltz and Borker argue that men and women have two distinct subcultures which originate in childhood, creating the different language styles responsible for misunderstandings between the sexes. The cornerstone of Maltz and Borker's hypothesis lies in the belief that people learn the rules for social conversation between the ages of five and fifteen from peer groups composed of same-sex children. Maltz and Borker claim that "girls learn to do three things with words: (1) to create and maintain relationships of closeness and equality, (2) to criticize others in acceptable ways, and (3) to interpret accurately the speech of other girls" (205). On the other hand, they claim that boys use speech "in three major ways: (1) to assert one's position of dominance, (2) to attract and maintain an audience, and (3) to assert oneself when other speakers have the floor" (207).

Adult norms for language, are, according to Maltz and Borker, extensions of behaviors learned in childhood. Thus, women are thought to operate more in a mode of cooperative friendship, sensitive to the feelings of others, sharing ideas and experiences. In contrast, men in a friendly atmosphere are thought to debate, argue, and engage in verbal posturing with less concern for the remarks or the turns of others. Five features of adult female speech, summarized in Maltz and Borker's essay but based on other studies, are that women: (1) ask more questions; (2) maintain social interaction by facilitating the flow of conversation; (3) display more positive minimal responses (such as "mmhmm"); (4) become silent after interruption or delayed response; and (5) use more pronouns such as "you" or "we" (which acknowledge others) (197-98).

Five features of male adult speech, again based on other studies but summarized in Maltz and Borker's essay, are that men: (1) interrupt others more often; (2) challenge or dispute other speakers; (3) ignore the comments of others; (4) use mechanisms to control topic of conversation; and (5) make more declarations of fact or opinion (198). In short, the study by Maltz and Borker links gender differences found in adult speech to patterns formed in childhood and points out direct associations between the ways girls and women use language and between the ways boys and men use language.

Assorted comments about the influence of an author's gender on his or her style of writing point to the need for additional research on this topic.[4] In "Some Notes on Defining a Feminist Literary Criticism" Annette Kolodny says that women's writing cannot be defined any more than men's writing. Mary Poovey argues in *The Proper Lady and the Woman Writer* that legal, economic, and political conditions greatly influence individuals' styles, and these conditions can affect men and women differently. In *Gender and the Writer's Imagination* Mary Suzanne Schriber traces the effects of cultural expectations for men and women on the imaginations of men and women writers. Linda Pickard's dissertation on "A Stylo-Linguistic Analysis of Four American Writers" concludes that writing styles are more a matter of conditioning than of sex. Writer Joyce Carol Oates (in "Why is Your Writing So Violent?") suggests that critics try to limit women writers to domestic subjects or pleasant themes on the grounds that war, murder, and other forms of violence are topics only men should address.

Rollande Ballorain concludes his study of American women writers with the following comment: "If for American men novelist [sic], the answer to the problem of identity is to *do*, or to *get*, and so, to become an *American man*; for American women novelist [sic], it is to *be*, an individual, a *person relating to others*" ("From Childhood to Womanhood" 109; Ballorain's emphasis). Ballorain thus connects distinctions in male and female writing styles to psychological differences between the sexes, and his remarks bear some similarities to points

118 The Voice of the Child

made in Maltz and Borker's study. Other critics, reacting against impressionistic characterizations of writing styles, have tried to be more concrete. Mary Hiatt's work ("The Sexology of Style," *The Way Women Write*, and "Women's Prose Style: A Study of Contemporary Authors"), for example, has used computers to examine fiction and nonfiction passages written by men and women. Overall, Hiatt finds that while men and women tend to use different rhetorical devices and may have some other stylistic differences, most cultural stereotypes about male and female writing are incorrect. For example, her studies show that female writers are slightly more terse, while male writers are slightly more verbose. Her work also establishes that, contrary to the stereotype, women writers do not have an exclamatory style.

Present research does not provide a comprehensive model for gender-related characteristics of language. The background information detailed here is diffuse because such is the current condition of knowledge about this aspect of linguistics. However, the linguistic research described above will provide a platform for examining aspects of children's conversations in selected works of American fiction.

Huck Finn's Feminine Disguise

Adventures of Huckleberry Finn contains many examples of role playing, with Huck disguising his identity in several episodes. In one early scene, shortly after Huck and Jim have discovered each other hiding on an island, Huck dresses as a girl and returns to town in hopes of hearing the latest news about his own "death" and about Jim's escape. Finding a shanty inhabited by a woman he does not know, Huck, posing as a girl, knocks on the door and is invited to enter. While Huck masquerades as a girl, his language assumes several characteristics not otherwise present in his speech.

In the Huck-as-girl scene, which lasts about six pages, not once does Huck introduce a topic; instead he allows the older woman to direct the conversation. He is extremely polite to her, calling her "mum" and answering discretely with "No'm" and "Yes'm." While Huck is kind to everyone, his polite language is otherwise reserved for older people of high status such as Judge Thatcher. Huck's speech in this episode also has a helpless tone because of the increased number of intensifiers he uses to express himself:

> "I've walked *all* the way and I'm *all* tired out."
> "Hungry, too I reckon. I'll find you something."

"No'm. I ain't hungry. I was *so* hungry I had to stop two mile below here at a farm; so I ain't hungry no more. It's what makes me *so* late. My mother's down sick, and out of money and everything, and I come to tell my uncle Abner Moore." [48, italics added]

While pretending to be a girl, Huck also asks many questions. In fact, each of his conversational turns either begins or ends with a question. (In the penultimate chapter, when Aunt Sally asks Tom Sawyer why he has engaged in intrigues to free Jim, Tom replies, "Well, that *is* a question, I must say; and *just* like women!" [226], showing plainly the author's perception of questions in female speech.) While disguised in girls' clothing, Huck qualifies even simple statements of intent, as in "I'll rest a while, *I reckon*, and go on" (49, italics added). He allows himself, most uncharacteristically for Huck, to be interrupted: "I'll—" (52) and "Why he—" (49). Some of his statements, such as "No—is that so?" (49) are made solely to facilitate the conversation. His speech has an aura of low self-esteem, especially when the woman confronts him with the idea that he must be a boy, for he says "Please to don't poke fun at a poor girl like me, mum" (52). Huck is usually humble and self-effacing, but not to the extent indicated in this exchange. All of these language features in Huck's speech are associated with female styles of talking.

Huck's speech patterns as a girl contrast with those in the next example of role playing when, during the scene immediately following the riverboat collision, Huck claims to be a boy named George Jackson. In his debut as George Jackson, Huck is direct, forthright, action-oriented, and uses no qualifiers, intensifiers, or questions, despite his helpless position:

"Who's there?"
I says:
"It's me."
"Who's me?"
"George Jackson, sir."
"What do you want?"
"I don't want nothing, sir. I only want to go along by, but the dogs won't let me."
"What are you prowling around here this time of night, for—hey?"
"I warn't prowling around, sir; I fell overboard off of the steamboat."

> "Oh, you did, did you? Strike a light there, somebody. What did you say your name was?"
>
> "George Jackson, sir. I'm only a boy." [79]

Huck's assertion that he is a boy is confirmed by his direct, unhesitating, and unintimidated style of language. Only his polite and deferential use of "sir" shows his predicament, though that could be interpreted as marking his young age. This passage contains none of the linguistic features which dominate Huck's speech while he poses as a girl.

The woman in the shanty eventually realizes Huck is a boy, but she does so only because of his behavior—his awkward needle-threading and his expert rock-throwing—and because of his inability to remember whether he'd given his name as Sarah Williams or Mary Williams. Linguistically, he has managed to pass as a girl, though the woman warns him, "don't go about women in that old calico. You do a girl tolerable poor, but you might fool men maybe" (53). Indeed, he might. With a little more practice, he could have fooled her.

Huck's language patterns vary throughout the novel, and his speech changes according to the social dynamics of his situation. His speech is different when he talks to Jim than when he talks to Judge Thatcher, just as it is different when he talks to his father or when he talks to Tom Sawyer. Huck is sensitive to the nuances of language to an extent that would be incredible if Clemens had not alternated direct discourse passages with indirect discourse and with narrative passages so that immediate juxtapositions of one speech style with another rarely occur. Huck's, or, rather, Clemens's, management of idiolects (that is, uniquely individual speech), dialects, and gender differences in language aids in characterizations, supports developments in the novel's plots and themes, and indicates a highly skillful and language-sensitive writer at work.

Faulkner's Fictional Children in a Time of Social Transition

Language, sexuality and gender, and children have all been recognized separately as important elements in William Faulkner's writing. Merging all three concerns, let us here examine gender issues in the language of Faulkner's fictional children. Specifically, let us look at the language of boys and girls in the generation between the Civil War and the turn of the century, a key time for Faulkner's personal family history and for his fictional characters' history. Whereas female characters of this generation begin to assume some traditionally male traits in their speech patterns, boys of this generation begin to develop some traditionally female traits in their speech patterns. Language use by Faulkner's characters thus serves as a barometer for assessing changes in a society and for measuring the responses of individuals to those changes.

By the end of The Unvanquished, Bayard Sartoris finds himself working toward a new mode of speech for a new age as a complex web of gender, language, and childhood interacts with issues of race and class. When the book opens, Bayard and his companion Ringo are twelve-year-old boys playing war games, staging mock battles, and shouting, "Kill the bastuds! Kill them! Kill them!" (8). Their aggressive and profane language invokes the rebuke of Granny, the matriarch of the family who upholds traditional standards of language and behavior, as women often do. When the Yankee army passes their home, the boys take down a rifle, and Bayard shoots as Ringo urges, "Shoot the bastud! Shoot him!" (29). Sharing the blame and the glory over the shot, they both say to Granny, "*We* shot the bastud" (30-31; my emphasis). Then, thinking they have killed him, they hide, literally, under Granny's skirts.

Though they have only caused the death of a horse, the offense is serious, so Granny lies to protect them. Her verbal act is magnified by the fact that lying is the only sin for which she has ever whipped the boys. After the Yankee colonel leaves without searching for the boys, Granny pounces on Bayard and Ringo. While she has herself violated her code of honor, she punishes them, not for shooting at people or for endangering the household, but rather for their language. When she says to her grandson, "You cursed. You used obscene language" (39), Bayard first responds, "Ringo did too," thus sharing the guilt, and then he adds with a masculine challenge, "And you told a lie. You said we were not here" (39). Acknowledging the charge, she drops to her knees in prayer, then rises to wash out their mouths with soap.

Despite the surface simplicity of The Unvanquished—it is the easiest of Faulkner's novels to read—the upheaval of war is intricately reflected in the reversal of the South's previous standards of gender, race, class, and language. Ringo, then a black adolescent, shrewdly outwits white men in the Union army. Drusilla goes away with the men to fight, while Granny assumes the responsibilities the men have left at home and even forms a business association with Snopes. Changes in language accompany these behavioral adaptations, as, for example, even Granny takes to calling the Yankees "bastuds" after they burn the house and steal the silver.

The ultimate break in the code comes years later when Bayard is called home to avenge his father's death. Even though he and Ringo earlier teamed up to avenge Granny's death, and even though everyone expects him to kill his father's enemy, he refuses. The narrative does not completely explain Bayard's change in attitude, but part of it is surely due to his recognition that a new code is necessary for civilized life. Perhaps he has arrived at this juncture because of his boyhood relationship with Ringo, for the two have shared a friendship of the type more characteristic of girls than of boys in its intimacy, sharing, and caring. To survive, the women Granny and Drusilla have become more like men in their language and behavior, while Bayard has taken on some traditionally feminine attributes.

A similar transformation occurs in "The Bear," the long central section of *Go Down, Moses*, where a changing relationship with the land is accompanied by distinctive gender characteristics in the young male protagonist's language.

Within the exclusively male environment of "The Bear," young Ike McCaslin is polite and deferential to the wisdom, experience, and age of the men in the hunting parties, and his language contains several features characteristic of some female speech. He uses more "we" and "you" pronouns than do the men. He does not try to outshine anyone else, and he even denies his own abilities. For instance, one year when Sam Fathers tells him that the only way they can get Old Ben is if he runs "by accident over somebody that had a gun and knowed how to shoot it," Ike says, "That wouldn't be me." Then he allows himself to be interrupted as Sam interjects, "It might" (201). Ike also asks more questions than do the other characters. Many of his sentences are left unfinished, especially those that center around the pronoun "I," as in the following examples: "You mean he already knows me, that I aint never been to the big bottom before, aint had time to find out yet whether I . . ." (201); "No," the boy said. "I—" (203); "I—" (206); and "I . . ." the boy said. I didn't . . . I never thought . . ." (206, all punctuation marked as in Faulkner's text). Though these traits could at first be explained by Ike's young age and powerless position in relation to the older men, his speech continues to contain the same characteristics during his adolescence and young manhood.

Laura Claridge in "Isaac McCaslin's Failed Bid for Adulthood" concludes that "Ike's inability to repudiate rather than relinquish . . . is a crucial weakness" (245) in his character. But Ike's decision about his land is no worse than that of the Yankee soldiers who destroy the land, or of the Sutpens who try to impose their will on the land, or of the Compsons who sell their land, or of the Snopeses who invade the land. Ike's other behavior is likewise no worse than that of his ancestors or his coevals. This does not make him a hero, but measured against others he is a survivor, not a failure. Like Bayard Sartoris's in *The Unvanquished*, the two being roughly of the same generation, Ike McCaslin's language and behavior breaks with that of the previous generation. The behavior of the Sartoris and McCaslin boys utilizes less action and domination and more concession and accommodation. Similarly, their language contains more characteristics of feminine speech than does that of older male characters, and this indicates the emergence of a new standard for masculine language and behavior.

Faulkner's only extended presentation of a female child is in the character Caddy Compson. In "Language and Act: Caddy Compson," Linda Wagner says Caddy's central role in *The Sound and the Fury* is that of language creator and language giver. Looking at her speech from the linguistic perspective of gender differences, we can further see that while Caddy's language does exhibit many characteristics of female speech, she also has a tough, independent, and assertive mode of talking.

In many sections of *Sound and Fury*, Caddy fills the void left by her emotionally withdrawn mother, providing nurture and love for her brothers. For example, in her first appearance in Benjy's memory, Caddy greets him as she arrives home from school:

> "Hello, Benjy . . . Did you come to meet me. . . . Did you come to meet Caddy. What did you let him get his hands so cold for, Versh." . . .
> "Did you come to meet Caddy. . . . What is it. What are you trying to tell Caddy." . . .
> "What is it. . . . What are you trying to tell Caddy. Did they send him out, Versh." . . .
> "What is it. . . . Did you think it would be Christmas when I came home from school. Is that what you thought. Christmas is the day after tomorrow. Santy Claus. Benjy. Santy Claus. Come on, let's run to the house and get warm." [5-6]

Caddy's juvenile language to her brother here and elsewhere is simple and repetitive. She calls people, including her retarded brother and his servant, by their first names. She asks questions to keep the conversation going. She is patient and kind and caring. She tries to explain Christmas and other concepts to Benjy. Her language contains specific characteristics of mother-to-child speech and general characteristics of female speech. Caddy's sensitivity to others and her affection for those who depend on her make her later estrangement from her own daughter all the more poignant.

At other times, as in the "muddy drawers" passage of *Sound and Fury*, Caddy can be aggressive. She defies Versh, who warns she will be spanked for getting wet, and orders him to unbutton her dress. She is undaunted when Quentin says, "I'm older than you," shooting back, "I'm seven years old," and, likewise, when he brags that he goes to school, she reminds him, "I'm going to school next year" (21). Neither Caddy's status as a second child nor her female gender keeps her from dominating others. She demands that her father order the other children to mind her during the night of Damuddy's death, and he complies.

In the "muddy drawers" episode, Jason Compson, two years younger than Caddy, is selfish and conniving, his adult self in miniature. He is concerned only with his own needs, his hunger and his sleepiness, and he withholds from the Caddy-Quentin-Versh-Benjy-Dilsey conversations. Caddy recognizes these qualities in Jason, for when Quentin says Jason will not tattle about them about getting their clothes wet and muddy, Caddy says, "I bet he does tell" (22), and indeed he does. In fact, though Quentin tries to bribe and cajole, Caddy will have none of it, saying, "Let him tell . . . I don't give a cuss" (23).

But, for all Caddy's caring and for all Jason's meanness, it is Caddy whom their parents scold and correct, though linguistic studies indicate that usually parents are verbally rougher on male children than on female. For instance, when Caddy comes home from school, Mrs. Compson can only say, "Why did you come in here. To give him [Benjy] some excuse to worry me again" (7). When Caddy fights with Jason because he has destroyed Benjy's dolls, her father rebukes her. She tries to explain with fierce language for a little girl, "He cut up all Benjy's dolls . . . I'll slit his gizzle," but Mr. Compson interrupts with a formal name command, "Candace" (79). Caddy, however, has the last word, promising Benjy she will make more dolls for him. She does not cry. She does not whine. She is action-oriented, and her focus is on positive, constructive action rather than, as in Jason's case, destructive action.

Despite the rejection in Faulkner's fiction of much that is associated with female sexuality, the language and behavior of male protagonists such as Bayard Sartoris or Ike McCaslin provide practical examples of the necessity of boys and men embracing certain feminine values and certain feminine patterns of speech and action. This is not to suggest that Faulkner advocated androgyny or asexuality, but rather that he recognized the need for flexible standards of masculinity and femininity. The old pre-Civil war codes of behavior simply do not work in later eras, as we see over and over in the demise of characters who cling to that code. By emphasizing children and childhood, Faulkner conveyed both literally and metaphorically the need for re-evaluating old ideas and for developing new ideas. Faulkner often dwelt on the universal, unchanging, abstract ideals of humanity, but he did not show narrowly defined gender roles and language behavior to be examples of those fixed ideals. Rather, in the period after the Civil War but just before the turn of the century, Faulkner's successful female characters assert themselves and challenge others when necessary, while his successful male characters add the more feminine traits of nurture and sensitivity to their penchant for action, bravado, and challenge.

In the samples of Huck Finn's language described earlier, we found Clemens using male and female patterns of speech to support Huck's role playing in male and female disguises. In other words, in Clemens's novel, set somewhat nostalgically before the Civil War, language use follows traditional lines: female characters use feminine language and male characters use masculine language. In contrast, in Faulkner's fictional characters growing up just after the Civil War, the gender patterns of speech are more variable, and those patterns have social and moral significance for the characters. The distinctions between Clemens's and Faulkner's use of gender in child characters' language indicate differences in the two writers' personal styles and perspectives. Their differing approaches to male and female language can be separated, at least in part, chronologically, with the Civil War standing between them as both imaginative and historical watershed.

Authors' Gender and the Presentation of Gender in Juvenile Characters' Language

Is a fictional character's manner of speaking influenced by the sex of the author who created the character and wrote the language? For example, does a female writer have better insight into female language, and, if so, can she better construct speech for female characters than, all else being equal, a male writer? In "The Language of the Novel" Derek Oldfield describes how George Eliot varied the speech of Dorothea in *Middlemarch*, altering her use of rhethorical questions, figurative speech, and negatives to indicate changes in Dorothea's self-image following her marriage. Could a male writer have executed such fine and subtle language variations in a female character? Or do writers with similar talents and experience have similar skills in creating speech for their male and female characters, regardless of the writers' gender? Or is gender just one of many features which may affect a writer's ability to create effective dialogue? We can begin to approach such questions by examining a limited set of gender-related variables in the fictional child speech of two twentieth-century writers, Willa Cather and John Steinbeck. Let us concentrate on some of their best and most characteristic work, Cather's *My Ántonia* and *Shadows on the Rock* and Steinbeck's *The Red Pony* and *The Grapes of Wrath*.

There are significant differences between Steinbeck and Cather. Cather (1873–1947) grew up a generation earlier than Steinbeck (1902–1968). Cather never married, whereas Steinbeck was married three times. The writings of the two authors are distinct, though both could be classified as realists. Some critics would say that Cather's fiction is marked by an undercurrent of nostalgia, while Steinbeck's fiction is permeated by a darker naturalism. Cather's characters typically exert a degree of control over their lives, but Steinbeck's characters are often helpless in the face of environmental circumstances.

Nevertheless, there are also substantial similarities between Cather and Steinbeck. Both novelists' writings have epic qualities and feature panoramic backdrops. Both center on characters seeking inner harmony and peace with their environments, and both emphasize ties between people and land. Both authors drew on the regional experiences of their younger years, Cather in Nebraska, Steinbeck in California. Both had keen social consciences with ambivalent attitudes toward ownership, property, and capitalism. Both wrote about immigrants or people on the move, and the protagonists of both are usually humble people. Steinbeck was awarded the Nobel Prize, and Cather the Pulitzer. While both are included in Jackson Bryer's *Sixteen Modern American Authors*, Cather as the only woman in the book, their critical reputations are disproportionately low to the honors their work has received. Though their imagery has been studied, especially Cather's analogs in visual art and Steinbeck's biblical parallels, their language use has otherwise been generally ignored.

Finally, as is appropriate for this study, both writers created many fictional children who are vital to their stories. *My Ántonia* (1918) is written from the point of view of a grown man, Jim Burden, telling about his boyhood in frontier Nebraska and about Ántonia, the daughter of a neighboring immigrant family. The novel shows Ántonia at various stages of her life, though in the first part of the story she is fourteen and Jim is ten. *Shadows on the Rock* (1931), written in third person and set in Quebec when the city was just a remote outpost, tells about twelve-year-old French-born Cecile who takes under her wing a small boy Jacques, age unstated, son of the town's prostitute. *The Red Pony* (1937) features a young boy of about ten growing up on a California ranch. As we have seen, *The Grapes of Wrath* (1938) traces the plight of the Joad family, which includes twelve-year-old Ruthie and ten-year-old Winfield. Both of Steinbeck's novels are written from the third person point of view with an invisible, omniscient narrator.

One possible gender difference which emerges immediately is that in these selections Cather's fiction contains more female protagonists and female children, while Steinbeck's contains more male protagonists and male children. True, Steinbeck's Ma Joad is a strong figure, and Cather's *My Ántonia* is told by a male narrator, but Ma Joad does not succeed in keeping her family together, and Jim Burden, though successful by worldly standards and in some ways aggressively masculine (as indicated by his choice of the possessive pronoun *my* in the title *My Ántonia*), remains in awe of the personal heroism and joie de vivre of Ántonia.

A related and surely not coincidental gender distinction appears in the fictional characterizations of parents. At least in these four novels, parental figures of the same sex as the author are portrayed negatively or weakly. In Willa Cather's fiction, Ántonia's mother is extremely disagreeable and Cecile's mother is dead. In the Steinbeck selections, the boy's father in *The Red Pony* exerts an excessively forceful and overbearing presence, while Pa Joad becomes as weak as his wife becomes strong. There are some problems with opposite sex parents, too, for Ántonia's father commits suicide and the mother in *The Red Pony* appears only in the kitchen and the bedroom; still, these suicidal fathers and subdued mothers are more loving and, arguably, more important than their spouses in their children's development. In these four works, Cather and Steinbeck have created more sympathetic portraits for parental figures not of their own sex. In Cather's two novels girls predominate among the child characters, but fathers are more pronounced in importance among the children's parents. In Steinbeck's selections the reverse is true, as male children and female parents receive more sympathetic attention.

All four novels contain direct discourse utterances by children. In Part I of *My Ántonia*, the section of the book portraying the characters' childhoods, Ántonia has 22 utterances, and Jim has 5.[5] In *Shadows on the Rock*, Cecile has 135 utterances, and Jacques has 28. In *The Red Pony*, Jody has 41 utterances in Part I and 38 in Part IV, sections of *The Red Pony* focusing on Jody. In *The Grapes of Wrath*, Ruthie speaks 78 times, and Winfield 58.

128   The Voice of the Child

To analyze possible gender differences in the language of these male and female child characters, we must identify features of communication which research suggests may be gender-related. Five aspects of language use which might be gender-related include: topic initiation, action orientation, other orientation, violence, and crying. Topic initiation refers to whether a child is initiating a conversation or a conversational topic as opposed to answering a query or responding to someone else's remarks. An action-oriented statement announces an intent to act or describes an act in progress. An other-oriented statement centers on the emotions or physical states of another person or animal. Violent speech promises or reports personal acts of violence. Crying is not exactly an utterance, but weeping might be considered, at least stereotypically, sex-linked.

These five categories are not mutually exclusive (an action-oriented statement could also be concerned with others, for example), so tallies of their occurrences will not exactly total the number of utterances each child makes. For instance, early in *Shadows on the Rock*, Cecile announces she is going to cook and serve dinner as she remarks about her father's tired and hungry condition, and this single utterance can be counted as both action-oriented and other-oriented since it expresses both an intent to act and a concern for others. These five features are not the only speech acts a child could perform, and they are not the only significant characteristics of child speech, but research suggests that these features might be gender-linked. In fact, although a child character's manner of speaking can be influenced by constraints other than gender, in these four novels patterns emerge among these five selected categories which could be gender-related.

In chronological order, *My Ántonia* begins the discussion. Ántonia's presentation as a survivor, a dominant personality, and the true heroine of the novel is reinforced by the strong language patterns she uses (see Table 13). She is imaginative and direct, for her 50 percent rate of topic initiation would be even higher if she did not often serve as the translator for her immigrant family. She has the highest rate of action-oriented utterances (45 percent) of any of the seven children in this review, yet she still has a high rate of other-oriented speech (59 percent). Through Ántonia's language, Cather shows that girls and women can be strong, independent, and caring at the same time. As a young boy, Jim frames his language in action-oriented statements twice as often (40 percent) as he utters other-oriented statements (20 percent); this pattern fulfills our cultural expectations for a boy's speech. Jim's relatively low rate of initiating topics (20 percent) makes sense because of his role as an observer within the novel.

Table 13. Gender-Related Characteristics of Speech in *My Ántonia*

Feature	Number	Percentage
Character: Ántonia, a fourteen-year-old girl		
Number of utterances	22	
Child initiates topic	11	50
Action-oriented	10	45
Other-oriented	13	59
Violent	1	5
Cries	1	5
Character: Jim, a ten-year-old boy		
Number of utterances	5	
Child initiates topic	1	20
Action-oriented	2	40
Other-oriented	1	20
Violent	0	0
Cries	0	0

In *Shadows on the Rock* Cecile's nurturing spirit is shown by the high percentage of her speech (62 percent) motivated by a concern for others. Yet she is also an independent thinker, as indicated by her high incidence of topic initiation (61 percent). The tallies of her speech in Table 14 are presented by chapter because her speech from chapter to chapter reflects her character development. The first chapter introduces Cecile with her father, the second shows Cecile taking care of the boy Jacques, the third tells of the long Canadian winter (the focus shifts from Cecile, and she is ill for part of the section), and the fourth presents Cecile with Pierre Charron, the man whom, the epilogue informs readers, she later marries. In the fifth Cecile interacts with adults in the community, and in the last chapter she turns to Pierre for comfort when all plans of returning to France are set aside. Cecile's rate of action orientation varies appropriately to her circumstances; during her illness she utters no direct action statements, in the chapter with the town's adults she utters very few, but when she is with the younger boy she has her most action-oriented speech behavior. As the novel progresses, Cecile becomes increasingly more other-oriented, a trait she might later need as the mother of four sons. Interestingly, in the chapter with Pierre Charron, Cecile's language reaches its highest rate of topic initiation (96 percent), its second highest rate of action-orientation (25 percent), but its lowest rate of other-orientation (still a high 50 percent). This implies that her initiative, independence, and sense of adventure appeal to the older outdoorsman, and also that a

Table 14. Gender-Related Characteristics of Speech in *Shadows on the Rock*

Feature	Count by Chapter						Total or Average
	1	2	3	4	5	6	
Character: Cecile, a twelve year old girl							
Number of utterances	15	49	19	20	20	12	135
Child initiates topic	10	28	9	19	12	5	83
% by chapter	67	57	47	96	60	42	61%
Action-oriented	2	15	0	5	1	1	24
% by chapter	13	31	0	25	5	8	18%
Other-oriented	8	28	13	10	15	10	84
% by chapter	53	57	68	50	75	83	62%
Violent	0	1	1	0	0	0	2
% by chapter	0	2	5	0	0	0	2%
Cries	0	0	1	1	1	1	4
% by chapter	0	0	5	5	5	8	3%

	Total Count	%
Character: Jacques, a younger boy		
Number of utterances	28	
Child initiates	13	46
Action-oriented	3	11
Other-oriented	9	32
Violent	0	0
Cries	0	0

Cather model for successful male-female relations includes assertive, independent, and caring language from both parties.

Looking at the data from *The Red Pony* (see Table 15) and comparing the fourth and final section of the story with the first, we see that Jody moves from a nurturing pattern of speech behavior to an aggressive pattern, doubling his percentage of action-oriented statements while halving his percentage of other-oriented remarks. His development toward traditional (or perhaps stereotypical) adult male behavior is likewise indicated by his lack of crying in the final section and by his great increase in violent utterances. These linguistic shifts coincide with thematic shifts: in "The Gift" Jody receives and cares for his own horse, while in "The Leader of the People" he is engaged by his grandfather's stories of earlier, tougher days which required strong leaders who acted decisively.

In *The Grapes of Wrath* (see Table 16), the selfish and undisciplined nature of the children is underlined by the low rate of concern for others in their speech. In the entire novel, Winfield utters

Table 15. Gender-Related Characteristics of Speech in *The Red Pony*

Character: Jody, a boy		
Feature	Number	Percentage
Part I: "The Gift" (age ten)		
Number of utterances	41	
Child initiates topic	25	61
Action-oriented	8	20
Other-oriented	20	49
Violent	1	2
Cries	1	2
Part IV: "The Leader of People" (age unstated)		
Number of utterances	38	
Child initiates topic	26	68
Action-oriented	17	45
Other-oriented	10	26
Violent	10	26
Cries	0	0

only one statement showing positive concern for others, and Ruthie utters only nine. Both children talk about their relatives and companions, but in a negative sense; that is, they make fun of, mock, and plot meanness against others. Their rates of initiating topics (Ruthie, 36 percent; Winfield, 33 percent) are also much lower than those of Ántonia, Jim, Cecile, Jacques, and Jody; this indicates that Ruthie and Winfield are comparatively impoverished in ideas and that communication within the Joad family is breaking down.

Actually, the whole Joad family is rendered inarticulate by their crisis, as children and adults alike replace verbal language with body language (pointing, slapping, and hugging) to a degree not apparent in Steinbeck's other fiction. However, the adult characters hold a regard for middle-class standards of language use. For example, in the aftermath of Ruthie's betrayal of Tom, Ma Joad does not scold Ruthie for what she has done, but rather she rebukes only Ruthie's foul language in calling the rival child a "big son-of-a-bitch of a girl" (457). The younger generation ignores traditional or middle-class standards of language, including those patterns associated with ladylike or gentlemanly language. Thus, Ruthie's speech is not only aggressive in a manner stereotypical of masculine behavior, but also her metaphor ("big son-of-a-bitch of a girl") attributes male characteristics to her female opponent.

So far, the statistical data about features of speech in these four novels have provided us with interpretive material for discussing the

Table 16. Gender-Related Characteristics of Speech in *The Grapes of Wrath*

Feature	Number	Percentage
Character: Ruthie, a twelve-year-old girl		
Number of utterances	78	
Child initiates topic	28	36
Action-oriented	23	29
Other-oriented	9*	12
Violent	5	6
Cries	2	3
Character: Winfield, a ten-year-old boy		
Number of utterances	58	
Child initiates topic	19	33
Action-oriented	14	24
Other-oriented	1*	2
Violent	5	9
Cries	3	5

*Figures include only positive references to others.

characterizations of the individual children. But does this information indicate any differences between male and female child speech? Table 17 presents the features of speech for all the girl characters compared with the speech features of all the boy characters.

On the surface, the information in Table 17 supports the conclusion that at least two speech features, topic initiation and action orientation, are not very different for girls and boys in these four novels. However, in the three works of fiction which include two child characters, the girl is the older child, and, overall, the average age of the girls is slightly more than twelve years, while the average age of the boys is under ten years. These age factors might have some bearing on the similar rates of topic initiation and action orientation. Information in Table 17 also shows that although the girls do cry more than the boys, the rate of crying is negligible for all the children. This lack of crying is remarkable given the traumas the children experience or witness: suicides, deaths, physical hardships, and social upheaval. Other data compiled in Table 17 indicate that two features of the children's speech reflect clear gender differences which we might expect, though the degree of difference is surprising. First, the boys are almost twice as likely to engage in violent talk. Second, the girls, on the other hand, are nearly twice as likely to gear their language toward the needs and concerns of others, though, again, their older

Table 17. Speech Differences between Male and Female Children

The figures represent the average percentage of the incidence of five designated features in the speech of children in all four selected fictional works by Cather and Steinbeck.

Feature	Percentage in Boys	Percentage in Girls
Child initiates topic	46	49
Action-oriented	28	31
Other-oriented	26	44
Violent	7	4
Cries	1	4

ages might place them in caretaker roles which require them to consider the needs of others.

More interesting differences appear in the presentation of gender in child language when the information is separated by sex of author (see Table 18). In Cather's fiction, only girls cry, even though the boys are younger. In Steinbeck's fiction, boys and girls both cry. In Steinbeck's work, Ruthie initiates more topics, is more action-oriented, and is more other-oriented than her brother Winfield, yet the boy Jody, the same age as Winfield, has a higher rate of incidence than Ruthie in all three categories. On the other hand, in Cather, the percentages for these three features (topic initiation, action-orientation, and other-orientation) are greater for the female children than for the male. Further, Cather's female children have higher rates of incidence in these features than either Steinbeck's female or male children. In fact, Cather's girls are three times more likely to be other-oriented than are Steinbeck's boys and thirty times more likely to be other-oriented than is Steinbeck's girl character. Male children in both authors' fiction have the same rate of orientation toward others, while Steinbeck's male children are more violent than Cather's male children.

The most striking difference between the language of the male and female child characters appears in two reversals of presentation by Cather and Steinbeck. As shown in Table 19, the figures for topic initiation and action-orientation by Cather's girls and Steinbeck's boys are nearly mirror images of each other, as are the figures for language by Cather's boys and Steinbeck's girl. Initiating topics and discussing action indicate strength, independence, assertiveness, and goal-direction. The language of Cather's female children contains these characteristics to a greater degree than does the language of her male children, and the reverse is true for Steinbeck's male and female children. Thus, these two authors in these four works portray child

Table 18. Speech Differences between Male and Female Children Created by Male and Female Authors

These figures represent the average percentage of the incidence of five designated features in the speech of children in four selected fictional works.

Feature	Percentage in Cather	Percentage in Steinbeck
Female Children		
Child initiates topic	56	33
Action-oriented	32	24
Other-oriented	61	2
Violent	3	9
Cries	4	5
Male Children		
Child initiates topic	33	54
Action-oriented	26	30
Other-oriented	26	26
Violent	0	12
Cries	0	2

characters of their own sex as stronger and more active than child characters of the opposite sex.

This study establishes that both male and female writers can create child characters with individualized and gender-realistic language. Despite some linguistic similarities, distinct differences exist between the speech of boys and the speech of girls in *My Ántonia, Shadows on the Rock, The Grapes of Wrath*, and *The Red Pony*. These differences follow paths we might expect based on what linguistic research tells us about real and stereotypic gender differences in language. Moreover, at least in these selected examples, differences exist in the child speech which form patterns related to the genders of the authors. Perhaps female authors tend to present stronger and more assertive female language than do male authors, and perhaps female writers create more young female characters than do male writers, but such conclusions cannot be firmly drawn from the limited body of evidence in this review. We can neither rule out nor prove that fictional children are projections of images the writer holds of himself or herself as a child, though this might be inferred from the prevalence of male children in our male-written literature and from Willa Cather's portrayal of female children exhibiting the strong and independent behaviors observed in Cather herself.

This chapter has explored the topic of gender in fictional chil-

Table 19. Gender Differences in Child Speech Related to Authors' Gender

These figures represent the average percentage of the incidence of two designated features in the speech of children in four selected fictional works.

Feature	Cather's girls	Steinbeck's boys	Cather's boys	Steinbeck's girl
Topic initiation	56	54	33	33
Action-orientation	32	30	26	24

dren's speech, applying the relevant linguistic data to literature in three ways. First, we looked at a passage from *Huckleberry Finn* in which Huck masquerades a girl, finding that Huck's language in the episode takes on the characteristics of feminine speech. This reinforces with concrete evidence the notions that Huck is an extremely sensitive and reliable individual for the job of narrator and that Clemens's ear for nuances of language, previously explored only in terms of dialect, is expert. The *Huck Finn* findings also prove that gender differences in language can be reflected in fictional child speech. Second, we examined the speech of William Faulkner's literary children, discovering that in the critical post-Civil War period male and female characters assimilate linguistic traits of the opposite sex into their language. This assimilation implies that survival in a time of social transition requires flexibility and creative adaptability; while new in its present application, this concept is consistent with other themes in Faulkner's work as summarized, for example, in Faulkner's Nobel Prize speech on the survival of the human race. Third, we compared the female and male child speech created by a female and male writer, Willa Cather and John Steinbeck, discovering patterns of differences which can be related both to the gender of the characters and to the gender of the authors. The discoveries in each section of this chapter show that various aspects of literary criticism can be enhanced by examining gender-related features of language.

8. Conclusion
"That Evening Sun"

This study has looked at how American writers portray the language of their child characters and has investigated this subject by applying linguistic principles drawn from child language acquisition research to the direct discourse of selected fictional children. Though not every young character in American literature nor every linguistic principle relevant to language acquisition has been exhaustively discussed, the consideration has been reasonably comprehensive in its use of linguistics and in its selection of literature. The speech of all major child characters in such classic fiction as *The Scarlet Letter* or *Adventures of Huckleberry Finn* has been reviewed. Many lesser-known novels and short stories such as *Call It Sleep* or "Angel Child" and some popular fiction such as *The Exorcist* have been discussed. Linguistically, the chapters have considered topics in phonology, morphology, and syntax and have set forth in-depth investigations of semantics and pragmatics, giving particular attention to role structures, speech functions, parent-child interaction, narrative structures, and gender differences. Analyzing literary children's speech has given us insight into formerly neglected areas of fictional technique and characterization, and the linguistic methodologies used have provided us with new avenues for interpreting specific texts and for understanding various textual issues.

Previous chapters have been organized around individual linguistic aspects of language acquisition as they are operative in several works of literature. To conclude, let us now see how one piece of fiction and the direct discourse of its child characters can be illuminated by the examination of phonological, morphological, syntactic, semantic, and pragmatic features of speech. This will establish that the combined application of all the linguistic topics introduced separately in earlier chapters—narrative structures, parent-child discourse, speech functions, case roles, and gender differences—can be helpful in reading and understanding a single text. The short story chosen for this final application is William Faulkner's "That Evening Sun."

Matters of language and children are central in Faulkner's writing, just as they are in American literature as a whole. While critics have long noted the significance of Faulkner's uses of language, they have been slower to acknowledge the special presence of children in his work except in a few studies such as Marvin Fisher's "The World of Faulkner's Children" and David Minter's "Faulkner, Childhood, and the Making of *The Sound and the Fury*." As Minter has shown, the direction of Faulkner's career was shaped by his rediscovery of childhood during a period of personal adult crisis. In 1927, after his third novel *Flags in the Dust* had been rejected by his editor, Faulkner wavered about whether to seek another career. He ultimately decided to continue writing, but for himself rather than for a publisher. In writing for himself, the subject to which Faulkner immediately turned was children, and he specifically drew on his own childhood as he wrote three short stories dealing with three youngsters, Quentin, Caddy, and Jason Compson. "That Evening Sun" was the first of these stories, and the third, called "Twilight," eventually grew into *The Sound and the Fury*.

Several features of their language mark Quentin, Caddy, and Jason Compson as children in "That Evening Sun." The three speak simply, expressing themselves with few syntactically complex structures. They frequently ask questions, and they constantly repeat themselves. Instances of nonstandard grammar abound in the children's and the servants' speech; for example, there are many double negatives and much use of the word *ain't*. Phonologically, Caddy calls her brother a "scairy cat" (293) rather than, as we might expect the word to sound, a *scairdy cat*, though a more interesting word construction and pronunciation comes from the servant Dilsey, who suggests that they "telefoam the marshall" (298). Both the content and the form of the children's speech are realistically presented, but, except for the questioning, which we have found typical of literary children, and the nonstandard grammar, which may be related to the children's modeling after the servants' dialects, the syntactic, morphological, and phonological features of the child language in "That Evening Sun" are unremarkable. As in much other American literature, the more interesting elements of the children's language lie outside phonology, morphology, or syntax.

The narrative features of "That Evening Sun" comprise its most notable qualities. The story is told by Quentin at age twenty-four as he remembers fifteen years earlier when he, his seven-year-old sister Caddy, and his five-year-old brother Jason were bystanders in a drama involving their servant Nancy. The first four paragraphs of the story form what appears to be a straightforward orientation for a traditional narrative structure. Unexpectedly, though, Quentin abandons his opening line of thought when he speaks of Nancy and her husband Jesus, who did not, as other husbands did, "fetch and deliver" (290) the clothes of white people for his wife to clean. At that point, Quentin's narrative dissolves into a series of mini-narratives about Nancy: Nancy and Mr. Stovall, Nancy with Jesus, Nancy alone in the kitchen, Nancy being walked home, Nancy sleeping with the children, Nancy with Dilsey, and, finally, the longest narrative, Nancy taking the children to her cabin. With each new story Quentin tells, his role as an adult narrator increasingly disintegrates; as Joseph Garrison says in "The Past and the Present in 'That Evening Sun,'" Quentin reenters the world of his childhood and does not emerge from it at the end.

Like the narrator in *Huckleberry Finn*, the narrator in "That Evening Sun" does not show himself very often as a speaker. As a child in the story Quentin tells no direct discourse stories, nor do any of the other children or adults tell stories. At one point Nancy starts to entertain the children in her cabin with a fairy tale, but she is so distraught that her tale is rejected by the children as nonsense. In fact, not only do the characters not communicate their experiences and feelings through personal narratives, they say very little to each other that is not a question or a rebuke. Most of the direct discourse in "That Evening Sun" consists of fragments of conversations which suggest fragmented lives and fragmented personal connections.

The breakdown of Quentin's narrative voice is demonstrated in several ways which are connected to the narrative framework of the story. For instance, though the story is divided into six sections marked off by Roman numerals, those sections do not correspond in any way to the six universal elements of personal narrative described in Chapter Six. None of the mini-stories contains all the elements of a fully finished narrative, either. Quentin's inability to complete a single narrative strongly hints at mental unbalance. The incompleteness in Quentin's narratives complements the situations in the surrounding society, as relationships between individuals and between classes of individuals are sadly incomplete. On an even larger scale, the lack of wholeness in Quentin's stories mirrors the breakdown of the Southern lifestyle, for the tale of Southern life had not turned out the way some individuals of Quentin's social class had hoped it would.

Furthermore, while the distinction between the narrator Quentin who in retrospect understands what happened and the child Quentin who did not is initially clear, that division becomes increasingly cloudy as he begins to describe people or events as he might have as a child. For instance, instead of a specific and logical explanation of time and temporal connection, he merely says of Dilsey's absence, "It was a long time" (292). With each new mini-narrative, the connections become looser, as when Nancy's perspiration is described in a childlike statement of nonunderstanding: "The water still ran down Nancy's face" (306). The organization of the mini-stories progressively becomes less conventional, less coherent, and less complete, paralleling the confusion and lack of connection which characterize Quentin's mental state and which support the essential themes of the fiction, fear and isolation. By the end of the story, the differentiation between adult and child understanding has collapsed into a single egocentric and childish point of view exemplified by Quentin's final remark about the possibility Nancy will be murdered: " 'Who will do our washing now, Father?' I said" (309).

The collapse of Quentin's adult self into his childish self is particularly important for his representation of Nancy. As a child, Quentin thinks of her in terms of his laundry, and his attitude typifies the mistreatment Nancy suffers at the hands of virtually everyone in the story except Dilsey. Some of the dehumanization is subtle; for instance, as Paula Sunderman notes in "Speech Act Theory and Faulkner's 'That Evening Sun,'" when Mr. Compson says to Nancy, "You'll be the first thing I'll see in the kitchen tomorrow morning" (308), he is reducing her to an object by his use of the word *thing* to describe her. Throughout the short story Nancy is abused, and Quentin's adult self cannot break through his childhood perspective to fight or even to recognize her suffering.

In "Faulkner's Three 'Evening Suns'" Norman Pearson has shown how Faulkner revised the short story by omitting passages of explicit comment. In doing this, Faulkner increased the importance of Quentin's narrative voice and of the narrowing gap between the adults' and children's perspectives on events of the story. In addition, while other aspects of "That Evening Sun" have remained more constant in all three versions, the reader's role in evaluating the significance of those other aspects has become more crucial because of the withdrawal of authorial comment.

The relationship between parents and children is vital in understanding all the characters in "That Evening Sun." Just as a lack of concern inhibits communication between races, so a lack of human kindness makes communication between the generations difficult. Nancy tries to kill herself while pregnant, and the father of her child cares nothing for her, kicking her teeth out when she demands payment for her sexual favors. In fact, though Quentin's narrative covers "a long time" (292), there is no discussion of what happens to that baby, the product of the union between Nancy and Mr. Stovall. Certainly Nancy has no child in her cabin, and it is not clear whether her pregnancy continued or whether a baby was ever born and, if so, what became of the child. The mystery of that child emphasizes Quentin's regression into a mode of thinking which does not connect a swelling female form with a baby, and the absence of explanation about the child also symbolizes the absence of human concern among and between generations, races, and sexes.

No desirable parent-child communication is shown in the story. Aunt Rachel, who is said to be the mother of Jesus, verbally rejects her maternal role: "Sometimes she said she was and sometimes she said she wasn't any kin to Jesus" (294). Mrs. Compson is too self-centered to become engaged in her children's lives. Mr. Compson speaks to and interacts with his children, but his attitude toward them is hardly positive, for when Mrs. Compson argues with him about the danger of Jesus ("You'll leave these children unprotected, with that Negro about?"), he responds as a man weary of fatherhood: "What would he do with them, if he were unfortunate enough to have them?" (294). Such a line might be spoken in jest, but even if his comment on fatherhood is not intended for literal interpretation, it contains too much truth not to be understood as an expression of harried paternity. Not surprisingly, since the parents say so little to their offspring, the children's speech resembles the servants' language more than the parents'. Because most of the adults ignore the children whenever possible, Nancy's close identification with them, sleeping with them, talking to them, and wanting them around her, seems deviant.

Problems associated with fatherhood are exacerbated by multiracial and multicultural complications in "That Evening Sun," just as they are in many other works of American literature. Mr. Compson is a prime example of a father under stress from conflicts of culture and of race, and the disharmony within his household reflects those conflicts. Mr. Stovall registers no responsibility for the mixed-race heirs

Table 20. Functions of Child and Adult Speech in "That Evening Sun"

Child Characters	Caddy		Jason		Quentin	
Function	Number	%	Number	%	Number	%
Instrumental	0	0	13	24	0	0
Regulatory	10	12	2	4	0	0
Interactional	2	2	0	0	0	0
Personal	4	5	3	6	0	0
Heuristic	35	41	3	6	2	20
Imaginative	1	1	0	0	0	0
Informative	17	20	14	26	6	60
Poetic	0	0	0	0	0	0
Interpretive	14	16	7	13	2	20
Performative	2	2	12	22	0	0

Adult Characters	Nancy		Mr. C		Mrs. C		Jesus		Dilsey	
Function	Number	%	Number	%	Number	%	Number	%	Number	%
Instrumental	10	9	5	14	0	0	0	0	0	0
Regulatory	13	12	8	23	0	0	0	0	7	37
Interactional	3	3	0	0	2	11	0	0	1	5
Personal	14	13	0	0	4	21	0	0	0	0
Heuristic	7	6	4	11	12	63	0	0	5	26
Imaginative	14	13	0	0	0	0	0	0	0	0
Informative	24	21	6	17	1	5	0	0	4	21
Poetic	1	1	0	0	0	0	0	0	0	0
Interpretive	20	18	11	31	0	0	1	50	0	0
Performative	6	5	1	3	0	0	1	50	0	0

These figures reflect an analysis of all the direct discourse utterances of each character. Numbers indicate the total occurrences of each function in each character's speech, and percentages represent the percentage of individual functions in an individual character's speech.

he might generate. Jesus, Nancy's husband, would be the legal but not the biological father of her biracial child, and he responds to that situation with violent threats and then, apparently, abandons his wife. Stovall does not speak at all to the Compson children, Jesus inappropriately lets them overhear his veiled threats and his metaphorical allusions to sex, and Mr. Compson does not take time to explain things to his children or to listen to their concerns.

As is the case with the narrative structures and the parent-child relationships, the speech functions in "That Evening Sun" also provide information useful for understanding the story and for appreciating its fictional techniques. An analysis of speech functions in the

Table 21. Self-Referencing Case Frames in "That Evening Sun"

	Agent		Experiencer		Patient		Beneficiary	
	Number	%	Number	%	Number	%	Number	%
Nancy	23	24	32	34	18	19	6	6
negative	3	3	12	13				
Quentin	0	0	0	0	0	0	0	0
negative	1	33			2	67		
Caddy	8	32	4	16	7	28	1	4
negative	1	4	4	16				
Jason	10	20	10	20	4	8	1	1
negative	2	4	23	46				
Mr. C.	5	63	3	38	0	0	0	0
Mrs. C.	1	14	2	29	2	29	1	14
negative			1	14				
Dilsey	4	67	2	33	0	0	0	0
Jesus	1	14	0	0	2	29	0	0
negative	2	29	1	14	1	14		

The first figure reflects a tabulation of all the direct discourse utterances in which characters refer to themselves. The second figure represents the percentage of individual case frames used in all of an individual character's self-references.

story reveals that the characters' language patterns are distinct and appropriate for the personalities of the individuals involved. Table 20 contains lists of the functions of each character's speech; the terms employed are those introduced in Chapter Four.

As shown in Table 20, the patterns of adult discourse in "That Evening Sun" are diverse. Of all the characters, Nancy alone expresses herself through every possible language function. This is a remarkable finding that underscores Nancy's difference and alienation from the other characters. In the context of the short story, Nancy's speech range might even be considered unhealthy, since Dilsey, a character who represents strength and reason, has a limited functional range. Nancy's sensitivity is illustrated by her concern for personal feelings (personal speech) and for interpreting behavior (interpretive speech), but these functions may be luxuries too costly for a poor, uneducated black woman in the early twentieth-century South. Jesus's nonconformity is also revealed by his speech; his two direct discourse utterances indicate thinking (interpretive speech) and promising (performative speech), qualities which, again, the surrounding community does not appreciate in a man of his circumstances. Mrs. Compson is childlike in her reliance on questions (63 percent of her speech is heuristic), and she is exaggeratedly feminine in her use of interactional and personal speech and in her nonuse of interpretive and performative language. In contrast, Mr. Compson's language has a distinctly masculine aura because it is heavily interpretive and regulatory and it contains no interactional or personal speech.

The functions of the younger characters' direct discourse also indicate the children's personalities (Table 20). Jason's frequent use of instrumental speech emphasizes his self-centered focus on his own needs and wants. In addition, he has a high rate of performatives; young children usually are not so aggressive in stating what they will or will not do. Jason asks surprisingly few questions for a five-year-old; only 6 percent of his speech is heuristic. His language behavior in "That Evening Sun" foreshadows or at least parallels the hostile, determined, and self-centered behavior he exhibits in The Sound and the Fury.

Quentin has little to say within the narrative of "That Evening Sun." Most of his speech is informative and interpretive, as befits a narrator, and his informative emphasis correlates with the lack of analysis within the story. The complete absence of instrumental, regulatory, interactional, personal, imaginative, poetic, and performative functions in Quentin's language places his speech in exact opposition to Nancy's, an interesting reversal given their respective social positions and given that he is telling the story. Quentin's language use disconnects and isolates him from the other children and adults in the story. This same pattern of behavior is seen in the Quentin of The Sound and the Fury who commits suicide.

Caddy, like many other literary children, continually asks questions; heuristic speech accounts for over 40 percent of her utterances. The motherliness she exhibits toward Benjy in The Sound and the Fury is also shown here by the absence of instrumental functions and the low rate of personal functions in her speech. Her language functions, not at all like her mother's, are similar to Dilsey's in that neither uses instrumental speech, both have similar rates of performative, interactional, and informative speech, and both have high rates of heuristic speech. Caddy's speech is also like Nancy's in its ratio of regulatory, interactional, informative, interpretive, and performative functions. The similarity of Caddy's speech patterns to Nancy's does not bode well for her, and, indeed, as an adult in The Sound and the Fury she is almost as unhappy and unsatisfied as Nancy is in this story. Further, the similarity between functions in the utterances of Caddy, Dilsey, and Nancy shows that the child models her language on that of the family's female servants, the adults with whom she interacts most frequently.

144 The Voice of the Child

Just as a review of the characters' language functions provides us with information about "That Evening Sun," so an examination of the case frames of the characters' speech reveals nuances of meaning in the story. Table 21 contains a list of the case frames of each character's references to himself or herself in "That Evening Sun"; restricting case analysis to statements of self-reference allows us to see how the characters view themselves. The terms employed are those introduced in Chapter Three.

The characters' language in this story contains an exceptional number of negative case constructions. All of the individuals except Dilsey and Mr. Compson place themselves in negative constructions. Quentin's self-reflective speech is entirely negative, Jesus's speech is more negative than positive, Jason's speech is half negative, and Caddy's reference to herself as an experiencer of feelings is as negative as it is positive. These negative feelings predict the characters' future courses either in this story or in *The Sound and the Fury*, as Quentin kills himself, Jesus runs away, Jason grows into a bitter man, and Caddy's bleaker characteristics eventually overshadow her more likeable traits. The gloomy outlook on self by so many characters in "That Evening Sun" promotes the general sense of hopelessness pervading the story.

Characters with positive self-references generally have a better outcome. For instance, Dilsey remains positive throughout her life in her acceptance of her circumstances, her determination to do good, and her Christian faith. Nancy's self-concept in "That Evening Sun," surprisingly more positive than negative, suggests an inner strength which may enable her to overcome her fears and to attain the curious moral stature she assumes in Faulkner's novel *Requiem for a Nun*.

The characters' depictions of themselves through their case frames raise some unexpected comparisons which cross lines of age, race, and sex. Both Dilsey and Mr. Compson, the only characters with no negative constructions in their self-references, portray themselves only as agents (related to performing action) or experiencers (related to having feelings), with their agency rates double that of their experiencer rates. Mrs. Compson and Jesus have similar negations of feelings (experiencer case), and both view themselves as the recipients of others' actions (patient case) at exactly the same rate. Caddy has a similar degree of self-references in the patient case as her mother and Jesus have, but many of Caddy's patient cases actually refer to all the children grouped under the umbrella *us*, as in, "Tell us a story" (302). Caddy's use of agent cases for herself is high for a child and high for a female character, and, though only half as high as the agency rate of her father and of Dilsey, her usage confirms that she is stronger and more self-reliant that either of her brothers. Mrs. Compson has far more opportunities and advantages in life than Nancy, yet Mrs. Compson places herself in patient cases (the recipient of others' actions) significantly more than Nancy.

The children's case role patterns are not at all like those of their parents. If anything, the negativity of Jason and Quentin is more like Jesus's, and Caddy's case frames are more like Nancy's; again, the children probably have learned much of their language from their servants. The role of the children in "That Evening Sun" is often said to be that of observers of an adult drama, but, as we have seen in *What Maisie Knew* and *Lolita*, when children are exposed to adult affairs, they inevitably become more than just observers. Quentin, Caddy, and Jason are, like Maisie, used by the adults around them, and they often serve as buffers between adults in conflict. Yet Caddy, much like Lolita, still presents herself as an agent, as one having power to act. The children in general do not view themselves as merely recipients of adult action, though they do not fully understand what the adults are doing. So, the case frames of Quentin, Caddy, and Jason Compson reveal their individual personalities, and they show evidence of the strength of children.

Because sexual issues are at the heart of this story, the gender-specific characteristics of the children's speech are of great interest. In the previous chapter on gender, we examined these same characters' speech in *The Sound and the Fury*, but the dynamics of their relationships are different here, mainly because of Benjy's absence. Without Benjy, the portrait of Caddy as mothering female is less strong. Also, here Quentin the narrator keeps his character in the background, reproducing few of his own utterances. What remains, then, is antagonism between Jason and Caddy, and the two bring out the worst qualities in each other. Quentin has deep feelings for his sister, so his silence in comparison with Jason's outbursts indicate a resigned and distant adoration of Caddy as opposed to Jason's rivalry and hatred. The sexuality of the children is less well delineated here because they function as innocent contrasts to the adults, who are directly involved in mature and violent sexual problems. The dread Nancy has of Jesus, the tension between Mr. and Mrs. Compson, and the sordid details of Nancy's relationship with Mr. Stovall all contribute to the steamy atmosphere of terror, but the children to not completely understand what happens around them. Their ignorance forms a filter through which Quentin's narrative lens must work, and as his narrative eye regresses to his childhood perspective, his knowledge of the sexual issues becomes increasingly uncertain.

A peculiar gender-related feature of the children's language occurs as Quentin and Caddy in at least one context seem to mirror the speech of their opposite-sex parents. Thus, Caddy says to Nancy, "Father says for you to come on and get breakfast" (290), while Quentin says to Nancy, "Mother wants to know if you are through" (292). Mr. Compson's orders for Nancy to fix breakfast are direct and explicit. Mrs. Compson's desire that Nancy finish her work and leave are phrased indirectly, and Mr. Compson must translate her "Isn't Nancy through in the kitchen yet?" to the clearer, "Let Quentin go and see.... Go and see if Nancy is through, Quentin. Tell her she can go home" (292). Notice that the female child Caddy echoes the more masculine declarative voice of her father, while the male child Quentin echoes the more feminine indirect speech of his mother. The reversal of gender identification in Quentin's and Caddy's speech may be associated with the special relationship between the two. That is, their incestual feelings might be related to their identification with parents of the opposite sex, seven and nine years being beyond the point at which most children cease such close cross-sex identification.[1] Caddy and Quentin's linguistic identifications might also be related to their atypical environment, for they play and talk only with opposite-sex siblings rather than with friends of their own sex and age. Or, the gender aspects of the children's speech patterns may indicate changing roles for males and females in their society, a finding noted in Chapter Seven.

Whatever the reason, in "That Evening Sun" Caddy's language is assertive in a male mode: she controls topics of conversation, she questions for information rather than for continuity of conversation, she seeks attention through her language use, she attempts to control the actions of others, and she is not too sensitive to taunt Jason with charges that he is a crybaby and a scairdy-cat. Quentin's discourse, on the other hand, is indirect and sensitive. Even as a young boy he understands the importance of language subtleties, and he knows how to interpret and respond to undercurrents in the speech of others. Quentin's sensitivity is shown in the following passage in which he describes his mother and her style of thinking and talking: "'Jason!' mother said. She was speaking to father. You could tell that by the way she said the name. Like she believed that all day father had been trying to think of doing the thing she wouldn't like the most, and that she knew all the time that after a while he would think of it. I stayed quiet, because father and I both knew that mother would want him to make me stay with her if she just thought of it in time" (294). At an early age, Quentin has developed an awareness of shades of language and, as women sometimes do, has learned to avoid spoken language in certain contexts. Though in Faulkner's fiction storytelling is often a male trait, Quentin's story, unlike, for example, V.K. Ratliff's yarns in *The Hamlet*, is built upon the more traditionally feminine characteristics of close attention to the subtleties of other people's speech rather than on a description of the actions of others.

The ending of "That Evening Sun" has already been mentioned in reference to the story's narrative structure, but another dimension to the ending has to do with the personalities, ages, and, especially, genders of the children. At the end Jason, with his aggressively self-centered demands for popcorn and chocolate cake, may be too young to understand Nancy's predicament. Caddy is too involved in asserting her position of dominance to be much concerned with Nancy. Only Quentin's line about "Who will do our washing now, Father?" shows a realization of the implications of events around him. His line does not end the story, though. The dialogue continues with Jason's constantly repeated self-vindication, "I'm not a nigger," Caddy's perceptive observation, "You're worse," and Mr. Compson's impotent reprimand, "Caddy." The taunts continue, so Mr. Compson strengthens his objection by uttering Caddy's full name in the last line of the story: "Candace!" And so, Caddy's name is left hanging in the air, reverberating in the memory of the narrator, her brother Quentin, who loves her as her parents and Jason do not, as Benjy cannot, and as the other men in her life will not. The use of Caddy's name in the final utterance and in the final line of "That Evening Sun" emphasizes her significance in the story and her importance in Quentin's mind.

"That Evening Sun," one of the earliest of Faulkner's best short stories, contains most of the themes prominent in the author's masterpieces, and it also contains many of the themes and motifs relating to children, childhood, and child language found elsewhere in American literature. An analysis of the story's child language, of its narrative structures, parent-child discourse, speech functions, case roles, and gender differences, gives us insight into the details of "That Evening Sun," its craft, its features, its meaning, its value within Faulkner's canon, and its place within the whole body of American literature.

Throughout this project we have seen that linguistic information taken from research in child language acquisition can be successfully applied to fictional children's discourse. We have found that such applications provide us with terms and methodologies useful for literary study and, furthermore, give us precise and concrete information about child characters, their language, and the fiction in which they appear. This information and these methodologies also lead to discoveries about the authors who have created speaking child characters and about the cultural and historical factors that have affected such authors. We have observed differences, for instance, in the ways children's narratives are used in *Call It Sleep* and in *Trout Fishing in America*, and our observations have, in turn, led to discoveries about the differing themes of the fictions and about the authors' differing attitudes toward children and toward life. We have seen in *Lolita* how a child's language can develop over the course of a novel, with speech changes paralleling the maturation of her character and the alteration of her self-image. We have discovered in Langston Hughes's "Father and Son" how friction inherent in multicultural situations manifests itself in and is increased by difficulties in parent-child communication. We have witnessed in the examples of Steinbeck and Cather how an author's gender may affect that author's portrayal of gender in children and in child language. These selected examples represent just a few of this study's specific conclusions.

More generally, we have determined that the language of fictional children effectively and vividly conveys their characterizations. Most American writers who have elected to portray children have done so in a lifelike way, giving child characters appropriate manners of talking. Of course, not all child speech is executed in a satisfying way, and very young children are virtually absent from our literature. We have also found that some features of language, such as poetic or imaginative speech, are not well represented in fictional children's utterances. On the whole, however, looking back over the text-specific findings of this project, we are left with an increased appreciation for the linguistic and psychological insight of most American authors who have chosen to write specifically about children or at least to include them in their casts of characters.

From beginning to end, this investigation underscores the fundamental importance of children's voices in American literature and the value of examining the intricate patterns of their speech. The results of this project have implications for the study and teaching of many aspects of literature, literary history, and literary criticism, especially but not exclusively criticism concerned with stylistics and linguistic approaches to literature. Both the general and the text-specific conclusions of this project establish that examining fictional child language is a worthwhile activity which can be pursued systematically and productively through linguistic approaches developed from research in child language acquisition.

Notes

1. Introduction

   1. The most notable articles giving broad consideration to children in American literature include: Alfred Kazin's 1964 "A Procession of Children" in *The American Scholar*; Daniel L. Guillory's 1978 "The Mystique of Childhood in American Literature" in *Tulane Studies in English*; L. Terry Oggel's 1979 "The Background of the Images of Childhood in American Literature" in *Western Humanities Review*; and Leslie Fiedler's 1958 series of five essays in the *New Leader*.
   2. The view that literary language violates the conventions of nonliterary language and is therefore outside the confines of proper linguistic inquiry predates the linguistic advances of the last two or three decades. Yet objections from within linguistics about linguistic approaches to literature persist, stemming in part from the discipline's usual focus on oral language. It is worthwhile to remember, however, that in speech as well as in writing language is an arbitrary and symbolic system. For purposes of basic definition and first-level examination, it may make sense to concentrate on oral communication. This should not mean, though, that the applications of linguistics must be restricted to oral systems.

   From a literary perspective, objections to linguistic studies of literature often include the argument that such research fails to take into account features of a text other than those under immediate consideration, that its methodology is flawed by rigidly compartmentalizing divisions of linguistics, and that its claims for objectivity are overstated. As indicated in Chapter One, the present project has been conducted with full knowledge of these criticisms, and this project aims to answer some of these criticisms.

   For fuller discussions of objections which have been raised against linguistic approaches to literature, see the following: Charles B. Wheeler's 1968 review of *Essays on Style and Language* in *Style*; Christian Mair's 1985 "The 'New Stylistics': A Success Story or the Story of Successful Self-Deception?" in *Style*; and Rei R. Noguchi's 1986 "Linguistic Description and Literary Interpretation" in *CLA Journal*. For a related critical examination of the portrayal of language in literature, see Brian McHale's 1984 "Speaking as a Child in *U.S.A.*: A Problem in the Mimesis of Speech" in *Language and Style*.

3. Case Grammar

1. The idea that children may model their case patterns on their mothers' usage might sound obvious, but it is, to the contrary, somewhat surprising. Previous conventional wisdom has held that mothers tune into their children's speech, modifying and simplifying speech according to the needs of their listening children, but Retherford, Schwartz, and Chapman argue that mothers use many role relationships, that children pick out roles from their mothers' speech, and that, over time, children develop patterns like their mothers'.

2. Further considerations of case frames in child speech have appeared, for example, in Olswang and Carpenter's "The Ontogenesis of Agent," Clark and Hecht's "Learning to Coin Agent and Instrument Nouns," Schmidt and Sydow's "On the Development of Semantic Relations between Nouns," Hardy and Braine's "Categories that Bridge between Meaning and Syntax in Five-Year-Olds," Maratsos's "Problems in Categorical Evolution: Can Formal Categories Arise from Semantic Ones?" and other publications.

3. For instance, Muriel Shine (*The Fictional Children of Henry James*) says that Maisie goes with the governess because Mrs. Wix needs her the most. Christopher Brown ("The Rhetoric of Closure") sees the final dialogue as a parody of closure rhetoric and part of the novel's satire on the wish-fulfilling conventions of romance comedy. Edward Wagenknecht believes that James himself is to blame for contradictory interpretations of the novel because he was unnecessarily ambiguous. A short summary of critical opinions about *Maisie* and its conclusion can be found in John McCloskey's "What Maisie Knows: A Study of Childhood and Adolescence."

4. Functions of Child Speech

1. A functionalist approach to language bears some similarities to Austin's and Searle's widely known work on speech acts. Speech act philosophy asserts, first, that to speak is to perform an act with intent to communicate and, second, that this intent lies behind and controls all the features of language. The exact relationship between speech acts and language functions depends upon how the terms are defined. In *Psychology and Language*, for instance, Clark and Clark consider speech acts to be one facet of language functions.

2. Fuller accounts of the interpretive controversy appear in *A Casebook on Henry James's "The Turn of the Screw"* (edited by Gerald Willen), in the Norton Critical Edition of *The Turn of the Screw* (edited by Robert Kimbrough), and in *An Anatomy of "The Turn of the Screw"* (edited by Cranfil and Clark).

3. In a few instances, a long block of speech was subdivided for classification purposes if obvious shifts in intent occurred within the block. Another reviewer using the same functional categories and the same speech samples might obtain slightly different counts and different percentages, depending on what was considered an utterance, how each function was defined, and how each passage of speech was interpreted. Since all determinations of functional categories in this study were made by one person applying the same criteria in every choice, the results are uniform. And, after all, in the present study, the numbers themselves are only raw material; what are important are the patterns suggested by the statistics and the comparisons which subsequently emerge.

4. In *Born to Talk* Weeks includes curses as performatives since many curses are acts of speech that could be loosely translated as, "I condemn you." However, most of the demon's curses in *The Exorcist* are either expressions of emotion or attempts to direct the behavior of others, so, in such cases, they have been counted as filling personal or regulatory functions.

5. Parent-Child Discourse

1. For example, Jacqueline Sachs's "Talking About the There and Then" illustrates the point that most mother-to-child conversations, at least those described in linguistic studies, deal with concrete and definite topics.

2. Numerous literary studies have identified the pivotal role fatherhood plays in American fiction. For example, Earl Rovit's "Fathers and Sons in American Fiction" and Irving Malin's "The Authoritarian Family in American Fiction" examine father-son relationships in American literature, though neither looks at the language of parents and children. Sometimes the absence of fathers makes an important literary statement. Discussing the frequency of characters who engage in a search for their fathers, John Daniel Stahl's essay on "American Myth in European Disguise: Fathers and Sons in *The Prince and the Pauper*" identifies orphanhood as the primary American condition. In "The Image of Fathers in Popular Adolescent Fiction," Eric Kimmel compiles an impressive list of "lost, stolen, or strayed" fathers who are well known to young American readers. None of this criticism has investigated the language exchanged between fathers and sons.

3. Books that de-emphasize or demean the role of women as mothers have even been celebrated, as Rosalie Black Kiah and Elaine Paige Witty note in "The Portrayal of the Black Mother in Fiction for Children and Adolescents."

4. Another sign of the coming of age of mother-daughter issues in literature is that in 1984 *Sage: A Scholarly Journal on Black Women* devoted an entire issue in its first volume to the topic of mothers and daughters in fiction.

6. Children's Narratives

1. In 1985 the Society for the Study of Narrative Literature began to publish *The Journal of Narrative Technique*, and several books, including

Wallace Martin's *Recent Theories of Narrative* and Shlomith Rimmon-Kenan's *Narrative Fiction*, have lately gained critical attention.

7. Gender and Fictional Children's Language

1. Though biological connections between language and gender are eagerly sought, research in this area is controversial. Classic sources for more information include Eric Lenneberg's *Biological Foundations of Language* and Norman Geschwind's "Anatomical Foundations of Language and Dominance." More technical information on children, sexual differences in language, and biology can be found in Kenneth Swaiman and Stephen Ashwal's *Pediatric Neurology Case Studies* and Francis Wright's "Disorders of Speech and Language." Part III of *Language, Gender, and Sex in Comparative Perspective* (edited by Susan U. Philips, Susan Steele, and Christine Tanz) contains two essays on sex differences in language and brain: "Cerebral Organization and Sex: Interesting But Complex" by Walter McKeever, and "Sex Differences in the Patterns of Scalp-Recorded Electrophysiological Activity in Infancy: Possible Implications for Language Development" by David W. Shucard, Janet L. Shucard, and David G. Thomas.

2. Culturally related gender differences in language are the subject of many articles and books. Some comprehensive considerations of the subject include the following: *Grammar and Gender*, by Dennis Baron; *Language and Sex: Difference and Dominance*, edited by Barrie Thorne and Nancy Henley; *Language, Gender, and Society*, edited by Barrie Thorne, Cheris Kramarae, and Nancy Henley; and *Women, Men, and Language*, by Jennifer Coates.

3. Reviewing hundreds of studies, Eleanor Maccoby and Carol Jacklin in *The Psychology of Sex Differences* have found slight evidence that, at least at certain ages, boys tend to be more aggressive and tend to be superior in visual-spatial abilities and in mathematics, while girls tend to excel verbally.

4. Although Annette Kolodny has said, in reference to published authors, that women's writing cannot be defined any more than men's writing, some writing teachers have begun to explore the idea that male and female students may write differently. The entire April 1979 issue of *College English* is devoted to gender-related subjects, and essays in it consider not only sexual differences involved in teaching literature and composition, but also sexual differences involved in composition styles of male and female college students. In this journal, Thomas Farrell observes in "The Female and Male Modes of Rhetoric" that men writers usually state their conclusion at the outset and then present the steps leading to the conclusion, whereas women writers often lead the reader through various steps and present the conclusion at the last possible moment. In another article, Margaret B. Pigott claims in "Sexist Roadblocks in Inventing, Focusing, and Writing" that male students prefer to draw universal conclusions in their compositions, whereas female students seem to be more comfortable when staying close to observations of personal experience. Of course, many teachers and critics are uncomfortable with such statements about male-female differences in language use.

5. In this case, an utterance may be understood as a turn in conversation. Most often, child speakers are attributed only a sentence or two at a time,

though occasionally they are given several sentences together in one paragraph. For present purposes, even these longer clusters of speech have been considered a single utterance unless the child changes the topic or otherwise alters the flow of dialogue in the middle of a turn, in which case the turn has been counted as two utterances. Such verbal behavior is rare and usually follows the pattern of a child making a statement on one subject and then, generally after a "he said" or "she answered" marker, the child asking a question about another subject.

8. Conclusion

1. Both Freud in *A General Introduction to Psychoanalysis* and Erikson in *Childhood and Society* indicate that children are ordinarily ready to resolve their Oedipal conflicts and to move beyond their immediate family attachments by age six.

Bibliography

This bibliography includes all works cited in the text along with a selection of additional articles, dissertations, and books on the topic of children and child language in American literature.

Abbott, Dorothy, ed. *Mississippi Writers: Reflections of Childhood and Youth.* Vol. 1: *Fiction.* Jackson: UP of Mississippi, 1985.

Abel, Darrel. "Hawthorne's Pearl: Symbol and Character." *English Literary History* 18 (1951): 50-66.

Adamowski, T.H. "Joe Christmas: The Tyranny of Childhood." *Novel* 4 (1971): 240-51.

Adrian, Arthur A. *Dickens and the Parent-Child Relationship.* Athens: Ohio UP, 1984.

Alcott, Louisa May. *Little Men.* 1871. New York: Grosset, 1947.

Allen, Suzanne. "Memories of a Southern Catholic Girlhood: Flannery O'Connor's *A Temple of the Holy Ghost.*" *Renascence* 31 (1979): 83-92.

Anderson, Elaine. "Young Children's Knowledge of Role-Related Speech Differences: A Mommy Is Not a Daddy Is Not a Baby." *Papers and Reports on Child Language Development* 13 (1977): 83-90.

Anderson, John. *The Grammar of Case: Toward a Localistic Theory.* New York: Cambridge UP, 1971.

Anderson, Sherwood. "I Want to Know Why." (1921.) *The Sherwood Anderson Reader.* Ed. Paul Rosenfeld. Boston: Houghton, 1947. 86-94.

———. *Tar: A Midwest Childhood.* 1926. Cleveland: P of Case Western Reserve, 1969.

———. *Winesburg, Ohio.* 1919. New York: Viking, 1966.

Andola, John A. "Pearl: Symbolic Link Between Two Worlds." *Ball State U Forum* 13 (1972): 60-67.

Aries, Philippe. *Centuries of Childhood.* (*L'Enfant et la Vie sous l'Ancien Regime.* France, 1960.) Trans. Robert Baldick. New York: Knopf, 1962.

Armstrong, Paul B. "How Maisie Knows: The Phenomenology of James' Moral Vision." *Texas Studies in Literature and Language* 20 (1978): 517-37.
Auchincloss, Louis. *Pioneers and Caretakers: A Study of Nine American Women Novelists*. Minneapolis: U of Minnesota P, 1965.
Austin, J. L. *How to Do Things with Words*. Cambridge: Harvard UP, 1962.
Bakhtin, Mikhail Mikhailovich. *The Dialogic Imagination: Four Essays*. Trans. Caryl Emerson and Michael Holquist. Ed. Michael Holquist. Austin: U of Texas P, 1981.
Ballorain, Rollande. "From Childhood to Womanhood (or From Fusion to Fragmentation): A Study of the Growing Up Process in XXth Century American Women's Fiction." *Revue Francaise d'Etudes Americaines* 11 (1981): 97-112.
Banerjee, Jacqueline. "Ambivalence and Contradiction: The Child in Victorian Fiction." *English Studies* 65 (1984): 481-94.
Bannan, Helen M. "Warrior Women: Immigrant Mothers in the Works of their Daughters." *Women's Studies* 6.2 (1979): 165-77.
Banta, Martha. "The Quality of Experience in *What Maisie Knew*." *New England Quarterly* 42 (1969): 483-510.
Barnett, Louise K. "Huck Finn: Picaro as Linguistic Outsider." *College Literature* 6 (1979): 221-31.
Baron, Dennis. *Grammar and Gender*. New Haven: Yale UP, 1986.
Bates, Elizabeth. *Language and Context: The Acquisition of Pragmatics*. New York: Academic, 1976.
Bawer, Bruce. "Capote's Children." *The New Criterion* 3.10 (1985): 39-44.
Baym, Nina. *Women's Fiction: A Guide to Novels by and about Women in America, 1820-1870*. Ithaca: Cornell UP, 1978.
Beck, M. Susan. *Kidspeak*. New York: NAL, 1982.
Beidler, Peter G. "The Governess and the Ghosts." *PMLA* 100 (1985): 96-97.
Beit-Hallahmi, Benjamin. "*The Turn of the Screw* and *The Exorcist*: Demoniacal Possession and Childhood Purity." *American Imago* 33 (1976): 296-303.
Benes, Peter, ed. *Families and Children*. Boston: Boston UP, 1987.
Bent, Nancy Pettengill. "Romance and Irony in Henry James's View of Women." *DAI* 42 (1981): 220A-221A.
Bier, Jesse. "'Bless You, Chile': Fiedler and 'Huck Honey' a Generation Later." *Mississippi Quarterly* 34 (1981): 456-62.
Billman, Carol. "Nathaniel Hawthorne: 'Revolutionizer' of Children's Literature." *Studies in American Fiction* 10 (1982): 107-14.
Bivens, William P., III. "Noun Phrase Case Schemes in the Deep Structure of Poems." *Style* 8 (1974): 305-21.
Bixler, Phyllis. "Idealization of the Child and Childhood in Frances Hodgson Burnett's *Little Lord Fauntleroy* and Mark Train's *Tom Sawyer*." *Research about Nineteenth Century Children and Books*. Ed. S.K. Richardson. Carbondale: U of Illinois Graduate School of Library Sciences, 1980. 85-96.
Black, Linda. "Louisa May Alcott's 'Huckleberry Finn.'" *Mark Twain Journal* 21.2 (1982): 15-17.
Blackall, Jean Frantz. "Cruikshank's *Oliver* and 'The Turn of the Screw.'" *American Literature* 51 (1979): 161-78.
Blasingham, Mary V. "Archetypes of the Child and of Childhood in the Fiction

of Flannery O'Connor." *Realist of Distances: Flannery O'Connor Revisited.* Ed. Karl-Heinz Westarp and Jan Nordby Gretlund. Aarhus, Den.: Aarhus UP, 1987. 102-112.

Blatty, William Peter. *The Exorcist.* 1971. New York: Bantam, 1972.

Bloomfield, Leonard. *Language.* 1933. Chicago: U of Chicago P, 1984.

Boas, George. *The Cult of Childhood.* London: Warburg, 1966.

Bode, Carl. *The Young Rebel in American Literature.* New York: Praeger, 1960.

Boose, Lynda E., and Betty S. Flowers, eds. *Daughters and Fathers.* Baltimore: Johns Hopkins UP, 1989.

Botvin, Gilbert J., and Brian Sutton-Smith. "The Development of Structural Complexity in Children's Fantasy Narratives." *Developmental Psychology* 13 (1977): 377-88.

Boutelle, Ann Edwards. "Hemingway and 'Papa': Killing of the Father in the Nick Adams Fiction." *Journal of Modern Literature* 9 (1981): 133-46.

Bowerman, Melissa. "Structural Relationships in Children's Utterances: Syntactic or Semantic?" *Cognitive Development and the Acquisition of Language.* Ed. Timothy E. Moore. New York: Academic, 1973. 197-214.

Braine, Martin D.S., and Judith A. Hardy. "On What Case Categories There Are, Why They Are, and How They Develop: An Amalgam of A Priori Considerations, Speculation, and Evidence from Children." *Language Acquisition: The State of the Art.* Ed. Lila R. Gleitman and Eric Wanner. New York: Cambridge UP, 1982. 219-39.

Brautigan, Richard. *Trout Fishing in America.* New York: Delta-Dell, 1967.

Bremner, Robert, et al., eds. *Children and Youth in America: A Documentary History.* 3 vols. Cambridge: Harvard UP, 1970-1974.

Brenzo, Richard. "Free Heron or Dead Sparrow: Sylvia's Choice in Sarah Orne Jewett's 'A White Heron.'" *Colby Library Quarterly* 15 (1978): 36-41.

Brooks, Cleanth. "Faulkner's 'Motherless' Children." *William Faulkner: Materials, Studies, and Criticisms* 7.1 (1985): 1-17.

Brown, Christopher. "The Rhetoric of Closure in *What Maisie Knew.*" *Style* 20 (1986): 58-65.

Brown, May Cameron. "The Language of Chaos: Quentin Compson in *The Sound and the Fury.*" *American Literature* 51 (1980): 544-53.

Brown, Penelope, and Stephen Levinson. "Universals in Language Usage: Politeness Phenomena." *Questions and Politeness.* Ed. Esther N. Goody. New York: Cambridge UP, 1978. 56-289.

Bryer, Jackson, ed. *Sixteen Modern American Authors: A Survey of Research and Criticism.* Rev. ed. New York: Norton, 1973.

Burke, Armand. "The Changing Family in American Fiction." *Contemporary Review* 208 (1966): 151-59.

Burroughs, Franklin G., Jr. "God the Father and Motherless Children: *Light in August.*" *Twentieth Century Literature* 19 (1973): 189-202.

Burton, Dolores. "Intonation Patterns of Sermons in Seven Novels." *Language and Style* 3 (1977): 205-20.

Calhoun, Arthur W. *A Social History of the American Family.* 2 vols. 1917. New York: Barnes, 1960.

Cardullo, Bert. "The Role of the Baby in *A Streetcar Named Desire.*" *Notes on Contemporary Literature* 14.2 (1984): 4-5.

Carlson, Larry A. "'Those Pure Pages of Yours': Bronson Alcott's *Conversations with Children on the Gospels.*" *American Literature* 60 (1988): 451-460.

Castagnino, Raul H. "Evocaciones de Infancia y Adolescencia en la Literatura Argentina." *Revista Interamericana de Bibliografia* 32 (1982): 338-46.
Cather, Willa. *My Antonia*. 1918. Boston: Houghton, 1949.
———. *Shadows on the Rock*. New York: Knopf, 1931.
Chafe, Wallace L. *Meaning and the Structure of Language*. Chicago: U of Chicago P, 1970.
Chapman, Raymond. *The Treatment of Sounds in Language and Literature*. New York: Basil Blackwell, 1984.
Cheung, King-Kok. "'Don't Tell': Imposed Silences in *The Color Purple* and *The Woman Warrior*." *PMLA* 103 (1988): 162-74.
Chomsky, Noam. *Aspects of the Theory of Syntax*. Cambridge: MIT P, 1965.
Christian, Barbara. *Black Feminist Criticism: Perspectives on Black Women Writers*. New York: Pergamon, 1985.
Claridge, Laura. "Isaac McCaslin's Failed Bid for Adulthood." *American Literature* 55 (1983): 241-51.
Clark, Eve V., and Barbara F. Hecht. "Learning to Coin Agent and Instrument Nouns." *Cognition* 12 (1982): 1-24.
Clark, Herbert H., and Eve V. Clark. *Psychology and Language*. New York: Harcourt, 1977.
Clark, Michael. "James Baldwin's 'Sonny's Blues': Childhood, Light and Art." *CLA Journal* 29.2 (1985): 197-205.
Clemens, Samuel Langhorne. *Adventures of Huckleberry Finn*. 1885. *Adventures of Huckleberry Finn: An Authoritative Text; Backgrounds and Sources; Criticism*. Ed. Sculley Bradley et al. 2nd ed. New York: Norton, 1977.
———. *The Adventures of Tom Sawyer*. 1876. Vol. 4 of *The Works of Mark Twain*. Ed. John C. Gerber, Paul Baender, and Terry Firkins. Berkeley: U of California P, 1980.
———. "The Celebrated Jumping Frog of Calaveras County." 1865. "Three Versions of the 'Jumping Frog.'" *Early Tales & Sketches, Vol. 2*. Vol. 15 of *The Works of Mark Twain*. Ed. Edgar Marquess Branch and Robert H. Hirst. Berkeley: U of California P, 1981. 262-288.
———. "Little Bessie Would Assist Providence." (Written 1908.) Unpublished ms. Mark Twain Papers. U of California, Berkeley. Excerpts appear in *The Innocent Eye: Childhood in Mark Twain's Imagination*. By Albert E. Stone. New Haven: Yale UP, 1961.
Coard, Robert L. "Tom Sawyer, Sturdy Centenarian." *Midwest Quarterly* 17 (1976): 329-49.
Coates, Jennifer. *Women, Men, and Language*. New York: Longman, 1986.
Coe, Richard N. *When the Grass Was Taller: Autobiography and the Experience of Childhood*. New Haven: Yale UP, 1984.
Cook, Walter A. "Role Structures in Context Analysis: A Case Grammar Approach to Literature." *Meaning: A Common Ground of Linguistics and Literature*. Proc. of the U of Northern Iowa Conference. 27-28 Apr. 1973. Cedar Falls: U of Northern Iowa, 1973. 179-87.
Coveney, Peter. *The Image of Childhood: The Individual and Society: A Study of the Theme in English Literature*. Rev. ed. Baltimore: Penguin, 1967.
Craig, Randall. "'Read[ing] the unspoken into the spoken': Interpreting *What Maisie Knew*." *Henry James Review* 2 (1981): 204-212.
Crane, Stephen. "The Angel Child." (1899.) *The Complete Short Stories and Sketches of Stephen Crane*. Ed. Thomas A. Gullason. Garden City: Doubleday, 1963. 558-65.

———. "The City Urchin and the Chaste Villagers." (1900.) *The Complete Short Stories and Sketches of Stephen Crane*. Ed. Thomas H. Gullason. Garden City: Doubleday, 1963. 756-62.

———. "A Little Pilgrimage." (1900.) *The Complete Short Stories and Sketches of Stephen Crane*. Ed. Thomas A. Gullason. Garden City: Doubleday, 1963. 765-68.

———. *Whilomville Stories*. 1900. *Tales of Whilomville*. Vol. 7 of *The Works of Stephen Crane*. Ed. Fredson Bowers. Charlottesville: UP of Virginia, 1969.

Cranfall, J.C. "Patriotism and Humanitarian Reform in Children's Literature, 1825-1860." *American Quarterly* 21 (1969): 3-22.

Cranfil, Thomas Mabry, and Robert Lanier Clark, Jr., eds. *An Anatomy of "The Turn of the Screw."* New York: Gordian, 1971.

Crews, Frederick. *The Sins of the Fathers: Hawthorne's Psychological Themes*. New York: Oxford UP, 1966.

Crowley, John W. "*Little Women* and the Boy-Book." *New England Quarterly* 58.3 (1985): 384-389.

Cuddy, Lois. "Mother-Daughter Identification in *The Scarlet Letter*." *Mosaic* 19.2 (1986): 101-15.

Cushman, Keith. "A Reading of Joyce Carol Oates's 'Four Summers.'" *Studies in Short Fiction* 18 (1981): 137-46.

Dalsimer, Katherine. *Female Adolescence: Psychoanalytic Reflections on Literature*. New Haven: Yale UP, 1986.

Davidson, Cathy N., and E. M. Broner, eds. *The Lost Tradition: Mothers and Daughters in Literature*. New York: Ungar, 1980.

Davis, Glenn. *Childhood and History in America*. New York: Psychohistory, 1977.

Dawe, Helen C. "An Analysis of 200 Quarrels of Preschool Children." *Child Development* 5 (1934): 139-57.

deMause, Lloyd, ed. *The History of Childhood*. New York: Psychohistory, 1974.

Demos, John. *Past, Present, and Personal: The Family and the Life Course in America*. New York: Oxford UP, 1986.

de Villiers, Jill G., and Peter A. de Villiers. *Language Acquisition*. Cambridge: Harvard UP, 1978.

Devlin, Albert. "Parent-Child Relationships in the Works of William Faulkner." Diss. U of Kansas, 1970.

Dolis, John. "Hawthorne's Letter." *Notebooks in Cultural Analysis I*. Ed. Norman F. Cantor. Durham: Duke UP, 1984. 103-24.

Donovan, Frank Robert. *Dickens and Youth: The Children of Charles Dickens*. London: Frewin, 1969.

Dore, John. "Children's Conversations." *Discourse and Dialogue*. Vol. 3 of *Handbook of Discourse Analysis*. Ed. Teun A. Van Dijk. New York: Academic, 1985. 47-65.

Dos Passos, John. *U.S.A.* New York: Modern Library, 1937.

Drotner, Kirsten. *English Children and Their Magazines, 1751-1945*. New Haven: Yale UP, 1988.

DuBois, John W. "The Discourse Basis of Ergativity." *Language* 63 (1987): 805-55.

Durkin, Kevin, D. R. Rutter, and Hilarie Tucker. "Social Interaction and Language Acquisition: Motherese Help You." *First Language* 3 (1982): 107-20.

Earle, Alice Morse. *Child Life in Colonial Days*. New York: Macmillan, 1899.
Early, Gerald. "Working Girl Blues: Mothers, Daughters, and the Image of Billie Holiday in Kristin Hunter's *God Bless the Child*." *Black American Literature Forum* 20.4 (1986): 423-42.
Eckley, Grace. *Children's Lore in Finnegan's Wake*. Syracuse, NY: Syracuse UP, 1984.
Edelsky, Carole. "Acquisition of an Aspect of Communicative Competence: Learning What It Means to Talk Like a Lady." *Child Discourse*. Ed. Susan Ervin-Tripp and Claudia Mitchell-Kernan. New York: Academic, 1977. 225-43.
Egan, Michael. *Mark Twain's Huckleberry Finn: Race, Class and Society*. Atlantic Highlands, NJ: Humanities, 1978.
Ehnmark, Anders. "Rebels in American Literature." *Western Review* 23 (1958): 43-56.
Elsen, Mary Mertz. "The Child Figure in Hawthorne's Fiction." Diss. U of Maryland, 1978.
Erikson, Erik. *Childhood and Society*. 2nd ed. New York: Norton, 1963.
Erlich, Gloria C. *Family Themes and Hawthorne's Fiction: The Tenacious Web*. New Brunswick: Rutgers UP, 1984.
Ervin-Tripp, Susan. "Wait for Me, Roller Skate!" *Child Discourse*. Ed. Susan Ervin-Tripp and Claudia Mitchell-Kernan. New York: Academic, 1977. 165-88.
Ervin-Tripp, Susan, and Amy Strage. "Parent-Child Discourse." *Discourse and Dialogue*. Vol. 3 of *Handbook of Discourse Analysis*. Ed. Teun A. Van Dijk. London: Academic, 1985. 67-78.
Fall, A.S. "The Child-Hero in African Folktales." *UNESCO Courier* 35 (1982): 23-25.
Farrell, James T. *Young Lonigan*. 1932. New York: Avon, 1972.
Farrell, Thomas J. "The Female and Male Modes of Rhetoric." *College English* 40 (1979): 909-21.
Faulkner, Howard. "Text as Pretext in *The Turn of the Screw*." *Studies in Short Fiction* 20.2-3 (1983): 87-94.
Faulkner, William. *Absalom, Absalom!* 1936. New York: Vintage, 1972.
———. *As I Lay Dying*. 1930. New York: Vintage, 1964.
———. "Barn Burning." (1939.) *Collected Stories of William Faulkner*. New York: Vintage, 1977. 3-25.
———. "The Bear." *Go Down Moses*. 1942. New York: Modern Library, 1955. 191-334.
———. *Flags in the Dust*. 1973. (First published in 1929 as *Sartoris*.) New York: Vintage, 1974.
———. *The Hamlet*. 1931. New York: Vintage, 1956.
———. *Light in August*. 1932. New York: Vintage, 1972.
———. "The Nobel Prize Speech." (1950.) *The Faulkner Reader*. New York: Random, 1953. 3-4.
———. *Requiem for a Nun*. 1950. New York: Vintage, 1975.
———. *The Sound and the Fury*. 1929. New York: Vintage, 1954.
———. "That Evening Sun." (1931.) *Collected Stories of William Faulkner*. New York: Vintage, 1977. 289-309.
———. *The Unvanquished*. 1938. New York: Vintage, 1954.
Fein, Richard J. "Fear, Fatherhood, and Desire in *Call It Sleep*." *Yiddish* 5.4 (1984): 49-54.

Bibliography

Fetterly, Judith. "Disenchantment: Tom Sawyer in *Huck Finn*." *PMLA* 87 (1972): 69-74.

———. "The Sanctioned Rebel." *Studies in the Novel* 3 (1971): 293-304.

Fiedler, Leslie. *Love and Death in the American Novel*. Rev. ed. New York: Stein, 1966.

Fiedler, Leslie A. "Boys Will Be Boys." *The New Leader* 41.17 (1958): 23-26.

———. "From Redemption to Initiation." *The New Leader* 41.21 (1958): 20-23.

———. "Good Good Girl and Good Bad Boy." *The New Leader* 41.15 (1958): 22-25.

———. "The Invention of the Child." *The New Leader* 41.13 (1958): 22-24.

———. "The Profanation of the Child." *The New Leader* 41.25 (1958): 26-29.

Fillmore, Charles J. "The Case for Case." *Universals in Linguistic Theory*. Ed. Emmon Bach and Robert T. Harms. New York: Holt, 1968. 1-88.

Finkelstein, Barbara, ed. *Regulated Children/Liberated Children*. New York: Psychohistory, 1979.

Fisher, Marvin. "The World of Faulkner's Children." *U of Kansas City Review* 27 (1960): 13-18.

Fishman, Pamela. "Interaction: The Work Women Do." *Language, Gender and Society*. Ed. Barrie Thorne, Cheris Kramarae, and Nancy Henley. Rowley, MA: Newbury, 1983. 89-102.

Fitzgerald, F. Scott. *The Great Gatsby*. New York: Scribner, 1925.

Fogle, Richard H. *Hawthorne's Fiction: The Light and the Dark*. Rev. ed. Norman, OK: U of Oklahoma P, 1964.

Fox, Vivian C., and Martin H. Quitt. *Loving, Parenting and Dying: The Family Cycle in England and America, Past and Present*. New York: Psychohistory, 1981.

Fraiman, Susan. "Mother-Daughter Romance in Charles W. Chestnutt's 'Her Virginia Mammy.'" *Studies in Short Fiction* 22.4 (1985): 443-48.

Freud, Sigmund. *A General Introduction to Psychoanalysis*. Garden City: Doubleday, 1938.

Galbraith, Mary. "What Everybody Knew Versus What Maisie Knew: The Change in Epistemological Perspective from the Prologue to the Opening of Chapter 1 in *What Maisie Knew*." *Style* 23.2 (1989): 197-212.

Gargano, James W. "The Turn of the Screw." *Western Humanities Review* 15 (1961): 173-79.

Garlitz, Barbara. "The Cult of Childhood in Nineteenth Century England and America." Diss. Radcliffe, 1959.

———. "Pearl: 1850-1955." *PMLA* 72 (1957): 689-99.

Garrison, Joseph M. "The Past and the Present in 'That Evening Sun.'" *Studies in Short Fiction* 13 (1976): 371-73.

Geher, Istvan. "A Child's Eye View of Tragedy: Faulkner's Mixed Metaphor." *Acta Litteraria Academiae Scientiarum Hungaricae* 23 (1982): 281-96.

Gehrki, Barbara Ann. "Willa Cather's Families." Diss. U of Nebraska, 1981.

Geller, Evelyn. "Tom Sawyer, Tom Bailey, and the Bad Boy Genre." *Wilson Library Bulletin* 51 (1976): 245-50.

Gerber, John C. *Twentieth Century Interpretations of The Scarlet Letter*. Englewood Cliffs: Prentice, 1968.

Gervais, Ronald J. "The Trains of Their Youth: The Aesthetics of Homecoming

in *The Great Gatsby, The Sun Also Rises,* and *The Sound and the Fury."* *Americana-Austriaca: Beitrase zur Amerikakunde* 6 (1980): 51-63.
Geschwind, Norman. "Anatomical Foundations of Language and Dominance." *The Neurological Bases of Language Disorders in Children: Methods and Directions for Research.* Ed. Christy L. Ludlow and Mary Ellen Doran-Quine. NINCDS Monograph No. 22. Bethesda, MD: US Dept. of HEW, 1979.
Giattino, Jill, and Jeanne G. Hogan. "Analysis of a Father's Speech to His Language-Learning Child." *Journal of Speech and Hearing Disorders* 40 (1975): 524-37.
Gilbert, Susan. "Children of the Seventies: The American Family in Recent Fiction." *Soundings: A Journal of Interdisciplinary Studies* 63 (1980): 199-213.
Ginsberg, Elaine. "The Female Initiation Theme in American Fiction." *Studies in American Fiction* 3 (1975): 27-38.
Gleason, Jean Berko. "Sex Differences in the Language of Children and Parents." *Language, Children and Society.* Ed. Olga Garnica and Martha King. New York: Pergamon, 1979. 149-57.
Gleason, Jean Berko, and Esther Blank Greif. "Men's Speech to Young Children." *Language, Gender and Society.* Ed. Barrie Thorne, Cheris Kramarae, and Nancy Henley. Rowley, MA: Newbury, 1983. 140-50.
Goodman, Charlotte. "Henry James, D.H. Lawrence, and the Victimized Child." *Modern Language Studies* 10 (1979): 43-51.
———. "The Sins of the Fathers and Mothers: The Child as Victim in Modern Literature." *Modern Language Studies* 15.2 (1985): 47-54.
Goodwin, Marjorie Harness. "Directive-Response Speech Sequences in Girls' and Boys' Task Activities." *Women and Language in Literature and Society.* Ed. Sally McConnell-Ginet, Ruth Borker, and Nelly Furman. New York: Praeger, 1980. 157-73.
Gordon, James S. "Demonic Children." *New York Times Book Review* 11 Sept. 1977: 3+.
Gordon, Jan B. "The *Alice* Books and the Metaphors of Victorian Childhood." *Aspects of Alice: Lewis Carroll's Dreamchild as Seen Through the Critics' Looking-Glasses.* Ed. Robert Phillips. New York: Vanguard, 1971. 107-28.
Greenleaf, Barbara Kaye. *Children Through the Ages: A History of Childhood.* New York: McGraw, 1978.
Greven, Philip J., ed. *Child-Rearing Concepts, 1628-1861: Historical Sources.* Itasca, IL: Peacock, 1973.
Grice, H. Paul. "Logic and Conversation." *Speech Acts.* Vol. 3 of *Syntax and Semantics.* Ed. Peter Cole and Jerry L. Morgan. New York: Academic, 1975. 41-58.
Griffin, Mary N. "Coming to Manhood in America: A Study of Significant Initiation Novels 1797-1970." Diss. Vanderbilt U, 1971.
Grimshaw, James A., Jr. *The Flannery O'Connor Companion.* Westport, CT: Greenwood, 1981.
Grove, James Paul. "Mark Twain and the Endangered Family." *American Literature* 57 (1985): 377-394.
Grylls, David. *Guardians and Angels.* London: Faber, 1978.
Guillory, Daniel L. "The Mystique of Childhood in American Literature." *Tulane Studies in English* 23 (1978): 229-47.

Hakak, John R. "The Juvenile Hero as a Literary Device in Selected American Novels." Diss. U of Texas, 1963.

Halliday, M.A.K. *Explorations in the Functions of Language.* London: Arnold, 1975.

———. "Linguistic Function and Literary Style: An Inquiry into the Language of William Golding's *The Inheritors.*" *Literary Style: A Symposium.* Ed. Seymour Chatman. London: Oxford UP, 1971. 330-68.

———. "The Linguistic Study of Literary Texts." *Essays on the Language of Literature.* Ed. Seymour Chatman and Samuel R. Levin. Boston: Houghton, 1967. 217-23.

Hamner, Eugenie Lambert. "The Unknown, Well-Known Child in Cather's Last Novel." *Women's Studies* 11.3 (1984): 347-57.

Hanson, John H. "The Child Archetype and Modern Primitivism: Kosinski's *The Painted Bird.*" *University of Hartford Studies in Literature* 14.3 (1982): 85-95.

Hardy, Judith Atkinson, and Martin D.S. Braine. "Categories That Bridge between Meaning and Syntax in Five-Year-Olds." *The Child's Construction of Language.* Ed. Werner Deutsch. New York: Academic, 1981. 201-22.

Harris, Natalie. "New Life in American Poetry: The Child as Mother of the Poet." *The Centennial Review* 31.3 (1987): 240-54.

Harris, Trudier. "Tiptoeing through Taboo: Incest in 'The Child Who Favored Daughter.'" *Modern Fiction Studies* 28 (1982): 495-505.

Hassan, Ihab. *Radical Innocence: Studies in the Contemporary American Novel.* Princeton: Princeton UP, 1961.

Hathaway, Richard D. "Hawthorne and the Paradise of Children." *Western Humanities Review* 15 (1961); 161-72.

Hawes, Joseph M. and N. Ray Hiner, eds. *American Childhood: A Research Guide and Historical Handbook.* Westport, CT: Greenwood P, 1985.

Hawthorne, Nathaniel. *The American Notebooks.* Ed. Claude M. Simpson. Vol. 8 of *The Centenary Edition of the Works of Nathaniel Hawthorne.* Ed. William Charvat, Roy Harvey Pearce, and Claude M. Simpson. Columbus: Ohio State UP, 1972.

———. "The Gentle Boy." 1832. *Twice-Told Tales.* Vol. 9 of *The Centenary Edition of the Works of Nathaniel Hawthorne.* Ed. William Charvat, Roy Harvey Pearce, and Claude M. Simpson. Columbus: Ohio State UP, 1974. 68-105.

———. *The Scarlet Letter.* 1850. Vol. 1 of *The Centenary Edition of the Works of Nathaniel Hawthorne.* Ed. William Charvat, Roy Harvey Pearce, and Claude M. Simpson. Columbus: Ohio State UP, 1962.

———. "The Snow-Image: A Childish Miracle." (1850.) *The Snow-Image and Uncollected Tales.* Vol. 11 of *The Centenary Edition of the Works of Nathaniel Hawthorne.* Ed. William Charvat, Roy Harvey Pearce, and Claude M. Simpson. Columbus: Ohio State UP, 1974, 7-25.

———. *A Wonder-Book for Girls and Boys.* 1852. *A Wonder Book and Tanglewood Tales.* Vol. 7 of *The Centenary Edition of the Works of Nathaniel Hawthorne.* Ed. William Charvat, Roy Harvey Pearce, and Claude M. Simpson. Columbus: Ohio State UP, 1972.

Hazlett, John D. "Repossessing the Past: Discontinuity and History in Alfred Kazin's *A Walker in the City.*" *Biography* 7.4 (1984): 325-340.

Heaton, C.P. "Style in *The Old Man and the Sea.*" *Style* 4 (1970): 11-28.

Heilman, Robert B. "Lure of the Demonic: James and Durrenmatt." *Comparative Literature* 13 (1961): 346-57.

Heininger, Mary Lynn Stevens, et al. *A Century of Childhood: 1820-1920*. Rochester: Margaret Woodbury Strong Museum, 1984.

Heldreth, Leonard G. "The Ultimate Horror: The Dead Child in Stephen King's Stories." *Discovering Stephen King*. Ed. Darrell Schweitzer. Mercer Island, WA: Starmont, 1985. 141-52.

Hemingway, Ernest. *In Our Time*. 1925. New York: Scribner's, 1970.

———. *The Old Man and the Sea*. New York: Scribner's, 1952.

Herbert, T. Walter. "Nathaniel Hawthorne, Una Hawthorne, and *The Scarlet Letter*: Interactive Selfhoods and the Cultural Construction of Gender." *PMLA* 103 (1988): 285-297.

Hiatt, Mary P. "The Sexology of Style." *Language and Style* 9 (1976): 98-107.

———. *The Way Women Write*. New York: Teachers College P, Columbia U, 1977.

———. "Women's Prose Style: A Study of Contemporary Authors." *Language and Style:* 13 (1980): 36-45.

Hiken, Arlin J. "Shakespeare's Use of Children." *Educational Theatre Journal* 15 (1963): 241-48.

Hildick, Wallace. *Children and Fiction: A Critical Study in Depth in the Artistic and Psychological Factors Involved in Writing Fiction for and about Children*. London: Evans, 1970.

Hill, Jane Bowers. "Ann Beattie's Children as Redeemers." *Critique* 27 (1986): 197-212.

Hill, Robert W., Jr. "A Counter-clockwise Turn in James' 'The Turn of the Screw.'" *Twentieth Century Literature* 27 (1981): 53-71.

Hiner, N. Ray, and Joseph M. Hawes, eds. *Growing Up in America: Children in Historical Perspective*. Urbana: U of Illinois P, 1985.

Hinz, John. "Huck and Pluck: 'Bad' Boys in American Fiction." *South Atlantic Quarterly* 51 (1952): 120-29.

Hinz, John P. "Restless Heir, The Boy in American Fiction." Diss. Columbia U, 1959.

Hodgin, Katherine Campbell. "The Child's Perspective of Sex and Death in Southern Literature." *DAI* 48 (1988): 1770A.

Hovet, Theodore R. "America's 'Lonely Country Child': The Theme of Separation in Sarah Orne Jewett's 'A White Heron.'" *Colby Library Quarterly* 14 (1978): 166-71.

Hughes, Langston. "Father and Son." *The Ways of White Folks*. 1933. New York: Vintage, 1971. 200-48.

———. "Red-Headed Baby." *The Ways of White Folks*. 1933. New York: Vintage, 1971. 121-28.

———. *Not Without Laughter*. New York: Knopf, 1930.

Hunter, Jim. "Mark Twain and the Boy Book in Nineteenth-Century America." *College English* 24 (1963): 430-38.

Hurst, Mary Jane. "Characterization and Language: A Case Grammar Study of William Faulkner's *As I Lay Dying*." *Language and Style*. 20.1 (1987): 71-87.

———. "Fire Imagery." Forum Section. *PMLA* 100 (1985): 236-37.

———. "The Language of Children in 'The Snow-Image.'" *Essex Institute Historical Collections* 125.1 (1989): 55-64.

Hymes, Dell. "The Ethnography of Speaking." *Readings in the Sociology of Language*. Ed. Joshua Fishman. The Hague: Mouton, 1968. 99-138.

Jackson, David Harold. "Robert Louis Stevenson and the Romance of Boyhood." Diss. Columbia U, 1981.

Jacobson, I. "Child as Guilty Witness." *Literature and Psychology* 24 (1974): 12-23.

Jacobson, Maria. "William Dean Howells' (Auto)biography: A Reading of *A Boy's Town*." *American Literary Realism* 16.1 (1983): 92-101.

Jakobson, Roman. *Child Language, Aphasia, and Phonological Universals*. The Hague: Mouton, 1968.

James, Henry. *The Notebooks of Henry James*. Ed. F. O. Mattheissen and Kenneth B. Murdock. New York: Oxford UP, 1947.

———. "The Turn of the Screw." (1898.) Vol. 10 of *The Complete Tales of Henry James*. Ed. Leon Edel. Philadelphia: Lippincott, 1964. 15-138.

———. *What Maisie Knew*. 1897. *What Maisie Knew; In the Cage; The Pupil*. Vol. 11 of *The Novels and Tales of Henry James*. New York: Scribner's, 1909. 1-363.

James, Sharon, and Martha Seebach. "The Pragmatic Function of Children's Questions." *Journal of Speech and Hearing Research* 25 (1982): 2-11.

Jewett, Sarah Orne. "The Dulham Ladies" (1899). *The Best Stories of Sarah Orne Jewett*. 2 vols. Gloucester, MA: Smith, 1965. 2: 64-89.

Johnson, James Weldon. *The Autobiography of an Ex-Coloured Man*. 1912. New York: Hill, 1960.

Johnson, Ronna. "Doctor Sax: The Origins of Vision in the Duluoz Legend." *Review of Contemporary Fiction* 3.2 (1983): 18-25.

Jonnes, Denis. "Family Pattern, Critical Method, Narrative Model." *The Journal of Narrative Technique* 17 (1987): 12-24.

Joseph, Gloria. "Black Mothers and Daughters: Their Roles and Functions in American Society." In *Common Differences: Conflicts in Black and White Feminist Perspectives*. Ed. Gloria Joseph and Jill Lewis. Garden City: Doubleday, 1981.

Kakutani, Michiko. "Changing Images of Childhood." *Time* 15 Jan. 1979: 50-51.

Kazin, Alfred. "A Procession of Children." *The American Scholar* 33 (1964): 171-83.

Kegan, Robert. *The Evolving Self: Problem and Process in Human Development*. Cambridge: Harvard UP, 1982.

Kelly, Erna Emmighausen. "Whitman and Wordsworth: Childhood Experiences and the Future Poet." *Walt Whitman Review* 23 (1977): 59-68.

Kernan, Keith T. "Semantic and Expressive Elaboration in Children's Narratives." *Child Discourse*. Ed. Susan Ervin-Tripp and Claudia Mitchell-Kernan. New York: Academic, 1977. 91-102.

Khattab, E.A. "Children in Nathaniel Hawthorne's Fiction." *University of Riyad Bulletin of the Faculty of Arts* 2 (1973): 7-30.

Kiah, Rosalie Black, and Elaine Paige Witty. "The Portrayal of the Black Mother in Fiction for Children and Adolescents." In *Adolescents, Literature, and Work with Youth*. Ed. J. Pamela Weiner and Ruth M. Stein. New York: Haworth, 1985. 81-91.

Kiefer, Monica Mary. *American Children Through Their Books 1700-1835*. Philadelphia: U of Pennsylvania P, 1948.

Kimbrough, Robert, ed. *The Turn of the Screw: An Authoritative Text; Backgrounds and Sources; Essays in Criticism*. New York: Norton, 1966.

Kimmel, Eric. "The Image of Fathers in Popular Adolescent Fiction." In *Adolescents, Literature, and Work with Youth*. Ed. Pamela Weiner and Ruth M. Stein. New York: Haworth P, 1985. 93-98.

King, Frances. "Treatment of the Mentally Retarded Character in Modern American Fiction." *Bulletin of Bibliography* 32 (1975): 106-14.
King, Stephen. *Firestarter*. 1980. New York: NAL, 1981.
King, Viola. "Dialect Awareness in Preschoolers." *Language Arts* 53 (1976): 248-50.
Kingston, Maxine Hong. *The Woman Warrior: Memoirs of a Girlhood among Ghosts*. 1976. New York: Random, 1977.
Kleederman, Frances. "A Study of Language in Henry Roth's *Call It Sleep*." Diss. New York U, 1974.
Kleinbard, David. "*As I Lay Dying*: Literary Imagination, the Child's Mind, and Mental Illness." *Southern Review* 22.1 (1986): 51-68.
Kolodny, Annette. "Some Notes on Defining a Feminist Literary Criticism." *Critical Inquiry* 2 (1975): 75-92.
Kondravy, Connie Ranck. "Faulkner's Study of Youth." Diss. Lehigh U, 1975.
Kosinski, Jerzy. *The Painted Bird*. Boston: Houghton, 1965.
Kramer, Cheris. "Women's Speech: Separate but Unequal?" *Language and Sex: Difference and Dominance*. Ed. Barrie Thorne and Nanby Henley. Rowley, MA: Newbury, 1975. 43-56.
Kuhn, Reinhard. *Corruption in Paradise: The Child in Western Literature*. Hanover: UP of New England, 1982.
———. "The Massacre of the Innocents: Mortality Among Fictional Children." *Michigan Quarterly Review* 19 (1980): 171-92.
Labov, William. *Language in the Inner City*. Philadelphia: U of Pennsylvania P, 1972.
Labov, William, and Joshua Waletsky. "Narrative Analysis: Oral Versions of Personal Experience." *Essays on the Verbal and Visual Arts: Proceedings of the 1966 Annual Spring Meeting of the American Ethnological Society*. Seattle: U of Washington P, 1967. 12-45.
Lakoff, Robin. *Language and Woman's Place*. New York: Harper, 1975.
Lattin, Patricia Hopkins. "Childbirth and Motherhood in Kate Chopin's Fiction." *Regionalism and the Female Imagination* 4.1 (1978): 8-12.
Lawrence, D.H. *Studies in Classic American Literature*. 1923. New York: Penguin, 1981.
Lederberg, Amy. "A Framework for Research on Preschool Children's Speech Modifications." *Language, Thought and Culture*. Vol. 2 of *Language Development*. Ed. Stan A. Kuczaj. Hillsdale, NJ: Erlbaum, 1982. 37-74.
Lee, Harper. *To Kill a Mockingbird*. 1960. New York: Warner, 1982.
Leish, David J. "From the Mists of Childhood: Language as Judgement of the Emerging Artist in Joyce's *A Portrait*." *James Joyce Quarterly* 12 (1975): 371-79.
Lenneberg, Eric. *Biological Foundations of Language*. New York: Wiley, 1967.
Leverenz, David. *The Language of Puritan Feeling*. New Brunswick: Rutgers UP, 1980.
Levine, Robert T. "'My Ultraviolet Darling': The Loss of Lolita's Childhood." *Modern Fiction Studies* 25 (1979): 471-98.
Lewis, R.W.B. *The American Adam: Innocence, Tradition, and Tragedy in the Nineteenth Century*. Chicago: U of Chicago P, 1955.
Libby, Anthony Peter. "Chronicles of Children: William Faulkner's Short Fiction." Diss. Stanford U, 1969.
Linder, Lyle Dean. "Children in the Literary Work of Stephen Crane." Diss. Duke U, 1976.

Ling, Daniel, and Agnes Ling. "Communication Development in the First Three Years of Life." *Journal of Speech and Hearing Research* 17 (1974): 146-59.
Lisca, Peter, ed. *John Steinbeck: An Introduction and Interpretation*. New York: Holt, 1963.
Long, Michael. *Marvell, Nabokov: Childhood and Arcadia*. New York: Oxford UP, 1984.
Lynn, Kenneth S. "Adulthood in American Literature." *Daedalus* 105 (1976): 49-59.
———. *The Scarlet Letter: Texts, Sources, Criticisms*. New York: Harcourt, 1961.
Macaigne, Bernard. "From Tom Sawyer to Penrod: The Child in American Popular Literature 1870-1910." *Revue Francaise d'Etudes Americaines* 17 (1983): 319-31.
Maccoby, Eleanor Emmons, and Carol Nagy Jacklin. *The Psychology of Sex Differences*. Stanford: Stanford UP, 1974.
Macnaughton, W.R. "Maisie's Grace Under Pressure: Some Thoughts on James and Hemingway." *Modern Fiction Studies* 22 (1976): 153-64.
Magistrale, Tony. "Inherited Haunts: Stephen King's Terrible Children." *Extrapolation* 26 (1985): 43-49.
Maillard, Denyse. *L'Enfant Americain au XXe Siecle d'apres les Romanciers du Middle-West*. Paris: Librairie Mizet et Bastard, 1935.
Mair, Christian. "The 'New Stylistics': A Success Story or the Story of Successful Self-Deception?" *Style* 19 (1985): 117-33.
Male, Roy R. "Hawthorne's Literal Figures." *Ruined Eden of the Present: Hawthorne, Melville, and Poe: Critical Essays in Honor of Darrel Abel*. Ed. G.R. Thompson and Virgil L. Lokke. West Lafayette: Purdue UP, 1981. 71-92.
Malin, Irving. "The Authoritarian Family in American Fiction." *Mosaic* 4 (1971): 153-73.
Maltz, Daniel N., and Ruth A. Borker. "A Cultural Approach to Male-Female Miscommunication." *Language and Social Identity*. Ed. John J. Gumperz. Cambridge: Cambridge UP, 1982. 196-216.
Maratsos, Michael. "Problems in Categorical Evolution: Can Formal Categories Arise from Semantic Ones?" *The Child's Construction of Language*. Ed. Werner Deutsch. New York: Academic, 1981. 245-61.
Marcus, Leah. *Childhood and Cultural Despair: A Theme and Variations in Seventeenth-Century Literature*. Pittsburg: U of Pittsburg P, 1978.
Marotta, Kenny. "*What Maisie Knew*: The Question of Our Speech." *Journal of English Literary History* 46 (1979): 495-508.
Marshall, Paule. *Brown Girl, Brownstones*. 1959. New York: Feminist P, 1981.
Martin, Wallace. *Recent Theories of Narrative*. Ithaca: Cornell UP, 1986.
Masback, Frederick Joseph. "The Child Character in Hawthorne and James." Diss. Syracuse U, 1960.
Mather, Cotton. *Diary of Cotton Mather, 1681-1724*. Boston: Massachusetts Historical Society, 1911-12.
Matheson, Annie. "George Eliot's Children." *Macmillan's Magazine* 46 (1982): 488-97.
Matthiessen, F.O. *American Renaissance*. London: Oxford UP, 1941.
Maxfield, James F. "The Child, the Adolescent, and the Adult: Stages of

Consciousness in Three Early Novels of William Maxwell." *Midwest Quarterly* 24.3 (1983): 315-35.

———. "Memory and Imagination in William Maxwell's *So Long, See You Tomorrow.*" *Critique* 24.1 (1982): 21-37.

McCloskey, John C. "What Maisie Knows: A Study of Childhood and Adolescence." *American Literature* 36 (1965): 485-513.

McCullers, Carson. *The Member of the Wedding*. 1946. New York: Bantam, 1975.

McCurry, Niki Alpert. "Concepts of Childrearing and Schooling in the March Novels of Louisa May Alcott." Diss. Northwestern U, 1976.

McHale, Brian. "Speaking as a Child in *U.S.A.*: A Problem in the Mimesis of Speech." *Language and Style* 17 (1984): 351-70.

McKay, Janet Holmgren. "Going to Hell: Style in Huck Finn's Great Debate." *Interpretations* 13 (1981): 24-30.

———. *Narration and Discourse in American Realistic Fiction*. Philadelphia: U of Pennsylvania P, 1982.

———. "'Tears and Flapdoodle': Point of View and Style in *The Adventures of Huckleberry Finn.*" *Style* 10 (1976): 41-50.

McKeever, Walter. "Cerebral Organization and Sex: Interesting but Complex." In *Language, Gender, and Sex in Comparative Perspective*. Ed. Susan U. Philips, Susan Steele, and Christine Tanz. New York: Cambridge UP, 1987.

McKenzie, Lee Smith. "Jane Austen, Henry James, and the Family Romance." Diss. U of Oklahoma, 1980.

McNamara, Anne Marie. "The Character of Flame: The Function of Pearl in *The Scarlet Letter.*" *American Literature* 27 (1956): 537-53.

McNamara, Eugene. "The Lost Innocence of Childhood." *Critic* 17 (1959): 15+.

Melville, Herman. *Moby-Dick*. 1851. *Moby-Dick: An Authoritative Text; Reviews and Letters by Herman Melville; Analogues and Sources; Criticism*. Ed. Harrison Hayford and Hershel Parker. New York: Norton, 1967.

Mesgaros, Patricia K. "Hero with a Thousand Faces, Child with No Name: Kosinski's *The Painted Bird.*" *College Literature* 6 (1979): 232-44.

Meyer, Kenneth. "Social Class and Family Structure: Attitudes Revealed by the Earliest American Novels, 1789-1815." Diss. U of Minnesota, 1965.

Miller, Edwin Haviland. "'Wounded Love': Nathaniel Hawthorne's 'The Gentle Boy.'" *Nathaniel Hawthorne Journal* 8 (1978): 47-54.

Miller, Mary Rita. "Attestations of American Indian Pidgin English in Fiction and Nonfiction." *American Speech* 42 (1967): 142-47.

Millhauser, Steven. *Edwin Mullhouse: The Life and Death of an American Writer, 1943-1954 by Jeffrey Cartwright*. New York: Knopf, 1972.

Milton, Dorothy. "The Unquiet Hearthside: A Study of the Parent-Child Relationship in the Fiction of Henry James." Diss. U of Chicago, 1968.

Minter, David. "Faulkner, Childhood, and the Making of *The Sound and the Fury.*" *American Literature* 51 (1979): 376-93.

Mitchell, Juliet. "*What Maisie Knew*: Portrait of the Artist as a Young Girl." In *Women: The Longest Revolution*. Ed. Juliet Mitchell. New York: Pantheon, 1984. 171-94.

Mitchell-Kernan, Claudia, and Keith T. Kernan. "Pragmatics of Directive Choice Among Children." *Child Discourse*. Ed. Susan Ervin-Tripp and Claudia Mitchell-Kernan. New York: Academic, 1977. 189-208.

Monteiro, George. "Innocence and Experience: The Adolescent Child in the Works of Mark Twain, Henry James, and Ernest Hemingway." *Estudos Anglo-Americanos* 1 (1977): 39-57.

Moorman, Mary. "Wordsworth and His Children." *Bicentenary Wordsworth Studies in Memory of John Alban Finch.* Ed. Jonathan Wordsworth. Ithaca: Cornell UP, 1970. 111-41

Morrison, Toni. *The Bluest Eye.* New York: Washington Square P, 1970.

Mundy, Jacqueline. "Hawthorne's Pervasive Child." Diss. Indiana U, 1975.

Murphy, John J. "Willa Cather's Children of Grace." *Willa Cather Pioneer Newsletter* 28 (1984): 13-15.

Nabokov, Vladimir. *Lolita.* 1955. New York: Berkley, 1977.

Nance, William L. "What Maisie Knew: The Myth of the Artist." *Studies in the Novel* 8 (1976): 88-102.

Nardin, Jane. "Children and Their Families in Jane Austen's Novels." *Women and Literature* 3 (1983): 73-87.

Nelles, William. "Theme and Frame in 'That Evening Sun.'" Unpublished paper presented at Narrative Literature Conference, Ann Arbor, 2 April 1987.

Nelson, Katherine. "Explorations in the Development of a Functional Semantic System." *Children's Language and Communication.* Ed. W. Andrew Collins. Hillsdale, NJ: Erlbaum, 1979. 47-81.

———. "The Syntagmatics and Paradigmatics of Conceptual Development." *Language, Thought, and Culture.* Vol. 2 of *Language Development.* Ed. Stan A. Kuczaj. Hillsdale, NJ: Erlbaum, 1982. 335-64.

Noguchi, Rei R. "Linguistic Description and Literary Interpretation." *CLA Journal* 30.2 (1986): 171-83.

Oates, Joyce Carol. "Why Is Your Writing So Violent?" *New York Times Book Review* 29 Mar. 1981: 15+.

O'Barr, William M., and Bowman K. Atkins. "'Women's Language' or 'Powerless Language'?" In *Women and Language in Literature and Society.* Ed. Sally McConnell-Ginet, Ruth Borker, and Nelly Furman. New York: Praeger, 1980. 93-110.

O'Connor, Flannery. "The Lame Shall Enter First." (1962.) *Everything That Rises Must Converge.* 1965. *Three by Flannery O'Connor.* New York: NAL, 1983. 371-404.

Oggel, L. Terry. "The Background of the Images of Childhood in American Literature." *Western Humanities Review* 33 (1979): 281-97.

———. "Twin Tongues of Flame: Hawthorne's Pearl and Barth's Jeannine as the Morally Redemptive Child." *Nassau Review* 4 (1980): 41-49.

Oldfield, Derek. "The Language of the Novel." *Middlemarch: Critical Approaches to the Novel.* Ed. Barbara Hardy. New York: Oxford UP, 1967. 63-86.

Olswang, Lesley Barrett, and Robert L. Carpenter. "The Ontogenesis of Agent." *Journal of Speech and Hearing* 25 (1982): 297-314.

Ong, Walter, S.J. *Orality and Literacy: The Technologizing of the Word.* New York: Methuen, 1982.

Opdahl, Keith M. "You'll Be Sorry When I'm Dead: Child-Adult Relations in *Huck Finn.*" *Modern Fiction Studies* 25 (1980): 613-24.

Opie, Iona, and Peter Opie. *The Lore and Language of Schoolchildren.* Oxford: Clarendon, 1959.

Orians, G. Harrison. "The Sources and Themes of Hawthorne's 'The Gentle Boy.'" *New England Quarterly* 14 (1941): 664-78.
Page, Norman. *Speech in the English Novel.* London: Longman, 1973.
Pair, Joyce M. "Growing Up Female: The Creative Pattern of Sylvia Wilkinson." *Southern Literary Journal* 19.2 (1987): 47-53.
Papovich, J. Frank. "Place and Imagination in Henry Crews's *A Childhood: The Biography of a Place.*" *Southern Literary Journal* 19.1 (1986): 26-35.
Pater, Walter. "The Child in the House." *English Prose of the Victorian Era.* Ed. Charles F. Harrold and William D. Templeman. New York: Oxford UP, 1938. 1469-78.
Pattison, Robert. *The Child Figure in English Literature.* Athens: U of Georgia P, 1978.
Payne, Alma J. "Duty's Child: Louisa May Alcott." *American Literary Realism* 6 (1973): 260-61.
———. "The Family in the Utopia of William Dean Howells." *Georgia Review* 15 (1961): 217-29.
Pearson, Michael. "*Edwin Mullhouse*: Re-flexing American Themes." *Critique* 27 (1986): 145-51.
Pearson, Norman Holmes. "Faulkner's Three 'Evening Suns.'" *Yale U Library Gazette* 29 (1954): 61-70.
Peck, Elizabeth. "Hawthorne's Nonsexist Narrative Framework: The Real Wonder of *A Wonder Book.*" *Children's Literature Association Quarterly* 10.3 (1985): 116-19.
Pers, Mona. *Willa Cather's Children.* Stockholm: Almqvist, 1975.
Person, Leland S., Jr. "Hawthorne's Love Letters: Writing and Relationship." *American Literature* 59 (1987): 211-227.
———. "The Scarlet Letter and the Myth of the Divine Child." *American Transcendental Quarterly* 44 (1979): 295-309.
Peterson, Carole, and Allyssa McCabe. *Developmental Psycholinguistics: Three Ways of Looking at a Child's Narrative.* New York: Plenum, 1983.
Petesch, Donald A. "Some Notes on Family in Faulkner's Fiction." *Notes on Mississippi Writers* 10 (1977): 11-18.
Pfeiffer, John Richard. "The Child in Nineteenth-Century British Fiction and Thought: a Typology." Diss. U of Kentucky, 1970.
Philips, Susan U., Susan Steele, and Christine Tanz, eds. *Language, Gender, and Sex in Comparative Perspective.* New York: Cambridge UP, 1987.
Phillipson, John S. "Character, Theme, and Symbol in *The Morning Watch.*" *Western Humanities Review* 15 (1961): 359-67.
Piacentino, Edward J. "Another Chapter in the Literary Relationship of Mark Twain and Joel Chandler Harris." *Mississippi Quarterly* 38 (1984/85): 73-85.
Piaget, Jean. *The Language and Thought of the Child.* 3rd ed. 1926. London: Routledge, 1967.
Pickard, Linda Kay Haskovec. "A Stylo-Linguistic Analysis of Four American Writers." Diss. Texas Women's U, 1976.
Pigott, Margaret B. "Sexist Roadblocks in Inventing, Focusing, and Writing." *College English* 40.8 (1979): 922-27.
Pitcher, Evelyn, and Ernst Prelinger. *Children Tell Stories: An Analysis of Fantasy.* New York: International Universities P, 1963.
Poe, Edgar Allan. "The Murders in the Rue Morgue." (1845.) Vol. 2 (*Tales and*

Sketches) of *The Collected Works of Edgar Allan Poe.* Ed. Thomas Ollive Mabbott. Cambridge: Harvard UP, 1969. 527-74.

Polanyi, Livia. "Conversational Storytelling." *Discourse and Dialogue.* Vol. 3 of *Handbook of Discourse Analysis.* Ed. Teun A. Van Dijk. New York: Academic, 1985. 183-201.

Pollock, Linda A. *Forgotten Children: Parent-Child Relations From 1500 to 1900.* Cambridge: Cambridge UP, 1983.

Poovey, Mary. *The Proper Lady and the Woman Writer: Ideology as Style in the Works of Mary Wollestonecraft, Mary Shelley, and Jane Austen.* Chicago: U of Chicago P, 1984.

Post, L.A. "Dramatic Infants in Greek." *Classical Philology* 34 (1939): 193-208.

Powers, Lyall H. "Hawthorne and Faulkner and the Pearl of Great Price." *Papers of the Michigan Academy of Science, Arts, and Letters* 52 (1967): 391-401.

Pratt, Mary Louise. *Toward a Speech Act Theory of Literary Discourse.* Bloomington: Indiana UP, 1977.

Prince, Gerald. *Narratology: The Form and Function of Narrative.* Berlin: Mouton, 1982.

Pryse, Marjorie, and Hortense J. Spillers, eds. *Conjuring: Black Women, Fiction, and Literary Tradition.* Bloomington: Indiana UP, 1985.

Psihalos, Theresia Erb. "An Analysis of Mark Twain's Concepts of the Child and Education." Diss. Loyola U, 1974.

Radden, Gunter. "Looking Back at Case Grammar." *Review of Applied Linguistics* 67-68 (1985): 185-99.

Ragussis, Michael. "Family Discourse and Fiction in *The Scarlet Letter.*" *Journal of English Literary History* 49.4 (1982): 863-88.

Raynor, Henry. "Little Victims." *Fortnightly* 174 (1954): 104-14.

Retherford, Kristine S., Bonnie C. Schwartz, and Robin S. Chapman. "Semantic Roles and Residual Grammatical Categories in Mother and Child Speech: Who Tunes into What?" *Journal of Child Language* 8 (1981): 583-608.

Rewak, William J. "James Agee's *The Morning Watch:* Through Darkness to Light." *Texas Quarterly* 16 (1973): 21-37.

Reyes, Pedro A. "A Difference of Grammar." *Diliman Review* 9 (1961): 117-23.

Ricou, Laurie. *Everyday Magic: Child Languages in Canadian Literature.* Vancouver: U of British Columbia P, 1987.

Rimmon-Kenan, Shlomith. *Narrative Fiction: Contemporary Poetics.* London: Methuen, 1983.

Robinson, Roselee. "Victorians, Children, and Play." *English Studies* 64 (1983): 318-29.

Roe, F. Gordon. *The Victorian Child.* London: Phoenix, 1959.

Roethke, Theodore. "Open Letter." *Mid-Century American Poets.* Ed. John Ciardi. New York: Twayne, 1950. 67-72.

Roller, Bert. "Children." *Sewanee Review* 37 (1929): 134-45.

———. "Children in American Poetry 1610-1900." Diss. George Peabody College for Teachers, 1930.

Ronda, Bruce Allen. "The Transcendental Child: Images and Concepts of the Child in American Transcendentalism." Diss. Yale U, 1975.

Rosen, Lois. "Sylvia Plath's Poetry about Children: A New Perspective." *Modern Poetry Studies* 10 (1981): 98-115.

Rossi, Philip, S.J. "Moral Imagination and the Narrative Modes of Moral Discourse." *Renascence* 31 (1976): 131-41.
Roth, Henry. *Call It Sleep*. 1934. New York: Avon, 1964.
Rovit, Earl. "Fathers and Sons in American Fiction." *Yale Review* 53 (1964): 248-57.
Sachs, Jacqueline. "Clues to the Identification of Sex in Children's Speech." *Language and Sex: Difference and Dominance*. Ed. Barrie Thorne and Nancy Henley. Rowley, MA: Newbury, 1975. 152-71.
―――. "Talking about the There and Then: The Emergence of Displaced Reference in Parent-Child Discourse." *Children's Language*. Vol. 4. Ed. Keith E. Nelson. Hillsdale, N.J.: Erlbaum, 1983. 1-28.
Salinger, J.D. *The Catcher in the Rye*. 1951. New York: Bantam, 1964.
―――. "For Esme—with Love and Squalor." *Nine Stories*. 1953. New York: Bantam, 1964. 87-114.
―――. "A Perfect Day for Bananafish." *Nine Stories*. 1953. New York: Bantam, 1964. 3-18.
―――. "Teddy." *Nine Stories*. 1953. New York: Bantam, 1964. 166-98.
―――. "Uncle Wiggly in Connecticut." *Nine Stories*. 1953. New York: Bantam, 1964. 19-38.
Santiago, Luciano. *The Children of Oedipus: Brother-Sister Incest in Psychiatry, Literature, History and Mythology*. Roslyn Heights, NY: Libra, 1973.
Satyanarayana, M.R. "'And Then the Child Became a Man': Three Initiation Stories of John Steinbeck." *Indian Journal of American Studies* 1.4 (1971): 87-93.
Schacht, Paul. "The Lonesomeness of Huckleberry Finn." *American Literature* 53 (1981): 189-201.
Schlesinger, Izchak M. "Semantic Assimilation in the Development of Relational Categories." *The Child's Construction of Language*. Ed. Werner Deutsch. New York: Academic, 1981. 223-43.
Schmidt, Hans-Dieter, and Hubert Sydow. "On the Development of Semantic Relations between Nouns." *The Child's Construction of Language*. Ed. Werner Deutsch. New York: Academic, 1981. 329-40.
Schorsh, Anita. *Images of Childhood: An Illustrated Social History*. New York: Mayflower, 1979.
Schrero, Eliot M. "Exposure in *The Turn of the Screw*." *Modern Philology* 78 (1981): 261-74.
Schriber, Mary Suzanne. *Gender and the Writer's Imagination: From Cooper to Wharton*. Lexington: UP of Kentucky, 1987.
Schulz, Gretchen and R.J.R. Rockwood. "In Fairyland, Without a Map: Connie's Exploration Inward in Joyce Carol Oates' Where Are You Going, Where Have You Been?" *Literature and Psychology* 30 (1980): 155-67.
Scudder, Horace. *Childhood in Literature and Art*. Boston: Houghton, 1895.
Searle, John R. *Speech Acts: An Essay in the Philosophy of Language*. New York: Cambridge UP, 1969.
Seelye, John D. "That Marvelous Boy—Penrod Once Again." *Virginia Quarterly Review* 37 (1961): 591-604.
Seib, Kenneth. "A Note on Hawthorne's Pearl." *Emerson Society Quarterly* 39 (1965): 20-21.
Sewell, David R. *Mark Twain's Languages: Discourse, Dialogue, and Linguistic Variety*. Berkeley: U of California P, 1987.

Shaw, Patrick W. "*My Antonia*: Emergence and Authorial Revelations." *American Literature* 56 (1984): 527-540.

Shine, Muriel G. *The Fictional Children of Henry James.* Chapel Hill: U of North Carolina P, 1969.

Shucard, David W., Janet L. Shucard, and David G. Thomas. "Sex Differences in the Patterns of Scalp-Recorded Electrophysiological Activity in Infancy: Possible Implications for Language Development." In *Language, Gender, and Sex in Comparative Perspective.* Ed. Susan U. Philips, Susan Steele, and Christine Tanz. New York: Cambridge UP, 1987.

Shulman, Irving. "A Study of the Juvenile Delinquent as Depicted in the Twentieth-Century American Novel to 1950." Diss. U of California at Los Angeles, 1972.

Sims-Woods, Janet, and Robert E. Staples. "Black Mother-Daughter Relationships: A List of Related Readings." *Sage* 1.2 (1984): 38-39.

Skaggs, Merrill Maguire. "A Good Girl in Her Place: Cather's *Shadows on the Rock*." *Religion and Literature* 17.3 (1985): 27-36.

Smith, Barbara Hernstein. *On the Margins of Discourse: the Relation of Literature to Language.* Chicago: U of Chicago P, 1978.

Smith, Betty. *A Tree Grows in Brooklyn.* New York: Harper, 1943.

Smith, Geoffrey D. "How Maisie Knows: The Behavioral Path to Knowledge." *Studies in the Novel* 15 (1983): 224-36.

Snow, Catherine. "Conversations with Children." *Language Acquisition.* Ed. Paul Fletcher and Michael Garman. New York: Cambridge UP, 1979.

———. "Mothers' Speech to Young Children Learning Language." *Child Development* 43 (1972): 549-65.

———. "Saying It Again: The Role of Expanded and Deferred Imitations in Language Acquisition." *Children's Language.* Vol. 4. Ed. Keith E. Nelson. Hillsdale, NJ: Erlbaum, 1983. 29-58.

Sokoloff, Naomi. "Discoveries of Reading: Stories of Childhood by Bialik, Shahar, and Roth." *Hebrew Annual Review* 9 (1985): 321-342.

———. "Interpretation: Cynthia Ozick's *Cannibal Galaxy*." *Prooftexts* 6 (1986): 239-57.

Sommerville, C. John. *The Rise and Fall of Childhood.* Beverly Hills: Sage Publications, 1982.

Spacks, Patricia Meyer. *The Female Imagination.* New York: Knopf, 1975.

Spaeth, Janet. "Language of Vision and Growth in the Little House Books." *Great Lakes Review* 8.1 (1982): 20-24.

Spiller, Robert E., et al., eds. *The Literary History of the United States.* 4th ed, rev. 2 vols. New York: Macmillan, 1974.

Stahl, John Daniel. "American Myth in European Disguise: Fathers and Sons in *The Prince and the Pauper*." *American Literature* 58 (1986): 203-16.

Stearns, Monroe M. "The Good Die Young." *Journal of the Rutgers University Library* 5 (1942): 71-77.

Steinbeck, John. *Cannery Row.* New York: Viking, 1945.

———. *The Grapes of Wrath.* 1939. New York: Penguin, 1976.

———. *The Red Pony.* (1937.) *The Portable Steinbeck.* Rev. ed. New York: Viking, 1971. 327-415.

Stella-Prorok, Elza M. "Mother-Child Language in the Natural Environment." *Children's Language.* Vol. 4. Ed. Keith E. Nelson. Hillsdale, NJ: Erlbaum, 1983. 187-230.

Stewart, Randall, ed. *The American Notebooks by Nathaniel Hawthorne.* New Haven: Yale UP, 1932.
Stone, Albert E. "Autobiography and the Childhood of the American Artist: the Example of Louis Sullivan." *American Character and Culture in a Changing World: Some Twentieth-Century Perspectives.* Ed. John A. Hague. Westport, CT: Greenwood, 1979. 293-322.
———. "Henry James and Childhood: 'The Turn of the Screw.'" *American Character and Culture in a Changing World: Some Twentieth-Century Perspectives.* Ed. John A. Hague. Westport, CT: Greenwood, 1979. 279-92.
Stone, Albert E., Jr. *The Innocent Eye: Childhood in Mark Twain's Imagination.* New Haven: Yale UP, 1961.
———. "Mark Twain's Joan of Ark: The Child as Goddess." *American Literature* 31 (1959): 1-20.
Stone, Lawrence. *The Family, Sex, and Marriage in England, 1500-1800.* New York: Harper, 1977.
Stowe, Harriet Beecher. *Uncle Tom's Cabin.* 1852. New York: Signet, 1966.
Strickland, Charles. "A Transcendentalist Father: The Child-Rearing Practices of Bronson Alcott." *Perspectives in American History* 3 (1969): 5-73.
———. *Victorian Domesticity: Families in the Life and Art of Louisa May Alcott.* University, AL: U of Alabama P, 1985.
Stroup, Sheila. "'We're All Part of It Together': Eudora Welty's Hopeful Vision in *Losing Battles.*" *Southern Literary Journal* 15.2 (1983): 42-58.
Stubbs, Michael. *Discourse Analysis: The Sociolinguistic Analysis of Natural Language.* Chicago: U of Chicago P, 1983.
Sunderman, Paula. "Speech Act Theory and Faulkner's 'That Evening Sun.'" *Language and Style* 14 (1981): 304-14.
Swaiman, Kenneth F., and Stephen Ashwal. *Pediatric Neurology Case Studies.* 2nd ed. New York: Medical Examination, 1984.
Tannen, Deborah. "Repetition in Conversation: Toward a Poetics of Talk." *Language* 63 (1987): 574-605.
Tanner, Tony. *The Reign of Wonder: Naivety and Reality in American Literature.* New York: Cambridge UP, 1965.
Thompkins, Jane P., ed. *Twentieth Century Interpretations of "The Turn of the Screw."* Englewood Cliffs: Prentice, 1970.
Thorne, Barrie, Cheris Kramarae, and Nancy Henley, eds. *Language, Gender and Society.* Rowley, MA: Newbury, 1983.
Thorne, Barrie, and Nancy Henley. "Difference and Dominance: An Overview of Language, Gender, and Society." *Language and Sex: Difference and Dominance.* Ed. Barrie Thorne and Nancy Henley. Rowley, MA: Newbury, 1975. 5-42.
Thota, Anand Rao. "The Concept of the Child in Whitman's Poetic Progress." *Osmania Journal of English Studies* 17 (1981): 61-71.
Tough, Joan. *The Development of Meaning.* New York: Halstead, 1977.
Traugott, Elizabeth Closs, and Mary Louise Pratt. "Role Structures and Literary Analysis." *Linguistics for Students of Literature.* By Elizabeth Closs Traugott and Mary Louise Pratt. New York: Harcourt, 1980. 210-19.
Tremblay, William A. "A Reading of Nathaniel Hawthorne's 'The Gentle Boy.'" *Massachusetts Studies in English* 2 (1970): 80-87.
Trensky, Anne. "The Bad Boy in Nineteenth-Century American Fiction." *Georgia Review* 27 (1973): 503-17.

Trensky, Anne T. "The Cult of the Child in Minor American Fiction of the Nineteenth Century." Diss. City College of New York, 1969.
Trensky, Anne Tropp. "The Saintly Child in Nineteenth-Century American Fiction." *Prospects* 1 (1975): 389-413.
Trilling, Lionel. "The Last Lover: Vladimir Nabokov's *Lolita*." *Encounter* 11.4 (1958): 9-19.
Troester, Rosalie Riegle. "Turbulence and Tenderness: Mothers, Daughters and 'Other Mothers' in Paule Marshall's *Brown Girl, Brownstones*." *Sage* 1.2 (1984): 13-16.
Trudgill, Peter. *Sociolinguistics: An Introduction to Language and Society*. Rev. ed. New York: Penguin, 1983.
Tumulty, Michael. "Youth and Innocence in the Novels of William Faulkner." Diss. U of Kansas, 1970.
Twain, Mark. See Clemens, Samuel Langhorne.
Vance, Jane Gentry. "Fat Like Mama, Mean Like Daddy: The Fiction of Sylvia Wilkinson." *Southern Literary Journal* 15.1 (1982): 23-36.
Von Abele, Rudolph. "Baby and Butterfly." *Kenyon Review* 15 (1953): 280-92.
Vygotsky, Lev Semanovich. *Thought and Language*. Cambridge, Mass.: MIT P, 1962.
Wade-Gayles, Gloria. *No Crystal Stair: Visions of Race and Sex in Black Women's Fiction*. New York: Pilgrim P, 1984.
―――. "The Truths of Our Mothers' Lives: Mother-Daughter Relationships in Black Women's Fiction." *Sage* 1.2 (1984): 8-12.
Wagenknecht, Edward. *The Novels of Henry James*. New York: Ungar, 1983.
Wagner, Linda. "Language and Act: Caddy Compson." *Southern Literary Journal* 14 (1982): 49-61.
Wall, Carey. "The Boomerang of Slavery: The Child, the Aristocrat, and Hidden White Identity in *Huck Finn*." *Southern Studies* 21.2 (1982): 208-221.
Walpole, Jane Raymond. "Eye Dialect in Fictional Dialogue." *College Composition and Communication* 25 (1974): 191-96.
Walsh, William. "Coleridge's Vision of Childhood." *The Listener* 53 (1955): 336-40.
Watkins, Floyd C., and William B. Dillingham. "The Mind of Vardaman Bundren." *Philological Quarterly* 39 (1960): 247-51.
Weeks, Thelma. *Born to Talk*. Rowley, MA: Newbury, 1979.
Weiner, J. Pamela, and Ruth M. Stein, eds. *Adolescents, Literature, and Work with Youth*. New York: Haworth P, 1985.
Weintraub, Sandra. "Parents' Speech to Children: Some Situational and Sex Differences." Diss. Boston U, 1978.
Welty, Eudora. *The Golden Apples*. New York: Harcourt, 1947.
―――. *Losing Battles*. 1970. New York: Vintage, 1978.
Wenke, John. "Sergeant X, Esme, and the Meaning of Words." *Studies in Short Fiction* 18 (1981): 251-59.
Wheeler, Charles B. Rev. of *Essays on Style and Language*, ed. Roger Fowler. *Style* 2 (1968): 231.
Whelan, Robert Emmet. "Hester Prynne's Little Pearl: Sacred and Profane Love." *American Literature* 39 (1968): 488-505.
White, Barbara. *Growing Up Female: Adolescent Girlhood in American Fiction*. Westport, CT: Greenwood P, 1985.
White, E.B. *Charlotte's Web*. 1952. New York: Scholastic, n.d.

Whitman, Walt. *Leaves of Grass*. 1891-92. *Leaves of Grass: Authoritative Texts; Prefaces; Whitman on his Art; Criticism.* Ed. Sculley Bradley and Harold W. Blodgett. New York: Norton, 1973.
Wilkinson, Louise Cherry, and Karen Rembold. "The Communicative Context of Early-Language Development." *Language, Thought, and Culture.* Vol. 2 of *Language Development.* Ed. Stan A. Kuczaj. Hillsdale, NJ: Erlbaum, 1982. 113-30.
Wilkinson, Sylvia. *Bone of My Bones.* New York: Putnam's, 1982.
Willen, Gerald, ed. *A Casebook on Henry James's "The Turn of the Screw."* New York: Crowell, 1960.
Willis, Susan. *Specifying: Black Women Writing the American Experience.* Madison: U of Wisconsin P, 1987.
Wilson, Angus. "Dickens on Children and Childhood." *Dickens 1970: Centenary Essays.* Ed. Michael Slater. London: Chapman, 1970. 195-227.
Wishy, Bernard. *The Child and the Republic.* Philadelphia: U of Pennsylvania P, 1968.
———. "Images of the American Child in the Nineteenth Century." Diss. Columbia U, 1958.
Witham, W. Tasker. *The Adolescent in the American Novel 1920-1960.* New York: Ungar, 1964.
Wolfe, Thomas. *Look Homeward, Angel.* 1929. New York: Scribner's, 1957.
Wolff, Cynthia G. "*The Adventures of Tom Sawyer*: A Nightmare Vision of American Boyhood." *Massachusetts Review* 21 (1980): 637-52.
Wright, Francis S. "Disorders of Speech and Language." *The Practice of Pediatric Neurology.* Ed. Kenneth F. Swaiman and Francis Wright. 2nd ed. 2 vols. St. Louis: Mosby, 1982. 1: 263-71.
Yaeger, Patricia S. "'Because a Fire Was in My Head': Eudora Welty and the Dialogic Imagination." *PMLA* 99 (1984): 955-73.
Yeazell, Ruth. *Language and Knowledge in the Late Novels of Henry James.* Chicago: U of Chicago P, 1976.
Zilversmit, Annette Claire Schreiber. "Mothers and Daughters: The Heroines in the Novels of Edith Wharton." Diss. New York U, 1980.
Zimmerman, Don H., and Candace West. "Interruptions and Silences in Conversation." *Language and Sex: Difference and Dominance.* Ed. Barrie Thorne and Nancy Henley. Rowley, MA: Newbury, 1975. 105-129.

Index

Included in the index are all child characters discussed in this study who have names. All such characters are listed by their first names (e.g., Huck Finn, not Finn, Huck).

adult point of view, 1, 3, 29, 34, 101, 108-13, 139-40
agent. See case grammar
Alcott, Louisa May: Little Men, 28
Anderson, Elaine, 115
Anderson, John, 20
Anderson, Sherwood: "I Want to Know Why," 63; Tar, 27; Winesburg, 27
Andola, John, 66
Ántonia Shimerda (in Cather's My Ántonia), 126-31
Ashwal, Stephen, 152 n 1
Atkins, Bowman, 115

baby talk, 69, 71
Bakhtin, Mikhail, 5
Ballorain, Rollande, 117
Bannan, Helen M., 83
Baron, Dennis, 152 n 2
Bates, Elizabeth, 42
Bayard Sartoris (in Faulkner's Unvanquished), 121-22, 124
Beck, Susan, 99
Beit-Hallahmi, Benjamin, 48

beneficiary. See case grammar
Benjy Compson (in Faulkner's Sound and Fury), 16, 18, 45, 123-24, 145
Bert Lewis (in Hughes's "Father and Son"), 79-80
biographical connections: in Halliday's linguistic analysis, 43; in literary criticism, 66-67; in Anderson's fiction, 27; in Cather's fiction, 126-35, 148; in Faulkner's fiction, 120, 137; in Hawthorne's fiction, 10-11, 67, 73-74; in King's fiction, 27; in Lee's fiction, 9; in Marshall's fiction, 86; in Roth's fiction, 11; in Steinbeck's fiction, 126-35, 148; in Wolfe's fiction, 27; in fiction generally, 3, 112-13, 117-18, 148. See also gender and language: writing styles
Bivens, William, 22
Blatty, William Peter: Exorcist, 48-56, 59, 61-62, 136, 151 n 4.4
Bloomfield, Leonard, 6
body language, 131
Borker, Ruth A., 116-18

Botvin, Gilbert, 99
Bowerman, Melissa, 21
Braine, Martin, 21-22, 150 n 3.2
Brautigan, Richard: *Troutfishing in America*, 108-10, 112, 148
Brown, Christopher, 150 n 3.3
Brown, Penelope, 45
Bryer, Jackson, 126
Burton, Dolores, 13

Caddy Compson: in Faulkner's "Evening Sun," 137-47; in Faulkner's *Sound and Fury*, 45, 123-24, 144
Carpenter, Robert L., 150 n 3.2
case grammar: definition of, 19-20; inadequacies of, 28; in linguistic studies of child language, 21-22, 150 n 3.1, 3.2; in literary child speech, 6, 7, 22-41, 136, 137, 144-45, 147; models of, 20-21; in prior literary studies, 22; significance of for literature, 28, 41
Cassie Morrison (in Welty's *Golden Apples*), 100
Cather, Willa: life and writings, 126, 148; *My Ántonia*, 126-35; *Shadows on the Rock*, 126-35
Cecile Auclair (in Cather's *Shadows on the Rock*), 127-31
Chafe, Wallace, 20
Chapman, Robin S., 21, 150 n 3.1
Charles (in Salinger's "For Esme"), 16
Charlie (in King's *Firestarter*), 26-27, 41
Cheung, King-Kok, 83
childhood: definition of, 7
child language: absence of, in literature, 12-13, 52, 60, 100-105, 112, 148; age-grading in, 9, 10, 11, 15-16; and cognitive development, 98; concreteness of, 1, 70, 151 n 5.1; as didactic, 16; first words, 22-28; freedom in, 9-10; freshness of, 27, 53; in literature, prior studies of, 4, 10, 17, 150 n 1.2; and moral development, 98-99, 107; older child to younger, 16, 23-24, 45, 78, 87, 123-24, 127, 132-33, 145-46; poetic, 60; simplicity of, 1, 15, 17-18, 51, 137. See also baby talk; crying; imitation; language; questions; realism; self-reflective speech; violence in language

children in literature: as artists, 27-28; as evil, 3, 47-56; and fire imagery, 82; as imaginative, 8-9, 12, 35, 46, 53-54, 108-9, 128, 148; as innocent, 2, 3; as observers, 25-28, 37, 128, 138, 145; in poetry, 1-2, 7, 12, 22; prior studies of, 3-4, 10, 17, 31, 35, 48, 49, 66-68, 137, 149, 150 nn 1.1, 3.3; retarded or damaged, 16, 46; romantic view of, 3, 11, 27; as symbols, 2, 3, 9, 66-67; very young, 12-13, 15-16, 66, 148; as victims, 28-40; as vulnerable, 9. See also child language; cultural attitudes; death; gender and language; racial/ethnic issues; realism/religious issues; sexual issues; individual characters by first name
Chomsky, Noam, 19
Civil War, 120, 125, 135
Claridge, Laura, 122
Clark, Eve V., 150 nn 3.2, 4.1
Clark, Herbert H., 150 n 4.1
Clark, Robert Lanier, Jr., 150 n 4.2
Clemens, Samuel: *Huck Finn* 15, 24-25, 103-5, 107-8, 113, 118-20, 125, 135, 136, 138; "Jumping Frog," 104; "Little Bessie," 63; *Prince and Pauper*, 151 n 5.2; *Tom Sawyer*, 15, 24-25
Coates, Jennifer, 152 n 2
Coe, Richard, 3
communicative and noncommunicative speech. See functions of speech
conversational analysis, 5, 6, 7, 13, 17-18, 103
Cook, Walter, 22
Cora (in Crane's *Whilomville Stories*), 100
Coveney, Peter, 3, 49
Craig, Randall, 29
Crane, Stephen: *Whilomville Stories*: "Angel Child," 100, 136; "City Urchin," 58-59, 61; "Little Pilgrimage," 58-59, 61
Cranfil, Thomas Mabry, 150 n 4.2
Crews, Frederick, 67
crying: by Benjy, 16; and gender, 116, 128, 130, 132, 133; by Norton, 78; by Pearl, 68, 70, 72; by possessed children, 54
Cuddy, Lois A., 82

cultural attitudes: and gender roles, 114-18, 120-25, 135, 146, 152 n 2; and miscommunication, 116-17; and parent-child interaction, 65-66, 75-94, 114-15; reflected in literature, 105, 112-13, 148. See also gender and language; racial/ethnic issues; religious issues

David Schearl (in Roth's Call It Sleep), 11-12, 17, 27, 41, 45, 80-82, 93, 110-12
Dawe, Helen C., 116
death: of children, 15, 49, 56-58, 77-80, 85; in children's conversations, 12, 17, 91, 106, 107, 110, 121, 132, 139; ends childhood, 7; of parents, 23, 30, 68, 77-80, 82, 88, 90, 92; of other adults, 50, 107, 139
Defoe, Daniel: Moll Flanders, 22
de Villiers, Jill G., 10
de Villiers, Peter A., 10
dialect: in linguistic studies, 66, 115; in Clemens's fiction, 120, 135; in Crane's fiction, 59; in Faulkner's fiction, 9, 137; in Lee's fiction, 9; in Roth's fiction, 11-12, 80, 110-12; in Steinbeck's fiction, 105-6. See also cultural attitudes; racial/ethnic issues
Dickens, Charles, 60
Dill (in Lee's Mockingbird), 23-24, 41
Dolis, John, 67-68
Dore, John, 43
Dos Passos, John: U.S.A., 112, 150 n 1.2
DuBois, John W., 42
Durkin, Kevin D., 64
dyslexia, 114. See also language: and biology

Edelsky, Carole, 115
Edwin Mullhouse (in Millhauser's Mullhouse), 46
Eliot, George, 125
Ella Ruth Higgins (in Wilkinson's Bone of My Bones), 46, 91-93
Erikson, Erik, 153 n 1
Ervin-Tripp, Susan, 45, 65
Esme (in Salinger's "For Esme"), 16
ethnic issues. See racial/ethnic issues

Eugene Gant (in Wolfe's Look Homeward, Angel), 27-28, 41
Eva (in Stowe's Uncle Tom's Cabin), 57-58, 61
experiencer. See case grammar

Farrell, James T.: Young Lonigan, 28
Farrell, Thomas, 152 n 4
fatherhood: compared to motherhood, 93-94; importance of, in American literature, 151 nn 5.3, 5.4; in linguistic studies, 65, 75-76; in multicultural literary settings 75-82; in Crane's "Angel Child," 100; in Faulkner's "Evening Sun," 140; in Faulkner's Light in August, 76-77, 82; in Hawthorne's "Gentle Boy," 23; in Hawthorne's Scarlet Letter, 67-68, 71-72, 73; in James's Maisie, 35; in Lee's Mockingbird, 106-7; in Marshall's Brown Girl, 87-88; in Morrison's Bluest Eye, 86; in O'Connor's "Lame Shall Enter First," 77-79, 82; in Roth's Call It Sleep, 80-82, 111-12; in Smith's Tree in Brooklyn, 90; in Wilkinson's Bone of My Bones, 91-93. See also motherhood; parents and children
Faulkner, Howard, 49
Faulkner, William: life, 120, 125, 137; Absalom, Absalom! 63; As I Lay Dying, 22; "The Bear" in Go Down Moses, 17-18, 122-24; "Evening Sun," 6, 136-48; Flags in the Dust, 137; The Hamlet, 9, 147; Light in August, 76-77, 82; Nobel Prize speech, 135; Requiem for a Nun, 144; Sound and Fury, 16, 18, 45, 123-24, 137, 143-45; "Twilight," 137; Unvanquished, 121-24
feminine. See gender
Fern Arable (in White's Charlotte's Web), 45
Fiedler, Leslie, 2, 31, 149 n 1
Fillmore, Charles J., 20
Fisher, Marvin, 137
Fishman, Pamela, 114-15
Flora (in James's "Turn of the Screw"), 48-56, 61
Fogle, Richard, 66
Fraiman, Susan, 83
framing devices. See narrative

Francie Nolan (in Smith's *Tree Grows in Brooklyn*), 47, 89-91, 93
Frankie (in Steinbeck's *Cannery Row*), 16
Frankie Addams (in McCullers's *Member of the Wedding*), 45-46, 101-3
Freud, Sigmund, 153 n 1
functions of speech: definition of, 42-43; in linguistic studies, 42-47, 151 n 4.4; in literary child speech, 6, 7, 45-63, 72-73, 136, 137, 141-44, 147; models of, 43-44; and speech acts, 150 n 4.1

Garrison, Joseph, 138
gender and language: biological influences on, 114, 152 n 1; cultural influences on, 114-15, 152 n 2; linguistic studies of, 99, 114-18; in literary dialogues in general, 6, 7, 59-60, 136, 137; stereotypes about, 115-18, 128, 130, 131, 134; and writing styles, 117-18, 125-35, 142-43, 148, 152 n 4; in Cather's fiction, 125-35; in Clemens's *Huck Finn*, 118-20, 135; in Faulkner's fiction, 120-25, 135, 142-43, 144-47; in Hawthorne's *Scarlet Letter*, 71-73; in James's "Turn of the Screw," 55-56; in McCullers's *Member of the Wedding*, 101-3; in Steinbeck's fiction, 125-35. *See also* crying: and gender; questions; sexual issues; violence in language
Geschwind, Norman, 152 n 1
Giattino, Jill, 65
Gleason, Jean Berko, 65, 73, 75, 116
Golding, William: *Inheritors*, 22
Goodwin, Marjorie Harness, 116
grammar. *See* syntax
Greif, Esther Blank, 65, 73, 75
Grice, H. Paul, 98
Guillory, Daniel L., 149 n 1

Halliday, M.A.K., 5, 42, 43-44
Hardy, Judith A., 21-22, 150 n 3.2
Hawthorne, Julian, 10-11, 67
Hawthorne, Nathaniel: *American Notebooks*, 10-11, 67, 73-74; "Gentle Boy," 23, 67; *Scarlet Letter*, 15, 17, 45, 60-62, 66-75, 82-83, 136; "Snow-Image," 10-11, 16; "Wonder-Book," 67
Hawthorne, Una, 10-11, 67, 73-74
Heaton, C.P., 17
Hecht, Barbara F., 150 n 3.2
Hemingway, Ernest: "In Our Time," 17, 61-62; *Old Man and Sea*, 17, 18, 22
Henley, Nancy, 152 n 2
heuristic. *See* functions of speech; questions
Hiatt, Mary, 118
Hogan, Jeanne G., 65
Holden Caulfield (in Salinger's *Catcher in the Rye*), 12
Huck Finn: in Clemens's *Huck Finn*, 24-25, 103-5, 108, 118-20, 125, 135; in Clemens's *Tom Sawyer*, 15, 24-25
Hughes, Langston: "Father and Son," 79-80, 148; *Not Without Laughter*, 26, 47; "Red-Headed Baby," 16
Hymes, Dell, 43

Ilbrahim (in Hawthorne's "Gentle Boy"), 23, 41, 67
imitation: in child language acquisition, 64-65, 115, 150 n 3.1; in literary child speech, 16, 137, 143, 146-47, 150 n 3.1; in literary language, 6
immigrants. *See* dialect; racial/ethnic issues; religious issues
intonation. *See* phonology
Isaac (Ike) McCaslin (in Faulkner's "The Bear"), 17-18, 122-23, 124
Izzy (in Roth's *Call It Sleep*), 111

Jacklin, Carol Nagy, 152 n 3
Jacques (in Cather's *Shadows on the Rock*), 127, 129-31
Jakobson, Roman, 10
James, Henry: critical studies of, 4, 35, 49, 150 n 3.3, 4.2; notebooks, 49; "Turn of the Screw," 48-56, 61-62; *What Maisie Knew*, 13-14, 28-40, 145
James, Sharon, 46
Jason Compson: in Faulkner's *Sound and Fury*, 45, 124, 144; in Faulkner's "That Evening Sun," 137-48
Jem Finch (in Lee's *Mockingbird*), 9, 23-24, 41, 106-7

Jewett, Sarah Orne: "Dulham Ladies," 61-62
Jim Burden (in Cather's *My Ántonia*), 126-31
Jimmie Trescott (in Crane's *Whilomville Stories*), 58-59, 61, 100
Jinny Love Stark (in Welty's *Golden Apples*), 100
Jody (in Steinbeck's *Red Pony*), 127, 130-31, 133
Joe Christmas (in Faulkner's *Light in August*), 76-77
John Henry West (in McCullers's *Member of the Wedding*), 102
Johnnie Hedge (in Crane's *Whilomville Stories*), 58
Johnson, James Weldon: *Autobiography of an Ex-Coloured Man*, 61

Kazin, Alfred, 149 n 1
Kegan, Robert, 99
Kernan, Keith T., 45, 99
Kiah, Rosalie Black, 151 n 5.3
Kimbrough, Robert, 150 n 4.2
Kimmel, Eric, 151 n 5.2
King, Stephen: life, 27; *Firestarter*, 26-27
King, Viola, 66
Kingston, Maxine Hong: *Woman Warrior*, 83-84
Kleederman, Frances, 11
Kolodny, Annette, 117, 152 n 4
Kosinski, Jerzy: *Painted Bird*, 75
Kramarae, Cheris, 152 n 2
Kramer, Cheris, 115
Kuhn, Reinhard, 3, 7
Kushy (in Roth's *Call It Sleep*), 111

Labov, William, 6, 95, 98, 102
Lady May (in Welty's *Losing Battles*), 15
Lakoff, Robin, 116
language: and biology, 4, 114, 152 n 1; child's acquisition of, 4, 8, 14-15, 21-22, 42-43, 64-66, 98-100, 115-17, 147; critical age for, 14-15; magical, and magical effect of, 44, 46, 47-56, 60; middle class standards of, 131. *See also* body language; case grammar; child language; cultural attitudes; functions of speech; gender and language; linguistics and literature; morphology; narrative; parents and children; phonology; power; questions; self-reflective speech; semantics; syntax; violence in speech
Lawrence, D.H., 69
Lederberg, Amy, 16, 65
Lee, Harper: *To Kill a Mockingbird*, 9, 23-24, 106-7
Lenneberg, Eric, 152 n 1
Leo (in Roth's *Call It Sleep*), 11, 12
Leverenz, David, 66
Levine, Robert, 31
Levinson, Stephen, 45
Ling, Agnes, 116
Ling, Daniel, 116
linguistics: definition of, 4
linguistics and literature: general theoretical issues, 4-6, 98, 149-50 n 1.2; present study of, 2-3, 5-7, 147-48, 150 n 1.2; prior studies of, 3, 4, 6, 10-11, 17, 22, 103, 150 n 1.2
Lolita (in Nabokov's *Lolita*), 28-41, 148
Long, Michael, 35

McCabe, Allyssa, 99-100
McCloskey, John, 150 n 3.3
Maccoby, Eleanor, 152
McCullers, Carson: *Member of the Wedding*, 45-56, 101-3
McHale, Brian, 150 n 1.2
McKay, Janet, 103
McKeever, Walter, 152 n 1
McNamara, Anne Marie, 67
Mair, Christian, 150 n 1.2
Maisie (in James's *What Maisie Knew*), 13-14, 28-41, 150 n 3.3
Male, Roy, 68
Malin, Irving, 151 n 2
Maltz, Daniel N., 116-18
mammy figure, 83
Maratsos, Michael, 150 n 3.2
Marshall, Paule: *Brown Girl*, 83-84, 86-88, 93-94
Martin, Wallace, 152 n 6.1
masculine. *See* gender and language
Mather, Cotton, 70
Matthiessen, F.O., 67
Melville, Herman: *Moby Dick*, 46

Miles (in James's "Turn of the Screw"), 48-56, 61
Miller, Mary Rita, 6
Millhauser, Steven: *Edwin Mullhouse*, 46
Minter, David, 137
Missie Spights (in Welty's *Golden Apples*), 100
Mitchell, Juliet, 35
Mitchell-Kernan, Claudia, 45
morphology, 4, 6, 7, 8-14, 136-37, 137-38
Morrison, Toni: *Bluest Eye*, 46, 83-86, 93-94
motherhood: linguistic studies of, 21, 64-65, 115, 151 n 5.1; as a literary theme, 82-84, 140, 151 nn 5.3, 5.4; in multicultural literary settings, 82-94; substitutes for, 87-88, 93; in Faulkner's "Evening Sun," 140; in Faulkner's *Light in August*, 76; in Hawthorne's *Scarlet Letter*, 68-75; in James's *Maisie*, 13, 35; in Marshall's *Brown Girl*, 86-86, 93-94; in Morrison's *Bluest Eye*, 84-86, 93-94; in O'Connor's "Lame Shall Enter," 77; in Smith's *Tree Grows in Brooklyn*, 89-91, 93-94; in Roth's *Call It Sleep*, 80-81, 111; in Salinger's "Uncle Wiggly," 8-9; in Steinbeck's *Grapes of Wrath*, 105-6, 127, 131; in Steinbeck's *Red Pony*, 127; in Welty's *Golden Apples*, 101; in Wilkinson's *Bone of My Bones*, 91-94. See also fatherhood; mammy figure; parents and children

Nabokov, Vladimir: *Lolita*, 28-40, 145, 148
narrative: absence of, in literature, 100-105, 112-13; crucial in literature, 105-7; definition of, 95; framing, 107-13; layering, 104-5, 112-13; natural, 95-98, 102; structures, 136, 137; purposes behind, 107-13; technique, 53, 127; temporal order in, 95-96, 99, 106; theory, 95-100, 151-52 n 6.1; in Brautigan's *Troutfishing*, 108-10, 112, 148; in Clemens's *Huck Finn*, 103-5, 107-8, 113; in Crane's *Whilomville Stories*, 100; in Faulkner's "Evening Sun," 138-40,

145, 147; in Lee's *Mockingbird*, 105-7; in McCullers's *Member of the Wedding*, 101-3; in Roth's *Call It Sleep*, 110-12, 148; in Steinbeck's *Grapes of Wrath*, 105-7, 108, 113; in Welty's *Golden Apples*, 100-101, 112
Nat (in Alcott's *Little Men*), 28, 41
Nelson, Katherine, 43
neurolinguistics. See language: and biology
Nick (in Hemingway's *In Our Time*), 17, 61-62
Noguchi, Rei, 150 n 1.2
Norton (in O'Connor's "Lame Shall Enter First"), 77-79

Oates, Joyce Carol, 117
O'Barr, William, 115
O'Connor, Flannery: "Lame Shall Enter First," 77-79
Oggel, L. Terry, 149 n 1
Oldfield, Derek, 125
Olswang, Lesley Barrett, 150 n 3.2
Ong, Walter, 44
Opie, Iona, 98
Opie, Peter, 98
orthography, 10-11, 13-14

Page, Norman, 6
parents and children: linguistic research about, 64-66, 116; as a literary theme, 6, 7, 11, 64-94, 124, 127, 140-41, 146-47, 148. See also fatherhood; motherhood
patient. See case grammar
Pattison, Robert, 49
Pearl (in Hawthorne's *Scarlet Letter*), 15, 17, 45, 60-62, 66-75, 82-83
Pearson, Norman, 139
Pecola Breedlove (in Morrison's *Bluest Eye*), 46, 85-86, 93
Peterson, Carole, 99-100
Peony (in Hawthorne's "Snow-Image"), 10, 16
Philips, Susan U., 152 n 1
phonology, 4, 8-14, 137, 138
Piaget, Jean, 7, 44, 60, 98, 99
Pickard, Linda, 117
Pigott, Margaret B., 152 n 4
Pip (in Melville's *Moby Dick*), 46
Pitcher, Evelyn, 98
Poe, Edgar Allan, 53
Polanyi, Livia, 97

politeness, 28, 45, 57, 116-17, 118-20
Poovey, Mary, 117
possession, demonic, 47-56
power: of language, 68; linguistic analysis of, 13-14, 45, 97, 114-15; reflected in literary dialogues, 23-27, 30-31, 34-35, 36-38, 45, 56-57, 103, 111
pragmatics, 4, 42, 136, 137
Pratt, Mary Louise, 6, 22, 98
Prelinger, Ernst, 98
Prince, Gerald, 95
pronunciation. See phonology
psycholinguistics, 42, 98
psychological reality, 22, 99. See also child language

Quentin Compson: in Faulkner's Absalom, 63; in Faulkner's "Evening Sun," 137-47; in Faulkner's Sound and Fury, 124, 143, 144
questions: importance in literary child speech, 1-2, 17, 58, 60-63, 69, 71, 73, 81, 137, 138, 143-44; linguistic analysis of, 46, 64; related to characters' gender, 119, 122, 123, 146

racial/ethnic issues, 11, 26, 56-57, 61, 65, 75-95, 138-40, 142, 147
Radden, Gunter, 20
Ramona (in Salinger's "Uncle Wiggly"), 8-9
realism: in characters' language, 5, 6, 24, 134, 148; lack of, 8, 13, 103; as literary movement, 126; in Pearl's presentation, 66-67, 74-75; significance or insignificance of, 2, 14, 51, 63, 148
Regan (in Blatty's Exorcist), 48-56, 59, 61
religious issues: absence of, in James's Maisie, 37; behind child figure, 3; in Clemens's Huck Finn, 103; in Clemens's "Little Bessie," 63; in Crane's "Little Pilgrimage," 58-59; in Faulkner's Light in August, 76-77, 82; in Hawthorne's "Gentle Boy," 23; in Hawthorne's Scarlet Letter, 66, 68, 69-70, 72; in Kosinski's Painted Bird, 75; in Marshall's Brown Girl, 87; in O'Connor's "Lame Shall Enter," 78-79; in Roth's Call It Sleep, 11-12, 80, 82, 111-12; in Smith's Tree Grows in Brooklyn, 47, 89; in Steinbeck's Grapes of Wrath, 126; in Stowe's Uncle Tom's Cabin, 57. See also possession, demonic
Rembold, Karen, 64
Retherford, Kristine S., 21, 150 n 3.1
Ricou, Laurie, 3
Rimmon-Kenan, Shlomith, 152 n 6.1
Ringo (in Faulkner's Unvanquished), 121-22
Roethke, Theodore, 12
role structures. See case grammar
Rossi, Philip, 98
Roth, Henry: Call It Sleep, 11-12, 17, 27, 45, 80-82, 93, 108, 110-12, 136, 148
Rovit, Earl, 4, 151 n 5.2
Rufus Johnson (in O'Connor's "Lame Shall Enter First"), 78-79
Ruthie Joad (in Steinbeck's Grapes of Wrath), 105-6, 127, 131-32, 133
Rutter, D.R., 64

Sachs, Jacqueline, 115, 151 n 5.1
Salinger, J.D.: Catcher in the Rye, 12; "For Esme," 16; "Perfect Day," 61-62, 46-47; "Teddy," 15; "Uncle Wiggly," 8-9
Sandy (in Hughes's Not Without Laughter), 26, 41
Schlesinger, Ischak M., 21
Schmidt, Hans-Dieter, 150 n 3.2
Schrero, Eliot M., 49
Schriber, Mary Suzanne, 117
Schwartz, Bonnie C., 21, 150 n 3.1
Scout Finch (in Lee's Mockingbird), 9, 23-24, 41, 106-7
Scudder, Horace, 3
Seebach, Martha, 46
self-reflective speech, 12, 15, 17-18, 23-28, 29-41, 144-45, 148
Selina Boyce (in Marshall's Brown Girl), 86-88, 93
semantics, 4, 19-22, 41, 42, 64, 136, 137
Sewell, David, 25
sexual issues: in children's dialogues, 29-41, 46, 47, 111; ending childhood, 7, 90; in literary settings, 13, 16-17, 29-41, 48-49, 85-86, 102, 140-41, 145, 147. See also gender and language

Shakespeare, William, 60
Shine, Muriel, 4, 49, 150 n 3
Shucard, David W., 152 n 1
Shucard, Janet L., 152 n 1
Smith, Barbara Hernstein, 98
Smith, Betty: *Tree Grows in Brooklyn*, 47, 83, 88-91, 93
Snow, Catherine, 64, 65
sociolinguistics, 4, 94
Sokoloff, Naomi, 4
sound in language, 6, 7, 10, 99, 137-38, 146. See also crying; phonology
Spacks, Patricia Meyer, 101
speech acts, 97-98, 150 n 4.1. See also functions of speech; narrative
Spiller, Robert E., 67
Stahl, John Daniel, 151 n 5.2
Steele, Susan, 152 n 1
Steinbeck, John: life and writings, 126, 148; *Cannery Row*, 16; *Grapes of Wrath*, 105-6, 108, 110, 113, 127-35; *Red Pony*, 127-35
Stella-Prorok, Elza, 64
Stewart, Randall, 67, 73
Stone, Albert, 4, 25
storytelling. See narrative
Stowe, Harriet Beecher: *Uncle Tom's Cabin*, 56-58, 61-62
Strage, Amy, 65
structure of language. See syntax
Stubbs, Michael, 43
Studs Lonigan (in Farrell's *Young Lonigan*), 28, 41
stylistics. See conversational analysis; linguistics and literature
Sunderman, Paula, 139
supernatural, 11. See also children: as evil; language: magical
Sutton-Smith, Brian, 99
Swaiman, Kenneth, 152 n 1
Sydow, Hubert, 150 n 3.2
syntax: definition of, 4; linguistic studies of, 14-15, 19-20, 41, 42; in literature, 6, 7, 15-21, 70-71, 136, 137-38

Tannen, Deborah, 5
Tanz, Christine, 152 n 1
Teddy (in Salinger's "Teddy"), 15
Thomas, David G., 152 n 1
Thorne, Barrie, 152 n 2
Tom Sawyer: in Clemens's *Huck Finn*, 24-25, 41, 103; in Clemens's *Tom Sawyer*, 25, 41
Topsy (in Stowe's *Uncle Tom's Cabin*), 57-58, 61
Tough, Joan, 43
Traugott, Elizabeth Closs, 22
Trensky, Anne Tropp, 3
Trilling, Lionel, 31
Trudgill, Peter, 115
Tucker, Hilarie, 64
Twain, Mark, 4. See also Clemens, Samuel

utterance: explanation of, 29, 35, 52, 151 n 4.3, 152-53 n 5

violence in language, 106, 121, 124, 128, 132. See also gender and language
Violet (in Hawthorne's "Snow-Image"), 10, 16
Virgie Rainey (in Welty's *Golden Apples*), 100
Vygotsky, Lev Semanovich, 44

Wade-Gayles, Gloria, 84
Wagenknecht, Edward, 150 n 3
Waletsky, Joshua, 95
Walker, Alice: *Color Purple*, 83-84
Walpole, Jane Raymond, 13
Weeks, Thelma, 43-44, 46, 60, 151 n 4.4
Weintraub, Sandra, 65
Welty, Eudora: *Golden Apples*, 100-101, 112; *Losing Battles*, 15, 101
West, Candace, 114-15
Wheeler, Charles B., 149-50 n 1.2
Whelan, Robert Emmet, 66
White, Barbara, 102-3
White, E.B.: *Charlotte's Web*, 45
Whitman, Walt, 1-2
Wilkinson, Louise Cherry, 64
Wilkinson, Sylvia: *Bone of My Bones*, 46, 83, 91-93, 98
Willen, Gerald, 150 n 4.2
Winfield Joad (in Steinbeck's *Grapes of Wrath*), 105-6, 108, 127, 130-32, 133
Wishy, Bernard, 66
Witty, Elaine Paige, 151 n 5.3

Wolfe, Thomas: *Look Homeward, Angel*, 27-28
word formation. *See* morphology
Wright, Francis, 152 n 1

Yeats, W.B., 22
Yeazell, Ruth, 35
Yussie (in Roth's *Call It Sleep*), 110

Zimmerman, Don H., 114-15

www.ingramcontent.com/pod-product-compliance
Lightning Source LLC
Chambersburg PA
CBHW032045150426
43194CB00006B/428